WITHDRAWN

JOHN MILTON
Odes, Pastorals, Masques

THE CAMBRIDGE MILTON FOR SCHOOLS AND COLLEGES

GENERAL EDITOR: J. B. BROADBENT

Already published

John Milton: introductions, edited by John Broadbent
Paradise Lost: introduction, John Broadbent
Paradise Lost: books I–II, edited by John Broadbent
Paradise Lost: books VII–VIII, edited by David Aers
and Mary Ann Radzinowicz
Paradise Lost: books IX–X, edited by J. Martin Evans

JOHN MILTON

Odes, Pastorals, Masques

Ode on the morning of Christ's nativity
The passion   Upon the circumcision
On time   At a solemn music
L'allegro   Il penseroso
Arcades   A masque: Comus
Lycidas

EDITED BY

DAVID AERS
University of East Anglia

PETER MENDES
Thames Polytechnic

WINIFRED MAYNARD
University of Edinburgh

LORNA SAGE
University of East Anglia

JOHN BROADBENT
University of East Anglia

Wehe, wo sind wir? Immer noch freier
wie die losgerissenen Drachen
jagen wir halbhoch, mit Rändern von Lachen,

windig zerfetzten. – Ordne die Schreier,
singender Gott! daß sie rauschend erwachen,
tragend als Strömung das Haupt und die Leier.

RAINER-MARIA RILKE *Sonnets to Orpheus* 1922 no. xxvi

Alas, where are we? Ever more free,
like loose kites, with edges of laughter,
we race through mid-air, wind-tattered.

– Singing god! set in order these criers,
so they may awaken roaringly,
as a river bearing the head and the lyre.

trans. C. F. MACINTYRE University of California Press,
Berkeley and Los Angeles 1960

Cambridge University Press

Published by the Syndics of the Cambridge University Press
Bentley House, 200 Euston Road, London NW1 2DB
American Branch: 32 East 57th Street, New York, N.Y.10022

© Cambridge University Press 1975

Library of Congress Catalogue Card Number: 73-94355

ISBN: 0 521 20456 9

First published 1975

Printed in Great Britain
at the University Printing House, Cambridge
(Euan Phillips, University Printer)

Acknowledgements

The photograph on the cover, of William Blake's *The sun at his eastern gate*, illustrating *L'allegro*, line 60, 'Where the great sun begins his state Robed in flames, and amber light', is reproduced by permission of The Pierpont Morgan Library, New York. The photograph of the Inigo Jones drawing of *Tethys or a nymph* (Devonshire Collection, Chatsworth) is reproduced by permission of the Trustees of the Chatsworth Settlement.

The general editor and publisher are grateful to the following for their permission to include substantial amounts of copyright material: Columbia University Press for the extract from C. L. Barber's essay, '*A mask presented at Ludlow castle*: the masque as a masque', in *The lyric and dramatic Milton: selected papers from the English Institute*, edited by J. H. Summers (1966); Faber and Faber Ltd for lines from Edwin Muir's poem *The Christmas*, in *One foot in Eden* (1956); Faber and Faber Ltd and Harcourt Brace Jovanovich Inc. for lines from Robert Lowell's poem, *New Year's Day*, in *Poems 1938–1949* and *Lord Weary's castle*; Faber and Faber Ltd and © Alfred A. Knopf Inc. for lines from Wallace Stevens's poem, *The paltry nude starts on a spring voyage*, in *The collected poems of Wallace Stevens*.

v

Contents

Pastorals and masques

The editors

DAVID AERS Cambridge, York, East Anglia. Doctorate on allegory and Langland, now working on Milton, Blake and social radicalism. Married to a schoolteacher, who is associated with him in editing *PL* VII in this series.

JOHN BROADBENT Edinburgh, Cambridge, East Anglia. Author of *Some graver subject: an essay on PL*; *Milton: Comus and Samson*; *Poetic love*; ed. Smart's *Song to David*. General editor of this series and author of *PL: introduction*, ed. *PL* I–II. Married to a social worker.

WINIFRED MAYNARD Durham, Oxford, Edinburgh; trained as a schoolteacher. Student of relations between lyric poetry and music, and herself a musician. Chapter on music in *John Milton: introductions* in this series.

PETER MENDES Reading, Manchester, Thames Polytechnic. Married to an assistant keeper at the Victoria and Albert Museum.

LORNA SAGE Durham, Birmingham, East Anglia. Writing a book on Platonism; author of general introduction to Milton's early poems, and of an essay on Milton in literary history, in *John Milton: introductions* in this series. Reviewer of contemporary fiction.

Foreword

This volume is part of the Cambridge Milton series. It can be used independently but we assume that you refer as appropriate to three other volumes in particular:

John Milton : introductions. A collaborative volume listed under the general editor's name. For Milton's life, times, ideas; music, visual arts, science, use of the Bible; place in literary history.

That volume also contains a *General introduction to the early poems* by Lorna Sage, which is intended to serve both for the poems published here, and for some of those in *Samson, sonnets &c.*

Samson, sonnets &c. This volume will contain most of the minor poems (mainly sonnets and occasional pieces) not included here, along with some of Milton's Latin and Italian poems (translated) and *Samson agonistes*. Each poem or group of poems will have its own introductory material.

Paradise Lost : introduction. J. B. Broadbent. General introduction to the poem as a whole with chapters on myth and ritual; epic; history of publication; ideology; structures; allusion; language; syntax; rhetoric; minor components of epic; similes; rhythm; style. This volume also contains a full list of resources (books, art, music etc.); a chronology of the Bible and biblical writings, epics, and other versions of the material of *PL* (this section constitutes a list of materials for projects); and a table of the contents of *PL* with cross-references.

The series will supersede A. W. Verity's Pitt Press edition of Milton's poetry published from Cambridge 1891 *et seq.* It is designed for use by the individual student, and the class, and the teacher, in schools and colleges, from about the beginning of the sixth form to the end of the first postgraduate year course in England. Introductions and notes aim to provide enough material for the reader to work on for himself, but nothing of a professionally academic kind. We hope that if any volume of text is prescribed for examination, some of its contents will not be set, but left for the student to explore at will.

In the face of the syllabus – heavy for many subjects – 'adventures of ideas' in wider fields, and the time-consuming operations of developing independence of thought . . . will be undertaken 'at risk'.

> Report of the Welsh Committee of the Schools Council, in Schools Council Working Paper 20, *Sixth form examining methods*, HMSO 1968

This edition assumes that risk.

See also the preface printed in other volumes of the Cambridge Milton.

This selection of Milton's earlier poems

The texts are based on the latest editions published in his lifetime: ie chiefly *Poems of Mr John Milton, both English and Latin* (the earlier poems) 1645; and the second edition 1673. But the text has no authority as such.

The spelling has been modernized (except where it would completely alter pronunciation, eg *anow* has been changed to *enow* but not to *enough*).

Stress marks (´) have been added where Milton seems to have intended a stress unusual for us. Grave accents (`) have been added to indicate voiced syllables in such cases as *blessèd* and in unfamiliar names.

Milton showed much elision of *e*'s, eg 'th'heavens'. These have been omitted because the elision comes more naturally if we read it with our usual neutral *e* sounds in such cases, than if we try to say *theavens*.

On the other hand, Milton's punctuation has been left almost untouched. It is not the same as ours, but you soon get used to it, and to tamper would alter the rhythm.

Bibliographical references. The place of publication is not cited for works published in London or New York.

Material printed below a double rule, and before the next ascription to an editor, is the sole responsibility of the general editor.

Introduction

JOHN BROADBENT

We suggest on the contents page of this volume a separation between *Early religious odes* and the slightly later *Pastorals and masques*. But that is merely for convenience; and there is a good deal of material contemporary with this volume which will be printed in *Samson, sonnets &c* and might need categories of its own. On the whole, however, all Milton's work before the Civil War of 1642 can take this motto:

> Schiksallos, wie der schlafende
> Säugling, atmen die Himmlischen;
> Kreusch bewahrt
> In bescheidener Knospe,
> Blühet ewig
> Ihnen der Geist,
> Und die seligen Augen
> Blicken in stiller
> Ewiger Klarheit.

FRIEDRICH HÖLDERLIN *Hyperions Schiksalslied* 1798

Immune as the sleeping Infant the celestials breathe; chaste in unopening bud it is their spirits that forever flower; and their blessed eyes gaze still in endless clarity.

These lines of Hölderlin's tie the link between *Nativity* and the dreaming mind of *Il penseroso*, the heavens of the epilogue to *Comus* and the apotheosis of *Lycidas*. All the poems in this volume search for some immunity, or 'chastity', of the body or of experience, that will liberate the spirit and keep its visions clear. They are 'adjuring verse' uttered to ward off the thickening of age, the closing down of intimations of immortality.

Milton's habitual tactic at this time was the expedition to another realm. In his Latin elegy *On the death of the bishop of Ely* written in 1626 when he was 17 he is 'borne aloft to the stars on

3

high' like Elijah being translated. In his Latin *Elegy V : On the coming of spring* of 1629 his 'soul is caught up into the limpid heights of the sky and, free of the body, I pass through the drifting clouds'. The year before, in his eulogy to the English language at Cambridge, he wanted words to express 'where the deep transported mind may soar Above the wheeling poles'.

Another tactic is to effect the epiphany of a god: if you can't go to heaven, bring it to earth. A third, of course, is chastity itself, both in his own life and in characters – making a human, heavenly. A fourth is the baptismal concern with waters.

The following passage, the Attendant Spirit's introduction of Sabrina, is representative of all the writing in this volume:

> Sabrina is her name, a virgin pure,
> Whilom she was the daughter of Locrine,
> That had the sceptre from his father Brute.
> The guiltless damsel flying the mad pursuit
> Of her enragèd stepdame Gwendolen,   5
> Commended her fair innocence to the flood
> That stayed her flight with his cross-flowing course,
> The water-nymphs that in the bottom played,
> Held up their pearlèd wrists and took her in,
> Bearing her straight to aged Nereus' hall,   10
> Who piteous of her woes, reared her lank head,
> And gave her to his daughters to imbathe
> In nectared lavers strewed with asphodel,
> And through the porch and inlet of each sense
> Dropped in ambrosial oils till she revived   15
> And underwent a quick immortal change
> Made goddess of the river; still she retains
> Her maiden gentleness, and oft at eve
> Visits the herds along the twilight meadows,
> Helping all urchin blasts, and ill-luck signs   20
> That the shrewd meddling elf delights to make,
> Which she with precious vialled liquors heals.
> For which the shepherds at their festivals
> Carol her goodness loud in rustic lays,
> And throw sweet garland wreaths into her stream   25
> Of pansies, pinks, and gaudy daffodils.   *Comus* 825

The concerns may be listed, with a few attempts at structural dyads, as:

genealogy and history *versus* metamorphosis (a quick immortal change) and myth. Instead of trying to incorporate the experience of ancestry, blood, time, environment, he tries to magic them into the visionary medium. It is as if the flesh and the flux were unacceptable.

sensuous detail (pearled wrists, vialled liquors) *versus* innocence, virginity, water, washing, worship by fresh flowers (mourning flowers) strewn on the stream. Obvious in *Lycidas* and the nymphs of *Nativity*; see Sir William Etty's breathtakingly sensuous painting of *Sabrina and her nymphs*. Blake's two illustrations of the dreaming poet explore this area delicately (Milton *Poems in English. With illustrations by Blake* 2 vols Nonesuch limited ed. 1926 vol 1).

solidity of the celestial world (nectared lavers) as if it were a 'real' alternative *versus* experiential and convincing rusticity of this world (herds along the twilight meadows). Whatever can be made of this? It is perhaps the same contrast as gods and goddesses versus fairies, urchins, magic.

The question is whether these dichotomies ever unite convincingly – not in the staged descent of a god, or apotheosis of a human, but in the language. It is a poetry of smooth continuousness, its sharp realizations chained in moulding emphasis – 'precious vialled liquors'. The experience attested by the words is of love poured out (despite the naughtiness of stepmothers and elves), poured out in liquids which are erotic – but only elsewhere (the inlets of the goddess are oiled beneath the river, by the nymphs). Like his masques, Milton's language is more serious and solid than all the recent Elizabethan midsummer night's dreams (how did that age come to be enchanted?). Yet, as Blake's illustration on the cover of this volume indicates, the divine sun remains separated from the 'hedgerow elms, on hillocks green', from which it is observed; and it appears like a figure in a masque.

> I know if I find you I will have to leave the earth
> and go on out
>   over the sea marshes and the brant in bays
> and over the hills of tall hickory
> and over the crater lakes and canyons
> and on up through the spheres of diminishing air
> past the blackset noctilucent clouds
>   where one wants to stop and look
> way past all the light diffusions and bombardments
> up farther than the loss of sight
>   into the unseasonal undifferentiated empty stark
>
>   .   .   .   .   .
>
> and if I find you I must go out deep into your far resolutions
> and if I find you I must stay here with the separate leaves

A. R. AMMONS *Hymn* 1963 *Collected Poems 1951–1971* Norton New York

The nativity ode

Edited by WINIFRED MAYNARD

['The nativity ode' is the common name for the poem titled *On the morning of Christ's nativity*, consisting of four 7-line stanzas introducing 'The hymn' of 27 8-line stanzas.]

Introduction

When Milton put together a collection of his early poems for publication, *Poems 1645*, he chose to put this poem first, although it was not the first he had written. In giving *Nativity* pride of place, he was so to speak making public affirmations to God, to his readers, and to himself. The poem, a birthday present offered to Christ, has the effect of dedicating the volume to God. It also declares to readers the kind of theme this poet values most highly, and as they read on, they will notice that other poems religious in theme or thought come next, and the secular poems later. Thirdly, the poem may have stood as a reminder to Milton of his own high seriousness about the use of his poetic gift when he wrote this poem in the month of his twenty-first birthday, December 1629. By 1645 he was enmeshed in writing controversial prose, and his life was sadder and harder, but the continuity of purpose and power is clear when he writes his three great later poems, all with religious themes.

Here is how he thought of the poem while he was writing it: he ends a Latin verse-letter to his friend Charles Diodati by saying what he is doing this Christmas:

I am writing about the King of heaven's dynasty, the bringer of peace and the ages of happiness promised in scripture – our God crying as a baby; he who with his Father governs heaven stabled in a shack. I am writing about the starry sky and the angels who sang in space and the gods suddenly smashed in their very shrines. These are my birthday-presents for Christ: gifts brought to me by the dawn of his nativity.

This tells us a lot about what Milton was doing, and also about what he was not doing. If you make a collection of poems about Christmas, you will find that although they nearly all refer to the birth of Christ (except for some secular carols and wassail-songs), they have a wide range of approaches. Some are devotional, some sentimental, others full of wit and paradox; some are lullabies, some are dancing-songs, some resound with joy and praise. The theme has so many facets and opens the way for so many possible responses, that no poet could show them all. As you read a nativity poem, ask, what aspects of the theme struck this poet, or were selected by him, and what has he made of these materials? Then you can read, say, Crashaw's *Hymn of the nativity*, and Ben Jonson's *I sing the birth was born tonight*, and see what each has to offer. Milton's account helps us adjust to his focus. It makes plain that his gaze is not fixed on earth, but keeps rising to heaven: phrase after phrase runs us upwards towards it. We shall not find here a tender description of the baby Jesus and his mother, as in Crashaw's poem, because Milton sees the scene in the stable in Bethlehem as the setting and sign of a drama encompassing earth, hell and heaven, in which the Son of God comes down from heaven as a man among men, to redeem them from sin and break the power of evil.

Form

Milton headed the poem simply *On the morning of Christ's nativity*. In the fourth stanza he urges his muse to offer her 'humble ode': it follows, headed *The hymn*. Clearly he is not concerning himself with strict definitions; he has asked his muse if she has 'no verse, no hymn, or solemn strain'; in referring to his poem as an ode, he is describing its nature, not defining its structure. He is indicating that it can figuratively be thought of as being sung or chanted. He did not intend it to be set to music, but it gains immensely by being delivered aloud, as if drawing the hearers into participation. It is not a poem to murmur like a prayer, privately, but to declaim exultantly, publicly; it celebrates the triumph of Christ, as the odes of the Greek poet Pindar, composed five hundred years before Christ's birth, celebrated victories in the Olympic and other games. (Milton's own copy of Pindar survives, annotated by him. On odes, see G. Highet *The classical tradition* 1954 chap 12.) Those were triumphs that all the winner's family and people rejoiced in: Christ's victory gives all mankind cause to rejoice.

An ode by Pindar is a tribute to the person or event it celebrates: Milton's is a tribute, a birthday gift to Christ, celebrating his coming on earth. But it has not the same formal structure as Pindar's odes. They are built up in complex units each of three verses, two corresponding in metre and the third contrasting. Milton's is closer in form to the odes of Horace. Each verse in this kind of ode has the same metrical pattern, but the pattern may be quite an elaborate one, specially evolved for a particular ode. Formally, the same could be said of a hymn, and it too is a song of praise, and can be quite large in scale.

The poem opens with four introductory stanzas each of seven lines, rhyming ababbcc. This is the rhyme-scheme Chaucer used for *Troilus and Criseyde* and several of the *Canterbury tales*, and Spenser for his *Four hymns*, but Milton here changes its effect by using an alexandrine, a twelve-syllabled line, to end each stanza. This makes the rhyming of the last two lines less insistent, and gives extra impressiveness to the last line. (Probably Milton had in mind the stanza Spenser evolved for *The fairy queen*.)

When one reads these verses aloud, it is natural to deliver them in a measured way, almost to declaim them. The hymn itself moves more lyrically, as if with his muse's aid the poet's utterance has risen from speech into song, and it invites great variety in delivery. Its flexible stanza is not quite like any known to have been used before: it has eight lines rhyming aabccbdd, giving the effect of three internal units.

The introductory stanzas

These verses form a porchway leading into the presence of the event. It is between night and the dawn of Christmas morning: still dark. Far off, the wise men are journeying with their gifts; but let the gift of this hymn be laid at Christ's feet before they reach the stable. So it is the first Christmas, and it is Christmas 1629: Milton has prepared us for a re-enactment of that once-for-all but forever valid event, and for the modulations between past and present tense that follow as he re-presents, re-enacts, the meaning of that birth. And what the core of its meaning is for

8

him is made clear in the terms of the very first verse: the *Son of heaven's eternal King* is bringing *redemption*, to *release* men from *deadly forfeit* and *work* our *peace* with God. Milton's mind is not on the localized earthly scene, but on the great transaction between heaven and earth it embodies: this child is the Son of God, who will work our peace with the Father and bring us redemption: the words run our minds forward to the crucifixion, the offering Christ will make of his own life to God to redeem our deadly forfeit. This is 'our Lord Jesus Christ, by whom we have now received the atonement' (*Romans* v 11); significantly, words of St Paul, not St Luke, come to mind: like Paul, Milton is thinking doctrinally. In this nativity, the second person of the Trinity leaves his throne and is born of 'mortal clay'. Contrast that, not only with the new-bloomed cheek of the babe in the balmy nest of Crashaw's *Hymn of the nativity*, but with the tenderness of almost any nativity play, any Christmas carol, and you begin to take the measure of Milton's distance from them, and of the adjustment of expectation you may have to make. Every man must offer his own kind of homage, as the shepherds brought what gifts they could, and the kings their richer presents: this hymn is to be Milton's offering, and he asks for divine inspiration so that his poetry may worthily celebrate this holy theme.

The hymn
stanzas I–XI : *the happening*

As Milton describes the happenings of that night, it is at first hard to get our bearings; incongruous figures appear to confuse the biblical scene. Here is the child in the manger, but the other figures are not Mary and Joseph, but Nature wooing the air, and Peace with wand and wings sliding down from the clouds as in a court masque; and the shepherds, when they appear, seem to be the idyllic sort who pipe to their flocks in Arcadia, not real ones around Bethlehem in Judaea. The poem will continue to produce for us clashes of this kind, if we respond to it as if it were a naturalistic nativity scene. But it is not: it is a celebration of the incarnation and its consequences, in the prologue introduced doctrinally, in the hymn presented symbolically. The cast is assembling, not for a domestic scene, but for a symbolic action. In it, such personages as Nature and Peace are not intruders, they are key figures.

Who, then, is Nature? She is all creation, so made as to

function by natural laws so that night follows day and spring follows winter without continual direct acts of God. She has 'doffed her gaudy trim' because it is winter; the trees are bare of leaves, the earth bare of flowers, and like Adam and Eve after the fall, she feels herself naked before her Maker's eyes, and longs for snow to cover her. But if she is God's creation, why has she 'foul deformities'? Why does she not greet her Lord with rejoicing? The parallel with the scene in the Garden of Eden points to the answer: 'cursed is the ground for thy sake', the Lord said to Adam (*Genesis* iii). Man's fall has cut Nature off from God, the disorder spreads as beast preys on beast and man wars with man. But now Peace descends and prevails: she is an allegorical figure but she represents a historical truth, the peace that prevailed, in the regions then known to history, at the time of Christ's birth.

Milton extends the sense of peace far beyond mere cessation of hostile activity until the universe is rapt into immobility. Winds and waves are still, the stars and the sun stop in their courses, the chatting shepherds will fall silent. The whole of creation holds its breath: and into the peace and silence falls the heavenly music and the singing shining angels appear.

XII–XVIII: *the music from heaven*

Such heavenly acclamation had rung out only once before, at the creation. Now it sounds again as the Creator enters his creation. From it Milton's thoughts move to that other celestial music, made by the stars themselves in their courses: the music of the spheres, forever sounding but inaudible to man. The concept of this music may have arisen as a metaphor, to express a fact about the structure of the creation, its mathematical order, or harmony;[1] but the additional fact that musical intervals are in mathematical ratios gave it more than metaphoric force. If the harmony of the spheres is actual sounding music, it must be audible; and if not to human ears, why not? Pliny discussed whether 'the sound caused by the whirling about of so great a mass be excessive, and, therefore, far beyond what our own ears can perceive';[2] Cicero

[1] For further discussion see the chapter on music in *JM: introductions* in this series.

[2] Pliny the Elder was a Roman administrator killed by the eruption of Vesuvius. His *Natural history* was an important source of scientific information for the middle ages.

considered this and the related view that the constant presence of the sound had made human hearing impervious to it.[1] Philo Judaeus, an Alexandrian Jew who lived in Christ's life-time but seems not to have known of him, and whose ideas about the sphere-music are in some respects close to Milton's, suggested that if man were ever to hear it, he would be seized with frantic desire for it alone, and would neglect even to eat or drink to keep himself alive.[2] Others foresaw the happier consequence of a return to the golden age if men heard the heavenly music, because they would aspire to virtue; and this is the vision unfolded in masque-like splendour in stanzas XIII–XV. Since human ears have already been allowed to hear heavenly music, the angelic song heard on earth at Christ's birth, the poet prays that once in this later age of time man may hear the sphere-music: then sin will fade away, and truth and justice and mercy reign among men. But the beautiful vision is brushed away: 'wisest Fate says no'. Why is this? The trail starts in Milton's own discussion of the sphere-music in *De sphaerarum concentu* (Of the harmony of the spheres), an academic discourse he delivered at Cambridge. In it he speaks of the tradition that one man, and one only in recorded history, had heard this music; and he perhaps was more than mortal: 'someone, both a good genius and an inhabitant of heaven, who perchance by command of the gods came down to fill the minds of men with sacred learning, and to recall them to virtue.' No one else, since Prometheus stole the sacred fire, has heard it: but if our hearts were pure, as Pythagoras's was, 'then indeed our ears should resound with that sweetest music of the circling stars and be filled with it. Then all things should return immediately as if to that golden age' (see *Private correspondence and academic exercises* [sometimes called prolusions] trans. and ed. Phyllis and E. M. W. Tillyard, Cambridge 1932). The words are those of classical fable, but Christian overtones are unmistakable. Prometheus's theft parallels Adam's disobedience with its consequence, the fall: the one virtuous man come down from heaven typifies Christ: the golden age is when man is in unbroken relationship with God.

The prose discourse stops short of explicit equations; it stays within the classical context. But Milton's mind has clearly been playing upon these ideas. By the time he writes *Nativity* he has seen that these are parallels that never meet; he has seen how far

[1] *The dream of Scipio* (*De republica* VI).
[2] *Of dreams* I.

Gramley Library
Salem College
Winston-Salem, NC 27108

they are valid, and where they fall short. In these stanzas he gives the fancy full play; and then sharply strips off the veil of illusion. The golden age will not be restored by man's hearing of heavenly, music, for it is sin – man's disobedience – that has made him unable to hear it by breaking the harmony between him and God, and the consequences can not be reversed by abstract virtues floating down from the skies: the way forward is *not* the way back. The bitter cross is the one road now to harmony with God, and judgement lies between man and bliss.

If one catches in 'the age of gold' not only the general reference to an early happy state, but a specific echo of the fourth eclogue of Virgil, one understands what is going on in these stanzas in another context of thought:

Time has conceived and the great Sequence of the Ages starts afresh. Justice, the Virgin, comes back to dwell with us, and the rule of Saturn is restored. The Firstborn of the New Age is already on his way from high heaven down to earth.

> VIRGIL *Eclogue* IV trans. in E. V. Rieu *The pastoral poems*
> Penguin Harmondsworth 1949

Virgil wrote that in Rome, shortly before the birth of Christ in Judaea. It is probably about the birth of a member of a royal family such as Caesar's, or Antony and Octavia's; but in the 4th century AD the Christian emperor Constantine declared it to be a prophecy of the birth of Christ. According to Virgil, a return of the golden age will follow; but in stanza XVI, Milton rejects this pagan vision in the light of Christian doctrine: no easy transition to bliss lies ahead. The rejection gains another level of meaning when Truth, Justice and Mercy appear in stanza XV: Peace has already descended, and here are the other three of the qualities that medieval allegory personified as the four daughters of God. The personification derives from *Psalm* lxxxv: 'Mercy and truth are met together, righteousness and peace have kissed each other.' Christ's self-sacrifice was seen as fulfilling this prophecy by reconciling their conflicting responses to man's sin. So in Langland's poem *Piers Plowman* they talk together of what the Crucifixion means (B text XVIII); and in Giles Fletcher's poem *Christ's victory in heaven* (1610), Justice and Mercy dispute about whether man deserves Christ's redemption. In *Nativity*, the vision of stanza XV is false, for Justice, Mercy and Truth would never agree together if Christ had not reconciled their claims: only he, by dying because of sin, won the right to forgive man for sin. The crucifixion is the true transformation scene.

XVIII–XXV: *the flight of the false gods*

The sequence of events in the Christian time-scheme to have in mind here is the creation of the world, the fall of man through sin, the redemption by Christ's life and death, and the last judgement when Christ will return, 'coming in the clouds of heaven with power and great glory' (*Matthew* xxiv; cf xvi, *Mark* xiii, *Luke* xxi); then the redeemed will be taken into heaven and the world will be brought to an end.

Only at the Last Judgement will evil be wholly destroyed, but from the moment of Jesus's birth its power is lessened: in the presence of the true God on earth the potency that illusion has lent to false gods ebbs from them. Not all of the old gods were evil: as the spirits with which classical legend had peopled the woods and streams depart, the tone is elegiac: the mountains and shore will be empty after their going. Greek and Roman mythology gave so much to mankind that we shall be poorer if we forget it wholly; but it pales into fable at the light of the 'dayspring from on high' (*Luke* i 78). Edwin Muir's Prometheus, chained to a rock for having stolen fire from the sun's chariot for men, muses on these events:

> The shrines are emptying and the peoples changing.
> It may be I should find Olympus vacant
> If I should return. For I have heard a wonder:
> Lands without gods; nothing but earth and water . . .
> A god came down, they say, from another heaven
> Not in rebellion but in pity and love . . .
> If I could find that god, he would hear and answer.

Prometheus in *One foot in Eden* 1956 *Collected Poems* Faber 1968

On the other hand, the eastern gods of XXII–XXV are a 'damnèd crew', bestial in form and worshipped with debasing, cruel rites: they are powers of darkness that must be routed. Milton attacks them again, as fallen angels in disguise, at *PL* 1 356–482.

XXVI–XXVII: *the final perspective*

The pageant of departing gods is ended, and the simile of XXVI completes the effect of their loss of all status and substance as they are likened to ghosts and moonlight shadows that vanish at the sun's first rays. The poem has been structured throughout in contrasting waves of sound and silence, successions of light and darkness, still tableaux and turbulent action. As the hymn opened the whole creation fell still and silent: then came the song of the angels, and the evocation of the harmony of the spheres: then the astounding trumpet of the Last Judgement heralded the end of the universe, the untuning of the spheres. Light beamed from heaven as the angels sang; but all was dimness, twilight, and livid flame as the false gods fell, in scenes of frenzy, flight, and disorder. Now the scene is empty of all false claimants, the clamour has died into silence: there is perfect stillness, as at the hymn's beginning, mirrored in the quietude of the verse. The baby sleeps, with the star that marked his birth above him, and angels keeping watch about him.

Like the Wise Men, we have not seen the birth. Milton does not describe it, for he, and we, were not there. The shepherds could gaze on the baby in his cradle: the Wise Men had to set out from afar and ponder the meaning, as Milton has done.

> . . . were we led all that way for
> Birth or Death? There was a Birth, certainly,
> We had evidence and no doubt. I had seen birth and death,
> But had thought they were different; this Birth was
> Hard and bitter agony for us, like Death, our death.
> We returned to our places, these Kingdoms,
> But no longer at ease here, in the old dispensation,
> With an alien people clutching their gods.

T. S. ELIOT *Journey of the Magi, Collected poems 1909–1962* Faber

The birth of Christ brought new joy and peace and love to the world, as the angels sang. It also brought death to the old mythologies, loosening the spell of beauty of the Greek and Roman fables as well as breaking the sinister power of eastern idols. Before the nativity, men wondered about the nature of the divine being or beings, and their imagination shaped their gods and their beliefs: now God makes himself known on earth in the person of Jesus Christ, and the clear light of this revelation shows earlier concepts of deity to be distorted shadows. So an old era ends, and a new era begins: this happening is both a coming to birth and a dying. Such long vistas of thought do not lead to a lullaby for the baby, but, as Milton wrote to Diodati, to a hymn for 'the heaven-descended King'.

On the morning of Christ's nativity

I

THIS IS THE MONTH, and this the happy morn
 Wherein the Son of heaven's eternal King,
 Of wedded maid and virgin mother born,
Our great redemption from above did bring;
For so the holy sages once did sing,   5
 That he our deadly forfeit should release
And with his Father work us a perpetual peace.

II

That glorious form, that light unsufferable,
And that far-beaming blaze of majesty
Wherewith he wont at heaven's high council-table   10
To sit the midst of trinal unity,
He laid aside; and here with us to be,
 Forsook the courts of everlasting day,
And chose with us a darksome house of mortal clay.

III

Say heavenly Muse, shall not thy sacred vein   15
Afford a present to the infant God?
Hast thou no verse, no hymn, or solemn strain,
To welcome him to this his new abode,
Now while the heaven by the sun's team untrod
 Hath took no print of the approaching light   20
And all the spangled host keep watch in squadrons bright?

3 **wedded maid** in *Luke* i Mary is a virgin engaged to Joseph. 5 **sages** Old Testament prophets eg Isaiah (liii) and Micah (iv). 6 **deadly forfeit** sin, and its penalty of death. 7 **work us** achieve for us. 10 **wont** was accustomed. 11 **trinal unity** the Trinity of Father, Son, Holy Ghost. 15 **Muse** Urania, muse of astronomy, inspirer of sacred poetry, which is the vein (kind) needed to provide (afford) a birthday hymn. 19 **team** winged horses of the sun-god. 21 **host ... squadrons** angels/stars; cf last stanza.

15

See how from far upon the eastern road
The star-led wizards haste with odours sweet,
O run, prevent them with thy humble ode,
And lay it lowly at his blessèd feet;   25
Have thou the honour first thy Lord to greet,
  And join thy voice unto the angel choir,
From out his secret altar touched with hallowed fire.

The hymn

I

It was the winter wild
While the heaven-born child   30
  All meanly wrapped in the rude manger lies;
Nature in awe to him
Had doffed her gaudy trim,
  With her great Master so to sympathize:
It was no season then for her   35
To wanton with the sun her lusty paramour.

II

Only with speeches fair
She woos the gentle air

23 wizards wise men, astrologers, the magi. They were not near
Bethlehem, like the shepherds, but understood from the appearance of
the new star in the east that the King of the Jews was born. They set out
from their eastern countries to find him and bring frankincense etc., led
to the stable by the star. Their coming is celebrated as the Epiphany
(6 January), the revelation of Christ to men of all races, 'A light to lighten
the Gentiles, and the glory of thy people Israel' (*Luke* ii). M urges his
Muse to *prevent*=arrive before them, with his gift. **28 out** out of. M's
muse is to be sanctified as Isaiah was in a vision when a seraph touched
his mouth with a live coal from the altar (*Isaiah* vi). **31 meanly** poorly
rude roughly made. **33 gaudy trim** leaves and flowers of summer.
36 paramour lover.

To hide her guilty front with innocent snow,
And on her naked shame,   40
Pollute with sinful blame,
The saintly veil of maiden white to throw,
Confounded, that her Maker's eyes
Should look so near upon her foul deformities.

III

But he her fears to cease,   45
Sent down the meek-eyed Peace,
    She crowned with olive green came softly sliding
Down through the turning sphere
His ready harbinger,
    With turtle wing the amorous clouds dividing,   50
And waving wide her myrtle wand
She strikes a universal peace through sea and land.

IV

No war, or battle's sound
Was heard the world around:
    The idle spear and shield were high up hung,   55
The hookèd chariot stood
Unstained with hostile blood,
    The trumpet spake not to the armèd throng,

39 guilty front shamed face.   **40 naked shame** the bareness of nature
is associated with the shame of Adam and Eve after eating the fruit.
Nature shares the consequences of the fall.   **41 Pollute** polluted.
43 Confounded embarrassed.   **46 Peace** having personified Nature,
M now depicts Peace as she was seen in masques, using traditional
symbolism such as the wand of myrtle, a plant sacred to Venus. Her
wing, like a turtle-dove's, and the amorous clouds, heighten the suggestion of pagan love: the description shares the attitude of created
nature, which does not yet understand the significance of the birth
of its Creator, bringing a new peace and love to earth.   **48 sphere** the
heavens, revolving concentrically round the earth as in the Ptolemaic
world-model.   **49 harbinger** Peace is Christ's prompt forerunner.
53 No war when Christ was born, there was peace in all parts of the
Roman empire, the Pax Romana under Augustus.   **56 hookèd** armed
with scythes.

And kings sat still with awful eye,
As if they surely knew their sovereign Lord was by.　　60

V

But peaceful was the night
Wherein the Prince of light
　His reign of peace upon the earth began:
The winds with wonder whist,
Smoothly the waters kissed,　　　　　　　　　　　　65
　Whispering new joys to the mild ocëan,
Who now hath quite forgot to rave,
While birds of calm sit brooding on the charmèd wave.

VI

The stars with deep amaze
Stand fixed in steadfast gaze,　　　　　　　　　　　70
　Bending one way their precious influence,
And will not take their flight,
For all the morning light,
　Or Lucifer that often warned them thence;
But in their glimmering orbs did glow,　　　　　　　75
Until their Lord himself bespake, and bid them go.

VII

And though the shady gloom
Had given day her room,

59 awful awed, reverent.　　**60 sovereign** Christ was a baby, yet 'King
of kings, and Lord of lords' (1 *Timothy* vi, *Revelation* xix).　　**61 But
peaceful** the sense follows from 53.　　**62 Prince** OT prophecies of
the Redeemer and the NT often use imagery of light: eg the Gospel
for Christmas Day *John* i 1–14.　　**64 whist** hushed, still.　　**67 rave**
roar.　　**68 birds** halcyons or kingfishers. In legend they made their nests
on the sea at the winter solstice, and wind and waves were calm until the
young birds were hatched and reared (hence halcyon days).　　**71 influence** astrologers taught that an ethereal fluid flowed from the stars
and affected man.　　**74 Lucifer** the morning star.　　**78 room** although
daylight had replaced darkness, the sun was reluctant to rise.

18

The sun himself withheld his wonted speed,
And hid his head for shame,   80
As his inferior flame
    The new enlightened world no more should need;
He saw a greater Sun appear
Than his bright throne, or burning axle-tree could bear.

VIII

The shepherds on the lawn,   85
Or ere the point of dawn,
    Sat simply chatting in a rustic row;
Full little thought they than,
That the mighty Pan
    Was kindly come to live with them below;   90
Perhaps their loves, or else their sheep,
Was all that did their silly thoughts so busy keep.

IX

When such music sweet
Their hearts and ears did greet,
    As never was by mortal finger strook,   95
Divinely-warbled voice
Answering the stringèd noise,
    As all their souls in blissful rapture took:
The air such pleasure loath to lose,
With thousand echoes still prolongs each heavenly close.   100

81 As as if.   **83 greater Sun** Christ, as in *Malachi* iv: 'unto you that
fear my name shall the Sun of righteousness arise with healing in his
wings'.   **85 shepherds** the birth of Christ transforms all meanings,
challenges all assumptions. Do these shepherds pasture their flocks outside Bethlehem in Judaea, or on the hillslopes of Arcadia in Greece?
M superimposes the one picture on the other, presenting the biblical
as real, the pagan pastoral as illusion: in a stroke the great shepherd-god
Pan is superseded and fades into myth because the Good Shepherd,
Christ, has come into the world. **lawn** grass.   **86 Or ere** before.
87 simply innocently.   **88 than** then.   **90 kindly** combines usual
meaning and that God, in Christ, was being born in mankind.
92 silly simple.   **95 strook** struck.   **97 noise** melodious sound.
98 As ... took in a way that captured.   **100 close** cadence, conclusion
of musical phrase.

X

Nature that heard such sound
Beneath the hollow round
　　Of Cynthia's seat, the airy region thrilling,
Now was almost won
To think her part was done,   105
　　And that her reign had here its last fulfilling;
She knew such harmony alone
Could hold all heaven and earth in happier union.

XI

At last surrounds their sight
A globe of circular light,   110
　　That with long beams the shame-faced night arrayed,
The helmèd cherubim
And sworded seraphim,
　　Are seen in glittering ranks with wings displayed,
Harping in loud and solemn choir,   115
With unexpressive notes to heaven's new-born heir.

XII

Such music (as 'tis said)
Before was never made,
　　But when of old the sons of morning sung,
While the Creator great   120
His constellations set,

102 **Beneath . . . thrilling** making the air between the moon's sphere
and the earth to quiver. Cynthia makes us aware, as in 85–9, of
classical deities as illusory. 104 **won** Nature was almost convinced
her task was done: this heavenly music could govern the universe more
harmoniously than her laws. 111 **shame-faced** shy, bashful (at being
clothed with light). 112 **helmèd** helmeted. **cherubim** second order
of angels; cf *Te Deum*. 113 **seraphim** highest order of angels.
114 **displayed** outspread. 116 **unexpressive** inexpressible. 119 **sons
of morning** stars/angels. 'Where wast thou when I laid the foundations
of the earth? . . . When the morning stars sang together, and all the
sons of God shouted for joy?' (*Job* xxxviii).

And the well-balanced world on hinges hung,
And cast the dark foundations deep,
And bid the weltering waves their oozy channel keep.

XIII

Ring out ye crystal spheres,   125
Once bless our human ears,
    (If ye have power to touch our senses so)
And let your silver chime
Move in melodious time;
    And let the base of heaven's deep organ blow,   130
And with your ninefold harmony
Make up full consort to the angelic symphony.

XIV

For if such holy song
Enwrap our fancy long,
    Time will run back, and fetch the age of gold,   135
And speckled vanity
Will sicken soon and die,
    And leprous sin will melt from earthly mould,
And hell itself will pass away,
And leave her dolorous mansions to the peering day.   140

---

125 crystal transparent. **spheres** the globes of the moon, sun, planets, fixed stars and, in medieval and later accounts, the *primum mobile*, making nine. **128 silver** silvery. **130 base** earth. Most accounts of sphere-music said the earth produced no sound, but in some it produced a note an octave below that of the celestial sphere, the *primum mobile*, so providing a base/bass to heaven. But since the fall, earth has been out of tune with the ninefold sphere-music which corresponds to the song of the nine orders of angels. See introduction to *Solemn Music*. **132 consort** term for a group of instruments, eg viols, playing together; also means accord. **symphony** harmony. **135 age of gold** age of happy innocence in the reign of Saturn in classical myth, so analogous to time before the fall in Christian myth. **136 speckled** spotted by sin. **138 earthly mould** the earth, and/or its creatures.

Yea, Truth and Justice then
Will down return to men,
   Orbed in a rainbow; and, like glories wearing,
Mercy will sit between
Throned in celestial sheen,   145
   With radiant feet the tissued clouds down steering,
And heaven as at some festival
Will open wide the gates of her high palace hall.

XVI

But wisest Fate says no,
This must not yet be so,   150
   The babe lies yet in smiling infancy
That on the bitter cross
Must redeem our loss,
   So both himself and us to glorify:
Yet first to those ychained in sleep   155
The wakeful trump of doom must thunder through the deep.

XVII

With such a horrid clang
As on Mount Sinai rang

141 Truth the whole stanza is like the transformation scene in a masque, with gods and goddesses appearing and all problems dissolving. It is beautiful but unreal, so our reason agrees when this shimmering vision is brushed away in line 149: in 'wisest Fate' we recognize the decree of God: 'what I will is fate' (*PL* VII 173). **143 like glories wearing** clothed in similar radiance. **145 sheen** brightness. **146 tissued** richly woven, as with gold or silver thread. **148** the line reverses 140. **151 infancy** unable to talk. **154 glorify** raise to the glory of heaven. **155 ychained** those chained (*ychained* was already obsolete) in the sleep of death must wake to the trump of the Last Judgement, as in *1 Thessalonians* iv, where it takes place 'in the air'; M has it in middle air, in classical theory the region between earth and moon inhabited by daemons, spirits both good and bad, including in some accounts spirits of the dead. **157 such** with a similar noise. M recalls a previous descent of God when the Ten Commandments were given to Moses (*Exodus* xix). The sound effects of these two events shatter the harmony of the preceding stanzas.

While the red fire, and smouldering clouds out brake:
The agèd earth aghast   160
With terror of that blast,
   Shall from the surface to the centre shake;
When at the world's last sessiòn,
The dreadful Judge in middle air shall spread his throne.

XVIII

And then at last our bliss   165
Full and perfect is,
   But now begins; for from this happy day
The old dragon under ground
In straiter limits bound,
   Not half so far casts his usurpèd sway,   170
And wroth to see his kingdom fail,
Swinges the scaly horror of his folded tail.

XIX

The oracles are dumb,
No voice or hideous hum
   Runs through the archèd roof in words deceiving.   175
Apollo from his shrine
Can no more divine,
   With hollow shriek the steep of Delphos leaving.
No nightly trance, or breathèd spell,
Inspires the pale-eyed priest from the prophetic cell.   180

163 sessiòn court of law.   **168 dragon** 'the dragon, that old serpent,
which is the Devil, and Satan' (*Revelation* xx).   **169 straiter** narrower.
170 sway rule.   **172 Swinges** lashes. **tail** the tail of the 'great red
dragon' of *Revelation* xiii 'drew the third part of the stars of heaven':
so Satan lured the angels that fell with him. Blake depicts Christ treading
on the dragon's tail, and the false gods falling, in his illustration of the
overthrow of Apollo and the pagan deities.   **173 oracles** an oracle was
both a place (often a cave or fissure) where the ancient Greeks sought
advice from a particular god (eg at Delphi, from Apollo); and the answer
given through the wild utterance of a priest or priestess there, often in
ambiguous terms. Plutarch (1st century AD) and many later writers
relate that oracles became silent from the date of Christ's birth.

23

XX

The lonely mountains o'er,
And the resounding shore,
   A voice of weeping heard, and loud lament;
From haunted spring, and dale
Edged with poplar pale,   185
   The parting genius is with sighing sent,
With flower-inwoven tresses torn
The nymphs in twilight shade of tangled thickets mourn.

XXI

In consecrated earth,
And on the holy hearth,   190
   The lars, and lemures moan with midnight plaint,
In urns, and altars round,
A drear and dying sound
   Affrights the flamens at their service quaint;
And the chill marble seems to sweat,   195
While each peculiar power forgoes his wonted seat.

XXII

Peor, and Baälim,
Forsake their temples dim,
   With that twice-battered god of Palestine,

186 parting genius departing local god, mourned by the nymphs, spirits of rivers, sea, hills and trees. The beauty of this stanza, with its intricate alliteration and sombre vowel-sounds, gives full value to the nymphs' mourning.   **189 consecrated** M is describing in turn the emptying of every dwelling-place of the old deities; in the previous two stanzas, oracles, and woods and waters; here, domestic shrines. These may be altars to the lars, protective deities of the home; or urns containing ashes of ancestors, whose spirits are the lemures; at both, services are held by **flamens,** priests. The deities of these three stanzas are Greek and Roman: XXII–XXIV describe eastern deities.   **197 Peor** see *PL* I 356–482, where M describes the fallen angels and how they got new names among men. Peor, or Baäl-Peor, was a sun-god of the Phoenicians and Canaanites. **Baälim** plural of Baal, other gods of the same cult.   **199 twice-battered** Dagon, god of the Philistines; see *1 Samuel* v.

And moonèd Ashtaroth,   200
Heaven's queen and mother both,
  Now sits not girt with tapers' holy shine,
The Libyc Hammon shrinks his horn,
In vain the Tyrian maids their wounded Thammuz mourn.

XXIII

And sullen Moloch fled,   205
Hath left in shadows dread,
  His burning idol all of blackest hue;
In vain with cymbals' ring,
They call the grisly king,
  In dismal dance about the furnace blue;   210
The brutish gods of Nile as fast,
Isis and Orus, and the dog Anubis haste.

XXIV

Nor is Osiris seen
In Memphian grove, or green,

200 Ashtaroth plural form of Ashtoreth, goddess worshipped by Canaanites and Phoenicians; among titles ascribed to her is 'creatrix of the gods'.
So she is described in terms sometimes applied to Mary, mother of
Christ: 'Heaven's queen and mother'. Ashtoreth was sometimes depicted
with horns; hence moonèd. **203 Libyc Hammon** or Ammon, an
Egyptian god worshipped in the Libyan desert, in the form of a ram.
204 Thammuz the same legend attaches to this Phoenician god as to
Adonis, of his slaying by a boar and annual revival. Now the ritual
mourning of the girls (from Tyre in Phoenicia) is in vain: after Christ's
birth, Thammuz will be reborn no more. **205 Moloch** an Ammonite
idol to whom children were sacrificed by fire, to the noise of cymbals to
drown their shrieks. The ruins of Ammon's capital city Rabbah survive
in modern 'Ammân. **211 brutish** the idols of many Egyptian gods,
including those next named, had the heads of animals. **212 Isis**
Egyptian goddess, sister and wife of Osiris: horned like a cow. **Orus**
Horus, son of Isis and Osiris, Egyptian god of light: hawk-headed.
Anubis son of Osiris and ruler of the dead: with the head of a jackal or a
dog. **213 Osiris** Osiris, chief god of Egypt (of which Memphis was the
ancient capital), was worshipped in the form of a living sacred bull;
also as an idol, carried in procession in a sacred chest or wooden box.
(Aaron let the Israelites make a golden calf while Moses was on Mount
Sinai receiving the commands of God, so reverting to Egyptian idolatry:
Exodus xxxii.)

Trampling the unshowered grass with lowings loud: 215
Nor can he be at rest
Within his sacred chest,
    Naught but profoundest hell can be his shroud,
In vain with timbrelled anthems dark
The sable-stolèd sorcerers bear his worshipped ark.   220

XXV

He feels from Judah's land
The dreaded infant's hand,
    The rays of Bethlehem blind his dusky eyn;
Nor all the gods beside,
Longer dare abide,   225
    Not Typhon huge ending in snaky twine:
Our babe to show his godhead true,
Can in his swaddling bands control the damnèd crew.

XXVI

So when the sun in bed,
Curtained with cloudy red,   230
    Pillows his chin upon an orient wave,
The flocking shadows pale,
Troop to the infernal jail,

219 timbrelled accompanied on tambourines.   **220 sable-stolèd**
black-robed.   **221 Judah's land** 'And thou Bethlehem, in the land
of Judah, art not the least among the princes of Judah: for out
of thee shall come a Governor, that shall rule my people Israel'
(*Matthew* ii). A further association, Christ as 'the Lion of the tribe of
Judah' (*Revelation* v), underlines the paradox developed in this stanza,
of the power of this apparently helpless baby.   **223 eyn** eyes.   **226
Typhon** the Egyptian god Typhon was brother of Osiris and killed him:
but snaky twine suggests the giant Typhon or Typhoeus of Greek mythology, human above the waist but serpent below. This serpent-monster
dominates Blake's illustration of the descent of Typhon and the gods into
hell.   **227 godhead true** genuine divinity.   **228 swaddling bands**
infant's clothing: again M is evoking Hercules, who as an infant strangled
two serpents; Christ, still a baby, can subdue the whole company of false
gods.   **229 So when** the false gods are routed by the coming of Christ
as ghosts vanish when the sun's face appears above the eastern sea,
between the dawn clouds that are likened to curtains round a four-
poster bed: the solidity of the simile emphasizes the insubstantiality of
the fleeing spirits.

Each fettered ghost slips to his several grave,
And the yellow-skirted fays,   235
Fly after the night-steeds, leaving their moon-loved maze.

XXVII

But see the virgin blest,
Hath laid her babe to rest.
  Time is our tedious song should here have ending:
Heaven's youngest-teemèd star,   240
Hath fixed her polished car,
  Her sleeping Lord with handmaid lamp attending:
And all about the courtly stable,
Bright-harnessed angels sit in order serviceable.

Appendix to The nativity ode

JOHN BROADBENT

Structure of the ode

The right-hand column (see p. 28) cites the first time some of the
recurrent words and concepts occur. It is worth tracing some of
them, with the question of their meaning or function in mind. What,

234 several separate.   **235 fays** fairies. John Selden, in his
study of gods, 1617, connected them with the classical goddesses
of childbirth; this birth ends their sway.   **236 night-steeds** the horses
of night's chariot.   **maze** winding dance, or fairy ring.   **237 But
see** from this eerie pageant of idols we are returned to a scene of
tranquillity and splendour, as at the poem's opening; the baby is sleeping,
while angels keep watch. Even here our gaze does not come to rest on
mother and child; our mind's eye must take in the night sky, the star,
and the angels. In Blake's illustration of the shepherds and the angels,
the stable, although it is at the centre of the picture, is tiny; in the fore-
ground the shepherds gaze upwards, directing our gaze too to the radiant
angels above.   **240 youngest-teemèd** most newly born. The new
star has stopped above the stable, waiting with the service of her light
like a handmaid.   **241 car** chariot.   **243 courtly stable** in earthly
terms nowhere could be more lowly: but it houses Christ, it is his court.
244 harnessed armoured. **serviceable** ready to serve.

for instance, is the place of shame in the poem? of snakes, dragons, tails? of the sun? The two chief symbolic powers are light and music; but both are varied. Consider the visual and aural characteristics of XIX–XXVI, as compared with IX–XV (which is where in various senses the poem's centre lies). Other significant structural features: times and seasons; globes; vertical–horizontal; fire. See Leach under *Commentaries on incarnation* below.

I–IV	*Proem*	4 × 7 = one lunar month?
	Hymn	27 octaves, or weeks of eternity?
I–II	winter	wild sun quiet shame air
III–V	Peace	green wing kings arm birds
	1st descent	ocean clouds sphere
VI–VII	light	stars Lucifer
	delayed dawn	
VIII	shepherds	Pan
IX–XIII	harmony	moon angels
XII	creation	sons of morning
	line 108 (union) or 122 (hinges) is the numerical middle of the poem	
XIV–XV	golden age	snake?
	Truth, Justice, Mercy hell heaven rainbow	
	2nd descent	
XVI–XVIII	discord	
XVI	Crucifixion	trump
XVII	Last Judgement	
XVIII	binding of Satan	dragon's tail
XIX–XXVI	dismissal of pagan gods	
XIX–XX	Greece	voices trees twilight
XXI	Rome	earth stone
XXII–XXIII	Palestine	horn
XXIV–XXV	Egypt	cymbals brutish grass
XXVI	England	graves
XXVII	conclusion	laid rest time

Values

In Eliot's *Journey of the Magi* the wise men admit

> There were times we regretted
> The summer palaces on slopes, the terraces,
> And the silken girls bringing sherbet.

There are intimations of naturalistic kinds of redemption – an old white horse, a fertile valley, vine-leaves and wine; but these are vain – 'there was no information, and so we continued'. There are some obvious parallels in Milton's ode – the divine

Egyptian bull in XXIV, for instance; the references to shame and sin. But what are the ode's great positives and negatives? And, if the centre is agreed to lie in the area IX–XV, what does that mean about the ode's 'placing' and valuation of the birth? It is sometimes said that the heroic quality of this ode necessarily excludes the intimacy of mother and child; then what sort of heroism is it? (There is a 17th-century painting, by Poussin, called *The nurture of Zeus*: it shows the king of gods as a naked baby lying with his rump between a woman's thighs and his head between the hindlegs of a nanny-goat, which is suckling him.)

Verse

There are some emphatic organlike passages where you can almost hear the finger or foot pressing down – 'This IS the MONTH ... SEE HOW from FAR ...' Against these, consider many lines of musical humility:

> He laid aside; and here with us to be
>
> Nature in awe to him
>
> Edged with poplar pale

Short lines can be powerful though:

> The hookèd chariot stood
>
> The helmèd cherubim

Consider the different modes of the final alexandrine in the hymn. The most difficult feature of the poem for most readers is the apparent naiveté, a clinking of rhythm and rhyme:

> Only with speeches fair
> She woos the gentle air
>
> With such a horrid clang
> As on Mount Sinai rang

They suggest a quattrocento or even medieval brightness and sharp outline. This is related to the definiteness of the poem: 'The oracles are dumb ... Nor can he be at rest ... Hath fixed her polished car'.

Carols

A carol is a poem for singing (and often dancing) which has a refrain. More loosely it is any song for Christmas (or Easter or other Christian festival). Most strict carols date from a hundred years either side of about 1450; no doubt many of them are versions of pre-Christian rites of the winter solstice. The best collection is Elizabeth Poston's *Penguin book of Christmas carols* 1965 (international) and *Second Penguin book* 1970 (carols of the USA), both with notes and music. *A selection of carols* ed. R. L. Greene 1962 (words only) consists wholly of carols in the strict sense; *Early English carols* ed. R. H. Robbins 1961 gives 30 of them with music for unaccompanied voices. The *Oxford book of carols* provides the largest selection.

Many of the 'carols' we know best were written in the 19th century and express a particular ethos about birth, children, animals, the poor, and God. Consider the differences in ethos between these two:

> And through all his wondrous childhood
>   He would honour and obey,
> Love and watch the lowly maiden
>   In whose gentle arms He lay;
> Christian children all must be
> Mild, obedient, good as He . . .

MRS C. F. ALEXANDER 1823–95 *Once in royal David's city*

> In the broom-cupboard, swaddled in dusters,
> Susan enacts the nativity, kneels by
> Stove-polish tins and mechanical sweepers,
> Clear-voices a carol, tuneful, but shapeless,
> Returning to no repeated form – endless, like
> Streams to the end of the landfall of childhood . . .

DAVID HOLBROOK *Christ in the cupboard* in his *Imaginings*
Putnam 1960

Traditions and themes of nativity poems

This section is concerned more, though, with the serious and individual poems which have been written about the nativity, so variously as to set up a series of emphases or traditions. These poems were begun by Aurelius Clemens Prudentius, a judge who was born in Spain AD 348. Prudentius was the first Christian poet of any note; he wrote in Latin, of course. His main nativity poems are *Kalendas ianuarius* and *Hymnus epiphaniae*. His poems (together with some much duller renaissance Latin poems)

contain almost all the traditions, as does this by Edwin Muir
from his *One foot in Eden*:

The Christmas

Now Christmas comes. The menial earth
Lays by its worn and sweaty gear
And strews with emblems of rebirth
The burial of the solar year.

Midnight strikes. One star awake
Watches the Mother and the Child
Who with his little hands will make
Spring blossom in the winter wild.

This star that left the ordered throng
Caused no confusion in the night,
Nor strayed to prove his brothers wrong,
But told that all the stars were right.

. . . .

Accomplishing the miracle,
The marriage feast of heaven and earth,
Of which on earth we cannot tell
Save in such words: a Death, a Birth.

The seasons and vegetation. The winter solstice is a death and a
birth, a standstill (longest night) and a breakthrough. The
Roman army worshipped a former Persian god, Mithras, as a
sacrificial bull and as *sol invictus*; his festival was 25 December
(which they regarded as the winter solstice); there are remains of
Mithraism in London.

He shall come down like rain upon the mown grass: as showers that
water the earth. *Psalm* lxxii

Dark and dull night, fly hence away
And give the honour to this day
That sees December turned to May.

. . . . .

Why does the chilling winter's morn
Smile like a field beset with corn?
Or smell like to a mead new-shorn
Thus on the sudden? Come and see

The cause why things thus fragrant be:
'Tis he is born whose quickening birth
Gives life and lustre, public mirth
To heaven and the under-earth.

We see him come and know him ours
Who, with his sunshine and his showers,
Turns all the patient ground to flowers . . .

HERRICK *A Christmas carol sung to the King in the presence at Whitehall.
The musical part was composed by Mr Henry Lawes*

That day which made immensity become
A little one; which printed goodly May
On pale December's face; which drew the sun
Of paradise into a bud; the day
    Which shrunk eternity into a span
      Of time, heaven into earth, God into man.

JOSEPH BEAUMONT Psyche 1648

The ox knoweth his owner, and the ass his master's crib . . . The beast
of the field shall honour me, the dragons and the owls . . . the mountains
and the hills shall break forth before you into singing, and all the trees
of the field shall clap their hands . . . and there shall come a rod out of
the stem of Jesse, and a Branch shall grow out of his roots . . .

Isaiah i 3, xliii 20, lv 12, xi

I sing of a maiden
    That is makëless;   [immaculate
King of all kinges
    To her son she ches.

He came also stillë
    There his moder was,
As dew in Aprille
    That fallyt on the grass;

He came also stillë
    To his moderës bower
As dew in Aprille
    That fallyt on the flower;

He came also stillë
    There his moder lay
As dew in Aprille
    That fallyt on the spray.

Moder and maiden
    Was never none but she;
Well may such a lady
    Goddës moder be.

15th-century carol

Þan myȝt þe mylde may singe,   [maiden þ = th
    Ysaye, þe woord of þee:
Þou seydest a yerd schulde sprynge   [stalk
    Oute of þe rote of jentill Jesse,
And schulde floure with florisschyng,
    With primeroses greet plente;
Into þe croppe schulde come a Kyng   [top
    Þat is a Lord of power and pyte –
My swete Sone I see!

I am þe yerde, þou art þe Flour!
My Brid is borne by beest in boure;   [bird, darling
My Primerose, my Paramour,   [lover
   With love I lulle þee.

At Cristemasse, mayde Mary

Sexuality

Tomorrow shall be my dancing day;
  I would my true love did so chance
To see the legend of my play,
   To call my true love to dance.
    Sing O my love, O my love, my love, my love;
    This have I done for my true love.
Then was I born of a virgin pure,
  Of her I took fleshly substance;
Thus was I knit to man's nature
   To call my true love to my dance.
In a manger laid and wrapped I was,
  So very poor, this was my chance,
Betwixt an ox and a silly poor ass
   To call my love to my dance.   Carol

Wit. The themes of seasonal and sexual revival were taken up by
the metaphysical poets of the earlier 17th century and worked into
characteristically witty patterns; but the wit is justified by the
paradox at the heart of the incarnation: 'The Word was made
flesh'. Beaumont's poem above is a good example; here are
others:

  . . . Ere by the spheres time was created, thou   [Mary
  Wast in his mind who is thy son, and brother;
  Whom thou conceiv'st, conceived; yea, thou art now
  Thy Maker's maker and thy Father's mother;
  Thou hast light in dark; and shut'st in little room
  Immensity, cloistered in thy dear womb.

DONNE *Annunciation*, part of his sequence of holy sonnets *La corona*

When Ben Jonson walked to Scotland in 1618 he visited William
Drummond of Hawthornden. Drummond published his own
Nativity in 1630:

Run, shepherds, run, where Bethlehem blest appears,
  We bring the best of news, be not dismayed:
A Saviour there is born, more old than years,
  Amidst heaven's rolling heights this earth who stayed;
  In a poor cottage inned, a virgin Maid,
A weakling, did him bear who all upbears;
  This is he, poorly swaddled, in a manger laid,
To whom too narrow swaddlings are our spheres.

Run, shepherds, run, and solemnize his birth,
  This is the night – no, day grown great with bliss,
  In which the power of Satan broken is;
In heaven be glory, peace unto the earth.
  Thus singing through the air the angels swam,
  And cope of stars re-echoèd the same

Mysticism. This poem is by Robert Southwell, a Roman catholic priest who was arrested on his way to celebrate mass in 1592, tortured, kept in prison for three years, and executed. He wrote it in prison.

The burning Babe

As I in hoary winter's night stood shivering in the snow,
Surprised I was with sudden heat which made my heart to glow;
And lifting up a fearful eye to view what fire was near,
A pretty Babe all burning bright did in the air appear;
Who, scorched with excessive heat, such floods of tears did shed,
As though his floods should quench his flames which with his tears
    were fed.
'Alas!' quoth he, 'but newly born in fiery heats I fry,
Yet none approach to warm their hearts or feel my fire but I.
My faultless breast the furnace is, the fuel wounding thorns;
Love is the fire, and sighs the smoke, the ashes shame and
    scorns;
The fuel justice layeth on, and mercy blows the coals.
The metal in this furnace wrought are men's defiled souls:
For which, as now on fire I am to work them to their good,
So I will I melt into a bath to wash them in my blood.'
With this he vanished out of sight and swiftly shrunk away,
And straight I called unto mind that it was Christmas day.

The Golden Age. Here is part of Ben Jonson's masque *The Golden Age restored*, performed at court 1615; it can be looked at under the heading of 'values' also.

Pallas Athene [goddess of wisdom]

> Descend, you long long wished and wanted pair,
> And as your softer times divide the air
> So shake all clouds off with your golden hair;
> For Spite is spent; the Iron Age is fled,
> And with her power on earth her name is dead.

[Astraea [Justice] and the Golden Age descending with a song . . .
the first dance . . . then]

Pallas Already do not all things smile?

Astraea But when they have enjoyed a while
  The Age's quickening power –

Golden Age That every thought a seed doth bring
  And every look a plant doth spring
  And every breath a flower –

Astraea Then earth unploughed shall yield her crop,
  Pure honey from the oak shall drop,
  The fountain shall run milk;
  The thistle shall the lily bear
  And every bramble roses wear
  And every worm make silk . . .

Crashaw. The English poems most like Milton's ode are by Richard Crashaw. Crashaw (1612–49) was the only son of a puritan minister and poet, but he sided with the king in the civil war, became a Roman catholic and went to Rome. What they have in common is 'the baroque': a style which conspicuously celebrates sensation, energy, and power; and which exhibits a strong sense of the 'European', and hence of the Latinate or Roman. It suited Milton temperamentally though it was also the style of the counter-reformation. Crashaw translated part of *Sospetto d'Herode*, an Italian epic on the massacre of the innocents:

> Below the bottom of the great abyss,
> There where one centre reconciles all things,
> The world's profound heart pants. There placed is
> Mischief's old master; close about him clings
> A curled knot of embracing snakes that kiss
> His correspondent cheeks; these loathsome strings
>   Hold the perverse prince in eternal ties
>   Fast bound, since first he forfeited the skies.

It is through Satan's eyes that we see the nativity:

> He saw a threefold sun with rich increase
> Make proud the ruby portals of the east;
> He saw the temple sacred to sweet peace
> Adore her prince's birth flat on her breast;
> He saw the falling idols all confess
> A coming deity . . .

Satan is appalled

> That the great angel-blinding light should shrink
> His blaze to shine in a poor shepherd's eye;
> That the unmeasured God so low should sink
> As prisoner in a few poor rags to lie;
> That from his mother's breast he milk should drink
> Who feeds with nectar heaven's fair family;
>   That a vile manger his low bed should prove
>   Who in a throne of stars thunders above.

35

That he whom the sun serves should faintly peep
Through clouds of infant flesh; that he, the old
Eternal Word, should be a child, and weep;
That he who made the fire should fear the cold;
That heaven's high majesty his court should keep
In a clay cottage by each blast controlled;
    That glory's self should serve our griefs and fears,
    And free eternity submit to years.

That was published in 1648. Here are some extracts from *In the holy nativity of our Lord God : a hymn sung as by the shepherds*:

> *Tityrus* [a shepherd]
>   Poor world (said I) what wilt thou do
> To entertain this starry stranger?
>   Is this the best thou canst bestow –
> A cold and not too cleanly manger?
>   Contend, the powers of heaven of earth,
>   To fit a bed for this huge birth.
>
> *Shepherds* Contend, &c.
>
> *Tityrus* I saw the curled drops, soft and slow,
>   Come hovering o'er the place's head,
>   Offering their whitest sheets of snow
>   To furnish the fair infant's bed.
>   Forbear, said I: be not too bold;
>   Your fleece is white but 'tis too cold.
>
> *Shepherds* Forbear &c.
>
> *Tityrus* I saw the obsequious seraphim
>   Their rosy fleece of fire bestow . . .

Crashaw's *In the glorious epiphany of Our Lord God, a hymn sung as by the Three Kings* is an essay on the decline of sunworship as the greater Son appears, particularly celebrated by the Three Kings as astronomers.

In relation to Crashaw, consider the diction and tone of Milton's Mary in *Paradise regained* II 66:

> O what avails me now that honour high
> To have conceived of God, or that salute
> 'Hail highly favoured, among women blest'?
> While I to sorrows am no less advanced,
> And fears as eminent, above the lot
> Of other women, by the birth I bore,
> In such a season born when scarce a shed
> Could be obtained to shelter him or me
> From the bleak air; a stable was our warmth,
> A manger his, yet soon enforced to fly

Thence into Egypt, till the murderous king
Were dead, who sought his life, and missing filled
With infant blood the streets of Bethlehem.

Christmas bells. Christmas is a birthday. Milton's was on
9 December and he was careful to date his composition 1629.

> The time draws near the birth of Christ:
>   The moon is hid; the night is still;
>   The Christmas bells from hill to hill
> Answer each other in the mist.
>
> Four voices of four hamlets round,
>   From far and near, on mead and moor,
>   Swell out and fail, as if a door
> Were shut between me and the sound:
>
> Each voice four changes on the wind,
>   That now dilate, and now decrease,
>   Peace and goodwill, goodwill and peace,
> Peace and goodwill, to all mankind.
>
> This year I slept and woke with pain,
>   I almost wish'd no more to wake,
>   And that my hold on life would break
> Before I heard those bells again:
>
> But they my troubled spirit rule,
>   For they controlled me when a boy;
>   They bring me sorrow touched with joy,
> The merry merry bells of Yule.

TENNYSON from In memoriam (1850)

Incarnation. Two poems which need to be looked at in full for
consideration of how the birth of Christ relates to his crucifixion
are Yeats's *The Magi* and Edwin Muir's *The incarnate one* (1956).
In another poem, *The second coming*, Yeats raises the question of
what was born at the nativity – or what else might be born.
'And what rough beast, its hour come round at last, Slouches
towards Bethlehem to be born?' What is the meaning, then, of a
myth in which a woman gives birth to a baby god? what is its
function for men? It is a peculiarity of Christendom that while
many mythologies have stories of gods inseminating women –
Zeus as a swan with Leda, as a bull with Europa – and even of
animals inseminating women (the bull with Pasiphäe), the
Christian emphasis has been not on the union of god with woman,
the act of conception, but the event of birth, the entry of the god
into manhood. It is also a peculiarity of Christianity that the god

eventually returns whence he came. Eliot touches on some of these issues in *The journey of the Magi* but his meditation on the incarnation is in *The dry Salvàges* (*Four Quartets* Faber 1944):

> to apprehend
> The point of intersection of the timeless
> With time, is an occupation for the saint
>
> . . . . .
>
> For most of us, there is only the unattended
> Moment, the moment in and out of time
>
> . . . .
>
> The hint half guessed, the gift half understood, is Incarnation.
> Here the impossible union
> Of spheres of existence is actual,
> Here the past and future
> Are conquered, and reconciled . . .

Dismissal of the gods. Swinburne regretted the historical dismissal of the pagan gods when Constantine (AD 306–37) made Christianity the official religion of the Roman Empire:

> ### Vicisti, Galilæe
>
> Wilt thou yet take all, Galilean? but these thou shalt not take,
> The laurel, the palm and the pæan, the breast of the nymph in the brake;
> Breasts more soft than a dove's, that tremble with tenderer breath;
> And all the wings of the Loves, and all the joy before death . . .
>
> *Hymn to Proserpine*

Christopher Smart's *Nativity hymn* grafts this theme onto the seasons and the paradoxes:

> Where is this stupendous stranger,
>   Swains of Solyma, advise,
> Lead me to my Master's manger,
>   Shew me where my Saviour lies?
>
> O most mighty! O MOST holy!
>   Far beyond the seraph's thought,
> Art thou then so mean and lowly
>   As unheeded prophets taught?
>
> O the magnitude of meekness!
>   Worth from worth immortal sprung;
> O the strength of infant weakness,
>   If eternal is so young!
>
> If so young and thus eternal,
>   Michael tune the shepherd's reed,
> Where the scenes are ever vernal,
>   And the loves be love indeed!

See the God blasphemed and doubted
    In the schools of Greece and Rome;
See the powers of darkness routed,
    Taken at their utmost gloom.

Nature's decorations glisten
    Far above their usual trim;
Birds on box and laurels listen,
    As so near the cherubs hymn.

Boreas now no longer winters
    On the desolated coast;
Oaks no more are riven in splinters
    By the whirlwind and his host.

Spinks and ouzles sing sublimely,
    'We too have a Saviour born!'
Whiter blossoms burst untimely
    On the blest Mosaic thorn.

Gold all-bounteous, all-creative,
    Whom no ills from good dissuade,
Is incarnate, and a native
    Of the very world he made.   1765

Other poems. Browning *Christmas Eve* (doctrinal); Hardy *The oxen*; Clement Paman *On Christmas Day to my heart* 1660; William Austin *All this night shrill chanticleer* before 1626; William Dunbar *On the nativity of Christ* (c. 1465–c. 1530); York mystery plays (which Milton knew).

Commentaries on incarnation, virgin birth, epiphany

'God is manifested in the flesh' [*I Timothy* iii] . . . In what flesh? What, in the pride and beauty of our nature? No: but in the most disgraceful estate of it that might be. . . The God whom 'the heavens and the heaven of heavens cannot contain' in a little child's flesh not a span long; and that flesh of a child not very well conditioned, as you may read in the 16th of Ezekiel.

So today, but after, much worse: today, in the flesh of a poor babe crying in the cratch, *in medio animalium*; after, in the rent and torn flesh of a condemned person hanging on the Cross, *in medio latronum*, in the midst of other manner persons than Moses and Elias.

LANCELOT ANDREWES, 'sermon preached before the King's majesty at Whitehall on Thursday 25 December 1607' [Andrewes at one time held a post at St Giles's, Cripplegate, where Milton and his father are buried; he became Bishop of Winchester and subject of an essay by T. S. Eliot.]

In this their coming we consider: (1) First, the distance of the place they came from. It was not hard by, as the shepherds' (but a step to Bethlehem over the fields): this was riding many a hundred miles, and cost them

39

many a day's journey. (2) Secondly, we consider the way that they came, if it be pleasant or plain and easy; for if it be, it is so much the better. (i) This was nothing pleasant, for, through deserts: all the way waste and desolate; (ii) nor, secondly, easy either: for over rocks and crags of both Arabies (specially Petraea) their journey lay. (3) Yet if safe – but it was not, but exceeding dangerous, as lying through the midst of the 'black tents of Kedar', a nation of thieves and cut-throats; to pass over the hills of robbers, infamous then and infamous to this day; no passing, without great troop or convoy. (4) Last, we consider the time of their coming, the season of the year. It was no summer progress. A cold coming they had of it, at this time of the year; just the worst time of the year to take a journey, and specially a long journey, in: the ways deep, the weather sharp, the days short, the sun farthest off *in solstitio brumali*, the very dead of winter.

LANCELOT ANDREWES 1622

Binary oppositions are intrinsic to the process of human thought . . . Religion seeks to deny the binary link between the two words [*alive* and *dead*]; it does this by creating the mystical idea of 'another world'. . . The attributes of this other world are necessarily those which are not of this world; imperfection here is balanced by perfection there. But this logical ordering of ideas has a disconcerting consequence – God comes to belong to the other world. The central 'problem' of religion is then to re-establish some kind of bridge between Man and God.

   This pattern is built into the structure of every mythical system; the myth first discriminates between gods and men and then becomes preoccupied with the relations and intermediaries which link men and gods together . . . So too with sex relations. Every human society has rules of incest and exogamy . . . But here again we are immediately led into paradox. How was it in the beginning?. . . In every myth system we will find a persistent sequence of binary discriminations as between human/ superhuman, mortal/immortal, male/female, legitimate/illegitimate, good/ bad . . . followed by a 'mediation' of the paired categories thus distinguished. 'Mediation' (in this sense) is always achieved by introducing a third category which is 'abnormal' or 'anomalous'. . . Thus myths are full of fabulous monsters, incarnate gods, virgin mothers. This middle ground is abnormal, non-natural, holy. It is typically the focus of all taboo and ritual observance.

EDMUND LEACH *Genesis as myth* 1962 repr in *Genesis as myth and other essays* Cape 1969

If we studied other examples of Virgin Birth [besides Indian, Australian, etc.] we should meet with the same variables in new combinations. We should also meet with new variables. For instance, in the Attis/Adonis mythology . . . there is a major reversal. The god is female and the recognized *genitor* a human being, but many of the other elements are similar to the Indian and Christian cases . . . themes of descent, filiation and sexual and/or marital alliance between gods and humans necessarily have basic relevance for the symbolization of time and for our topographical apprehension of the other world . . . The crux is this. From many sources we learn of legends, traditions, ritual practices which seem to imply a belief that women may sometimes be made pregnant by means other than insemination by a human male. The simplest way of 'explaining' such a belief is to say that it is due to the ignorance of the believer ... An alternative way ... is to say that it is a species of religious dogma ... Christians who say that they 'believe' in the doctrine of the Virgin Birth ... are not ordinarily arguing from a position of ignorance; on the contrary these are doctrines which are compatible with positions of extreme philosophical sophistication ... The problem ... lies at the core of speculative philosophy. What is the difference between the physical and the metaphysical? One way of viewing the matter is to equate the not-now with the other world; in that case past and future coalesce as attributes of the other in contrast to the present which is the factual experience of real life. The relationship between the 'here-now' and the 'other' can then be seen as one of *descent*. My ancestors belong to the 'other' category and so do my descendants. Only *I* am in the here and the now ... But the disjunction of the two worlds is not enough, there must also be continuity and mediation. Crosscutting the idea that impotent men are the descendants of potent gods we have the incestuous dogma that gods and men may establish sexual connection. Dogmas of virgin birth and of the irrelevance of human male sexuality appear as by-products of such a theology.

EDMUND LEACH Virgin birth 1966 repr in ibid

In the light of those extracts from Leach you might consider the place in the ode, and in the myth generally, of (a) anomalous beings (eg seraphim, floating birds . . .), and (b) transactions across boundaries of space-time (eg floating birds, solstice, spring-in-winter) and efforts to control them (eg fixed star, stanza xii, 'In straiter limits bound').

Suppose the event true. Supposing there were a star
Steered over a barn, and a frail avatar
Labour thrust through her pelvis, upside down, angel seed
Or virgin cell division become real, prompted by human need –

Who Made All become budded cauled growth
Roped to a belly wall; a woman's breath
Reddens His blood; a woman's lilting voice
Who Knows All hears confined, glad of such half-heard grace,

Glad of a man's delivering hand, blunt bite of teeth,
Nose-freeing finger, slap to make bawl, make breathe –
Ah! Jesus lives! And is straight put to breast,
Glad of colostrum, comfort, coarse-twisted shawl, and rest.

.   .   .   .

Suppose so. Shall we be glad that He was born
Of our imagination, or our flesh? Forlorn
At the age of thirty-four what firmed so in mould
Of His mother's crook of arm, dies, clotted, cold,

.   .   .   .

What can we make of it? Human love rears, but hate
Inevitably counterblights? Everlasting rewards await
The victims of our inability to live and let live?
Await us too, for being true imperfection? Can we believe

Atonement, grace (does it matter?) those subjects of faction
Between church and church? Is it not merely for our self-satisfaction
We say God cropped Himself like fatstock for oblate destruction,
While each child's raised to rood still from the angelic first seduction?

DAVID HOLBROOK *Doubts about Messiah* in *Imaginings* Putnam 1960

Commentaries on the ode

The 'Ode' begins with an induction in which time is negated so that the
discord between the past and the present, which we plainly understand,
may be altered into a concord of eternity, or into an essence of time,
which is timelessness. To this end the poem is carefully dated. The
title and the induction inform us that it was written in the small hours
of December 25, 1629... This is a matter that Milton does not want the
reader to miss because he is about to invent the fable that this fact is
untrue, that the real time is the last hour of the pre-Christian era and
that he is himself present in a land of palms and snow, a seventeenth
century interloper between the events of the Nativity and the Epiphany.
This is the temporal conflict, but what Milton does is to reconcile it by
pressing towards the eternal consequences of the Incarnation. By annul-
ling the chronology of this event, he extracted the everlasting from the
conflict between the past and the present.

DON CAMERON ALLEN *The harmonious vision* © The Johns Hopkins
University Press Baltimore 1970

In connection with Milton's innumerable suggestions, often barely caught
in an echoed cadence or a connotative linking, we should emphasize one
important way in which such uses were nourished and made powerful:
the Scriptural lections for the season. For the *life* of symbols is very dependent on their being constantly *met*, and their *depth* is very dependent
on constant re-use in varied *contexts*. Through five or more years of
school and seven years of university we know exactly what Scriptural
images Milton heard read, daily, December after December, and even the
reader (now rare) to whom for similar reasons these large bodies of material are familiar to the point of rote-memory will experience surprise if
he reads with daily rigor the full seventeenth-century Calendar. Not
exactly source-study, this concerns the apprehension of symbolic force,
by Milton and ourselves; whole chapters count, not 'parallel passages',
as the mere reminders which follow will indicate. The reading of Isaiah
complete began November 23 and continued through December; the
familiar Advent Sunday lessons (Isa. i, ii, v, xxiv, xxv, xxvi, xxx, xxxii)
are but a few among the many showing the unceasing stress on *peace* and
light (uncountable references like those to the light of the sun that shall be
sevenfold in the day that the Lord bindeth up the breach of his people;
the moon shall be confounded and the sun ashamed), so also the December second lessons (Heb.; Peter; 1, 2, 3 John; also of course the Epistles,

Gospels and collects for the season). Our peace is the theme of Isaiah lvii, lix (December 23, 24) and the theme is put in terms of Light, as we are so familiar with it in the Christmas lessons (Isa. ix: the people that walked in darkness have seen a great light . . . the Prince of Peace; and Luke ii), and in the Christmas Eve lesson from Isaiah lx (Arise, shine . . . The sun shall be no more thy light . . . but the Lord . . . Thy sun shall no more go down). So also St. John's Day, December 27 (Rev. i; xxii: and they need no candle, neither light of the sun . . . I am the bright and morning star), and Innocents' Day, December 28 (Jer. xxxi).

ROSEMOND TUVE *Images and themes in five poems by Milton* Harvard University Press Cambridge Mass. 1957

Milton, faced with the rude fact of a god being born, is confused and falls . . . into the worst kind of imagery – personification, which is extremely figurative but not in the least natural . . . what is the nexus between the defeated fear and lust, and the victorious peace and harmony? It is not the babe in the stable. It seems intended to be . . . the salvific *policy* implicit in the proem and in stanzas xv–xviii . . . But this theoretical connection is not felt in the hymn so strongly as the two climaxes of the greater sun and the dragon . . . These are the poem's hinges. Symbolizing the conquest by hard-edged right reason of the soft dim liquid allures of passion, they make the poem Miltonic . . . the same dark illusions are defeated in *Comus*, the same weltering waves and tangled hair of nymphs are transcended in *Lycidas*, the same mystical rays of solid light dazzle error in the prose and *Paradise Lost*, the same gigantic force ruins idolatry in *Samson* . . . What, consistently, would be the concomitants of a life whose energies were directed as they symbolically are in this poem?

J. B. BROADBENT in *The living Milton* Routledge and Kegan Paul 1960

Resources

Editions and criticism

The most helpful editions of *Nativity* are by Verity in the old Pitt Press series; Isabel MacCaffrey in Signet (*Samson . . . and . . . shorter poems* 1956); and F. T. Prince in *Milton: Comus and other poems* (Oxford 1968). The effective criticism of the poem is small in quantity but contained (except for G. Wilson Knight's) in essays of a very demanding kind:

ALLEN, DON CAMERON 'The higher compromise' in his *Harmonious vision* Baltimore 1970.

BARKER, ARTHUR 'The pattern of M's Nativity Ode' *University of Toronto Quarterly* X 1941.

BROADBENT, J. B. 'The Nativity Ode' in *The living M* ed F. Kermode 1960.

COOK, ALBERT S. 'Notes on M's Ode' *Transactions of the Connecticut Academy of Arts and Science* XV 1909. The ideal annotator.

KNIGHT, G. WILSON 'The frozen labyrinth: an essay on M's poetry' in his *The burning oracle* Oxford 1939.

MADDISON, CAROL *Apollo and the Nine : a history of the ode* 1960.
ROSS, MALCOLM M. 'M and the protestant aesthetic: the early poems'
University of Toronto Quarterly XVII 1948.
TUVE, ROSEMOND 'The *Hymn* . . .' in her *Images and themes in five
poems by M* Cambridge, Mass. 1957. Liturgy, iconography, theology.

Music, speech, drama

See 'Carols' and 'Traditions and themes' above. Some of the poems
cited there are read by Robert Dona in *Poems at Christmas* Argo RG192.
One or two incidental poems that link with Christmas are available for
singing, such as *The prayer of the donkey* from *Prayers from the ark*, and
The camel from *The beasts' choir*, both by Carmen Bernos de Gasztold
trans. Rumer Godden 1967.

Heinrich Schutz 1585–1672 *Christmas oratorio*; Purcell Christmas
anthems; Handel *Messiah*, and *Samson* which includes lines from the
Ode; Archangelo Corelli 1653–1713 *Christmas concerto*; J. S. Bach
Christmas oratorio and *Magnificat* for the Christmas vespers (original
version). More recently, Gordon Jacob *The newborn king* cantata; Malcolm Arnold *Song of Simeon* cantata; Vaughan Williams *The first nowell*
choral nativity play, *This day* cantata, *Fantasia on Christmas carols*;
Britten *Ceremony of carols*. Argo's catalogues list various programmes of
Christmas material.

To grasp the ritual structure of the nativity, go to the advent and
Christmas Eve carol services of a great church such as King's College
Chapel, Cambridge, and collect their programmes (they vary slightly
from year to year and church to church).

Art

The iconography is so rich that the first act must be to ask why? Distinguish between the parts of the myth, and their rituals – annunciation,
annunciation to the shepherds, nativity, adoration of the shepherds,
adoration of the magi, flight into Egypt. Select an area, or a collection, for
study. Collections run from Christmas cards (in which case the issue is
why those scenes for greeting?) to the National Gallery, London, which
has a large number of paintings on these themes, and holds a special
exhibition of some of them at Christmas with an illustrated booklet
The Christmas story. The standard art textbooks also contain plenty of
material, notably Berenson *Italian painters of the renaissance* 1961 repr
Penguin 1964 and Plumb ed. *The Horizon book of the renaissance* 1952.

Nativity art tends to polarize at the artificial, majestic, political,
mystical (eg Gentile de Fabriano *Adoration of the kings*; Botticelli) or
simple, natural (Bruegel's *Adoration of the magi* satirizes its own pomp).
With some, notably Piero della Francesca and Poussin, it is as though
the painting were dipolar.

For illustrations see the list of resources in *PL : introduction* in this
series. The most important are Blake's, reproduced in *On the morning
of Christ's nativity* ed. G. Keynes Cambridge 1923.

The passion

Edited by DAVID AERS

Introduction

Luke's gospel claims 'it behoved Christ to suffer' (xxiv) and the
passion narrative is the account of his suffering, culminating in
the crucifixion (see also *Matthew* xxvii, *John* xviii). Meditation on
the passion focussed on the details of Christ's human suffering
in an attempt to stir men to passionate involvement in the situation which revealed God's love for man and was seen as the
means of redeeming man from death ('Rejoice, inasmuch as ye are
partakers of Christ's sufferings' *1 Peter* iv).

Milton shows a tendency to fuse Christ's life, and his own
response, with nature and the necessity of an impersonal fate
(see lines 5–7, 20). But one of the crucial points about Christ's
'later scenes' is the way he retains spiritual initiative in the face of
the most recalcitrant events (eg *Matthew* xxvi 44 on the Mount
of Olives). The conclusion of the first stanza, which reduces the
context to the cycles of nature, launches this depersonalization of
the crucifixion.

In this connection, the play and disguise images are relevant
(2, 13, 17). They are traditional and common enough models for
exploring the theology of the incarnation and redemption. As
Milton's royalist and anglican contemporary Robert Herrick
wrote:

> The cross shall be thy stage; and thou shalt there
> The spacious field have for thy theatre.
> Thou art that Roscius, that marked-out man,
> That must this day act the tragedian . . .

> *Good Friday : Rex tragicus*

Theologically, however, the model could encourage an ancient
gnostic heresy in which Christ's humanity was only an appearance, his manhood, and hence his suffering, being unreal. It

certainly encourages Milton to maintain a comfortable aesthetic distance from the suffering Servant (the suffering does seem unreal) and helps him avoid any personal involvement in the drama of sin and redemption which is his explicit subject. Rather, he manages to transform the events and theological perspectives to an indulgent melancholy (27–28 and stanza v). When he fancies himself transported to behold a 'holy vision' he again evades the passion and turns to a pleasing meditation on the Ruins of Time (40–2). At *PL* III 476 Milton was to mock those pilgrims who 'strayed so far to seek In Golgotha him dead, who lives in heaven', and he shows great reluctance to follow those pilgrims now.

Having reached the tomb ('Why seek ye the living among the dead?' *Luke* xxiv 5) he manufactures secular conceits of no theological value – to what purpose *are* they? (45–6, 54–6).

C. A. Patrides has shown (*Milton and the Christian tradition* Oxford 1966 chap v) the emphasis on the divine wrath of God in protestant views of the atonement (see *Circumcision*). We can also see it in Bunyan's spiritual autobiography *Grace abounding to the chief of sinners*:

I remember that one day, as I was travelling into the country and musing on the wickedness and blasphemy of my heart, and considering of the enmity that was in me to God, that scripture came in my mind, 'He hath made peace by the blood of his cross', *Col*. i. 20, by which I was made to see both again, and again, and again, that day, that God and my soul were friends by this blood; yea, I saw that the justice of God and my sinful soul, could embrace and kiss each other through this blood: this was a good day to me, I hope I shall not forget it.

Section 115

For 'the blood of his cross' to have the existential significance it does for Bunyan, there must be awareness of 'the enmity that was in me to God', a sense of personal sin and alienation which puts man 'under wrath' (*PL* III 275). Milton mentions this wrath elsewhere and it is central in *PL* III (264ff), but in *The passion* there is no sense of personal 'sin' nor of God's 'wrath': there is no felt *need* for atonement or the passion of Christ. Without emotional and intellectual concentration on these issues it was surely impossible to write an impressive protestant poem on the passion.

One other question should be considered, though not in this brief Introduction: why did Milton publish this poem when 'nothing satisfied' with it?

The passion

I

EREWHILE OF MUSIC, and ethereal mirth,
  Wherewith the stage of air and earth did ring,
  And joyous news of heavenly infant's birth,
My muse with angels did divide to sing:
But headlong joy is ever on the wing,   5
  In wintry solstice like the shortened light
Soon swallowed up in dark and long out-living night.

II

For now to sorrow must I tune my song,
And set my harp to notes of saddest woe,
Which on our dearest Lord did seize ere long,   10
Dangers, and snares, and wrongs, and worse than so,
Which he for us did freely undergo.
  Most perfect hero, tried in heaviest plight
Of labours huge and hard, too hard for human wight.

III

He sovran priest stooping his regal head   15
That dropped with odorous oil down his fair eyes,

1 **Erewhile** recently (ie *Nativity*).   2 **stage** here the 'play' image
begins: see 13–24, and Introduction.   4 **divide to sing** punning on
divide – 'share' (perhaps 'separate' too?) and also perform with 'divi-
sions' – descant.   6 **wintry solstice** December 22 (why the inversion?).
6–7 fear of what Elizabethan Campion calls 'one ever-during night' –
does Milton follow this up?   11 What *is* worse than so? Out of control
already?   14 **wight** man (14–15 hint at Hercules, a figure of Christ: see
Nativity 227–8).   15 Christ traditionally seen as priest (*Genesis* xiv
18–19, *Hebrews* v 6–10, vii): 'Wherefore in all things it behoved him to
be made like unto his brethren, that he might be a merciful and faithful
high priest in things pertaining to God, to make reconciliation for the
sins of the people' (*Hebrews* ii). Christ also traditionally seen as king –
Revelations xvii 14, *Zechariah* ix 9.   16 **oil** Christ is prefigured in the
OT ceremonies – see the consecration of priests in *Exodus* xxix and
Leviticus xvi (the annointed priest 'shall make the atonement').

Poor fleshly tabernacle enterèd,
His starry front low-roofed beneath the skies;
O what a mask was there, what a disguise!
    Yet more; the stroke of death he must abide,   20
Then lies him meekly down fast by his brethren's side.

IV

These latest scenes confine my roving verse,
To this horizon is my Phoebus bound,
His godlike acts, and his temptations fierce,
And former sufferings otherwhere are found;   25
Loud o'er the rest Cremona's trump doth sound;
    Me softer airs befit, and softer strings
Of lute, or viol still, more apt for mournful things.

V

Befriend me night, best patroness of grief,
Over the pole thy thickest mantle throw,   30
And work my flattered fancy to belief,
That heaven and earth are coloured with my woe;
My sorrows are too dark for day to know:
    The leaves should all be black whereon I write,
And letters where my tears have washed a wannish   35
    white.

VI

See see the chariot, and those rushing wheels
That whirled the prophet up at Chebar flood!

17–19 See Introduction, and *Nativity* 1–14.   21 see *Hebrews* ii 16–17.
23 **Phoebus** Apollo, god of sun and poetry. **bound** both meanings relevant.
The passion and crucifixion not 'godlike' and Milton finding himself in
fetters *says* so! What *is* congenial to him? (See *Vacation Exercise* 29ff,
Nativity.) Phoebus *also* figures Christ: Milton would rather he too were
not bound to this horizon.   26 **Cremona's trump** Vida (1485–1566)
born in Cremona wrote Latin *Christiad* with Christ as 'heros'.   27–8
And *Nativity* written recently? **still** quiet.   29–35 What kind of grief
here? He doesn't believe 'heaven and earth' are affected by his woe, but
hopes his deceived (**flattered**) fancy will be convinced that they are (or,
could he imply his fancy is beguiled in *not* believing this?): the supposed
object of his woe seems of no concern.   34–5 !!   38–42 See host of

My spirit some transporting cherub feels,
To bear me where the towers of Salem stood,
Once glorious towers, now sunk in guiltless blood;   40
　　There doth my soul in holy vision sit
In pensive trance, and anguish, and ecstatic fit.

VII

Mine eye hath found that sad sepulchral rock
That was the casket of heaven's richest store,
And here though grief my feeble hands up-lock,   45
Yet on the softened quarry would I score
My plaining verse as lively as before;
　　For sure so well instructed are my tears,
That they would fitly fall in ordered characters.

VIII

Or should I thence hurried on viewless wing,   50
Take up a weeping on the mountains wild,
The gentle neighbourhood of grove and spring
Would soon unbosom all their echoes mild,
And I (for grief is easily beguiled)
　　Might think the infection of my sorrows loud,   55
Had got a race of mourners on some pregnant cloud.

*This subject the author finding to be above the years he had,
when he wrote it, and nothing satisfied with what was begun,
left it unfinished.*

Easter 1630

17c paintings of visionaries and saints being propelled aloft by cherubs
(eg in A. Blunt *N. Poussin* plates vol, plates 21b, 202, 204, or E. Male
L'art religieux du 17s 1951, chap 4). **Salem** Jerusalem (*Genesis* xiv 18–19
and note to 15 above). **41–2** Milton as baroque (Roman catholic?)
seer in this stanza? What does he actually see in his ecstasy (*fit*) and what
relation to his subject? **43 sepulchral rock** *Luke* xxiii 53, *Matthew*
xxvii 58–61. **46 quarry** rock. **50 viewless** invisible. **52–3** Cf
Nativity 181ff. **54** ! Now the 'pathetic fallacy' sought for in stanza v
is found. **56 got** conceived; cf Ixion's attempt to rape Jove's wife
Hera – he is deceived by a cloud in her shape and on this he begets a race
of centaurs. Does Milton want to exclude this allusion?

49

Appendix to The passion

RICHARD ROLLE d. 1349 *Meditations on the passion*

Efte, swet Jhesu, thy body is like to a dufhouse. For a dufhouse is ful of holys, so is thy body ful of woundes. And as a dove pursued of an hauk, yf she mow cache an hool of hir hous she is siker ynowe, so, swete Jhesu, in temptacion thy woundes ben best refuyt to us. Now, swet Jhesu, I beseche the, in euche temptacion graunt me grace of some hoole of thy woundes, and lykynge to abide in mynd of thy passioun.

Also, swete Jhesu, thi body is like to a honycombe. For hit is in euche a way ful of cellis, and euche celle ful of hony, so that hit may nat be touched without yeld of swetnesse. So, swet Jhesu, thy body is ful of cellys of devocion, that hit may nat be touched of a clene soule without swetnesse of lykynge. Now, swet Jhesu, graunt me grace to touche the with criynge mercy for my synnes, with desyre to gostly contemplacion, with amendynge of my lyf and contynuynge in goodnes, in stody to fulfille thy hestes and delicatly to abyde in mynde of thy passioun.

RICHARD CRASHAW (Roman catholic, d. 1649), four stanzas from *Sancta Maria dolorum*:

> In shade of death's sad TREE
>   Stood Dolefull SHEE.
> Ah SHE! now by none other
> Name to be known, alas, but SORROW'S MOTHER.
>   Before her eyes
> Her's, & the whole world's ioyes
> Hanging all torn she sees; and in his woes
> And Paines, her Pangs & throes.
> Each wound of His, from euery Part,
> All, more at home in her owne heart.

>   What kind of marble than
>   Is that cold man
>   Who can look on & see,
> Nor keep such noble sorrowes company?
>   Sure eu'en from you
>   (My Flints) some drops are due
> To see so many vnkind swords contest
>   So fast for one soft Brest.
> While with a faithfull, mutuall, floud
> Her eyes bleed TEARES, his woundes weep BLOOD.

>   O costly intercourse
>   Of deaths, & worse,
>   Diuided loues. While son & mother
> Discourse alternate wounds to one another;
>   Quick Deaths that grow
>   And gather, as they come & goe:

His Nailes write swords in her, which soon her heart
   Payes back, with more then their own smart
Her SWORDS, still growing with his pain,
Turn SPEARES, & straight come home again.

   O teach those wounds to bleed
   In me; me, so to read
   This book of loues, thus writ
In lines of death, my life may coppy it
   With loyall cares.
   O let me, here, claim shares;
Yeild somthing in thy sad praerogatiue
   (Great Queen of greifes) & giue
Me too my teares; who, though all stone,
Think much that thou shouldst mourn alone . . .

W. B. YEATS (d. 1939) first stanza of *Two songs from a play*
         I saw a staring virgin stand
         Where holy Dionysus died,
         And tear the heart out of his side,
         And lay the heart upon her hand
         And bear that beating heart away;
         And then did all the Muses sing
         Of Magnus Annus at the spring,
         As though God's death were but a play . . .

See also the *Towneley Plays* on the passion, a brilliant medieval
contrast to M's poems; and Rosemary Woolf *English religious
lyrics of the middle ages* 1968 chap 2.

Upon the circumcision

Edited by DAVID AERS

Introduction

In the OT God orders Abraham, 'Ye shall circumcise the flesh of your foreskin; and it shall be a token of the covenant betwixt me and you' (*Genesis* xvii): as all Jews, Christ too was circumcised to signify his membership in the race of Abraham (see *Luke* ii).

Why a poem on the circumcision? When God led Adam and Eve out of their paradise of pleasure they were clothed in skins (*Genesis* iii), and according to Gregory of Nyssa (d. 394) 'the circumcision symbolizes the stripping off of dead skins with which, when we were stripped of life after our disobedience, we clothed ourselves' (quoted in J. Daniélou *The Bible and the liturgy* 1960 p. 274). The OT understanding of circumcision is explained in *Genesis* xvii, where it symbolizes the total commitment of man to God in new life and personal faith. Its *obedient* performance is an act of faith sealing man's covenant with God, as it seals the promises God makes to Abraham.

As Calvin emphasized in his *Institutes of the Christian religion* (IV xvi 3–4), circumcision is the OT forerunner of baptism, both being symbols of 'regeneration', and circumcision figuring 'both forgiveness of sins and the mortification of the flesh'. This connection could point to a rich symbolic matrix: the waters of baptism recall Israel's deliverance from Egyptian slavery towards God's promised land (Egyptian pursuers being drowned in the Red Sea), recall the chaotic primeval waters out of which God created the world (just as through Christ's work and baptism he re-creates the chaotic individual), recall the flood which destroyed the 'sinful' men of the first world, and suggest that these waters are now mysteriously transformed into the waters of life, grace. Furthermore, circumcision took place on the eighth day, and this symbolized the eternal sabbath (see *On time*) which follows the seven ages of the world's history.

These then are the basic areas which answer the question 'why write a poem on the circumcision?': but you should now go on to ask how much, if any, of this traditional material Milton deploys (compare especially Cartwright's and Southwell's poems in the Appendix), and what aspects does he find congenial? What does this suggest about his mind and religious sensibility at this time?

Milton certainly focusses on Christ's *satisfaction* of the covenant which man disobeys, so preparing himself for eternal death (*PL* IX 679–x 909, XII 402): the subjective aspects of regeneration are not central here (see Introduction to *Passion*). The legalistic model used in thinking about Christ's atonement for man was completely normal: for instance, '[Christ] fulfils the law in suffering punishment for us. This punishment has to be paid, and his suffering is a payment for us because he is innocent' (Melancthon *Loci communes* 1555 chap 17 trans. C. L. Manschreck 1965). Or, 'Our acquittal is in this – that the guilt which made us liable to punishment was transferred to the head of the Son of God. We must specially remember this substitution in order that we may not be all our lives in trepidation and anxiety, as if the just vengeance, which the Son of God transferred to himself, were still impending over us' (Calvin *Institutes* II xvi 5).

This is the context in which to place lines 11–28. Although such information prevents us taking Milton's view and expression as unusual or idiosyncratic, it cannot govern our response to the God of 'vengeful wrath', so severely handled by Blake. In his own epic *Jerusalem*, Blake comments on this view of the atonement and forgiveness:

Doth Jehovah forgive a debt only on condition that it shall
Be paid? Doth he forgive pollution only on condition of purity?
That debt is not forgiven! That pollution is not forgiven!
Such is the forgiveness of the gods, the moral virtues of the
Heathen, whose tender mercies are cruelty. But Jehovah's salvation
Is without money and without price, in the continual forgiveness of sins,
In the perpetual mutual sacrifice in great eternity! for behold!
There is none that liveth and sinneth not! And this is the covenant
Of Jehovah: If you forgive one-another, so shall Jehovah forgive you.

Jerusalem LXI 17–25

Upon the circumcision

YE FLAMING powers, and wingèd warriors bright,
    That erst with music, and triumphant song
    First heard by happy watchful shepherds' ear,
So sweetly sung your joy the clouds along
Through the soft silence of the listening night;   5
Now mourn, and if sad share with us to bear
Your fiery essence can distil no tear,
    Burn in your sighs, and borrow
    Seas wept from our deep sorrow,
He who with all heaven's heraldry whilere   10
Entered the world, now bleeds to give us ease;
Alas, how soon our sin
    Sore doth begin
        His infancy to seize!
O more exceeding love or law more just?   15
Just law indeed, but more exceeding love!
For we by rightful doom remédiless
Were lost in death, till he that dwelt above
High throned in secret bliss, for us frail dust
Emptied his glory, even to nakedness;   20
And that great covenant which we still transgress
    Entirely satisfied,
    And the full wrath beside
Of vengeful justice bore for our excess,
And seals obedience first with wounding smart   25
This day, but O ere iong
Huge pangs and strong
    Will pierce more near his heart.

January 1631 or later

1 powers angels.   **2 erst** formerly (see *Nativity*).   **6–9 if . . . sorrow**
if your heavenly nature can't weep (fire and water are mutually exclusive)
then burn in sighs and as the sun sucks up water from earth so draw up
our seas of tears.   **10 heraldry** heraldic pomp (see *Nativity*).   **11–26**
see Introduction.   **20** Literal translation of *Philippians* ii 7.

Appendix to Upon the circumcision

WILLIAM CARTWRIGHT 1611–43 'the most florid and seraphical preacher in the university' of Oxford, royalist and anglican, *On the circumcision : for the king's music* (ie set to music)

Gently, O gently, Father, do not bruise
That tender vine that hath no branch to lose;
Be not too cruel, see the Child doth smile,
His blood was but his Mother's milk erewhile.
   Fear not the pruning of your vine,
   He'll turn your water into wine;
   The Mother's milk that's now his blood,
Hereafter will become her food.
'Tis done; so doth the balsam tree endure
The cruel wounds of those whom it must cure.
   'Tis but the passion's essay: this young loss
   Only prelúdes unto his riper cross.
Avert, good heaven, avert that fate
To so much beauty so much hate.
   Where so great good is meant
   The blood's not lost, but spent.
Thus princes feel what people do amiss;
The swelling's ours, although the lancing his.
   When ye fair heavens white food bled,
   The rose, say they, from thence grew red,
   O then what more miraculous good,
   Must spring from this diviner flood?
   When that the Rose itself doth bleed,
   That blood will be the Church's seed.

ROBERT SOUTHWELL Jesuit priest and martyr d. at Tyburn 1595 *The sequence on the Virgin Mary and Christ* section 7 *His* [Christ's] *circumcision*

The head is lanced to work the body's cure,
With angering salve it smarts to heal our wound,
To faultless Son, from all offences pure
The faulty vassals' scourges do redound,
The Judge is cast the guilty to acquit,
The sun defaced to lend the star his light.

The vein of life distilleth drops of grace,
Our rock gives issue to an heavenly spring,
Tears from his eyes, blood runs from wounded place,
Which showers to heaven of joy a harvest bring,
This sacred dew let angels gather up,
Such dainty drops best fit their nectared cup.

With weeping eyes his Mother rued his smart,
If blood from him, tears ran from her as fast,

55

The knife that cut his flesh did pierce her heart,
The pain that Jesus felt did Mary taste,
His life and hers hung by one fatal twist,
No blow that hit the Son the Mother missed.

See also Crashaw's *Hymn for the circumcision*; and depiction in *Complete woodcuts of Albrecht Dürer* ed. W. Kurth, Dover paperback plate 184.

ROBERT LOWELL *New Year's Day*

> . . . Under St Peter's bell the parish sea
>
> Swells with its smelt into the burlap shack
> Where Joseph plucks his hand-lines like a harp
> And hears the fearful *Puer natus est*
> Of Circumcision, and relives the wrack
> And howls of Jesus whom he holds. How sharp
> The burden of the Law before the beast:
> Time and the grindstone and the knife of God.
> The Child is born in blood, O child of blood.

On time

Edited by DAVID AERS

Introduction

An astonishingly confident and single-minded poem: so confident
is Milton that he doesn't even invoke a Christian God to terminate temporal process – it will inevitably terminate itself (10). Nor,
in this poem, does he have any suspicion that a centrally human
task might be

> Creating space, creating time according to the wonders divine
> Of human imagination . . .
> Blake Jerusalem IV 31

His imagination is exultingly absorbed by the consummation
hereafter and he 'does not hesitate to use abstract nouns conveying
a large elemental meaning . . . as though the ultimate in virtue
and divinity cannot be expressed in any other way' (D. Daiches
Milton 1968).

The subject of the poem has always teased men out of thought.
Originally Milton wrote his poem 'To be set on a clock case',
and this encourages one to ask *how* and *why* does man reduce the
process of events, the personal strivings of the process to the
static circle of a clock face? In *As you like it* when Rosalind asks,
'I pray you, what is't o'clock?', Orlando replies, 'You should ask
me what time o' day; there's no clock in the forest' (III ii). What
images and work patterns does the clock impose on us, and with
what effect? Compare Augustine's, 'It is in thee, my mind, that I
measure time' (*Confessions* XI). How does Milton's poem face 'time'?

Consider that Book of Augustine's, a magnificent meditation
on time; Shakespeare Sonnet 65 *Since brass nor stone* and others;
George Herbert *Time*; Donne *Good Friday 1613 : riding westward*.

On time

FLY ENVIOUS TIME, till thou run out thy race,
  Call on the lazy leaden-stepping hours,
    Whose speed is but the heavy plummet's pace;
And glut thyself with what thy womb devours,
Which is no more than what is false and vain, 5
And merely mortal dross;
So little is our loss,
So little is thy gain.
For when as each thing bad thou hast entombed,
And last of all thy greedy self consumed, 10
Then long eternity shall greet our bliss
With an individual kiss;
And joy shall overtake us as a flood,
When every thing that is sincerely good
And perfectly divine, 15
With truth, and peace, and love shall ever shine
About the súpreme throne
Of him, to whose happy-making sight alone,
When once our heavenly-guided soul shall climb,
Then all this earthy grossness quit, 20

1–3 'Fly . . . race', but also 'lazy leaden-stepping hours': depends on
subjective perspective? **plummet** lead weight for setting clock's works
going – before pendulums – see cuckoo clocks.   4 Time here as the
devourer = Death: read *PL* x 264–81. Wombs (naturally) life-making,
and though Milton uses **womb** in primary sense of stomach here, does
he also exploit sexual resonances? (read *PL* II 149–51, 438ff, 765–7;
v 299–302).   5–9 'It is characteristic of Renaissance art that it produced an image of Time the destroyer by fusing a personification of
"Temps" with the frightening figure of Saturn [who devoured his own
children, compare line 4] . . . Only by destroying spurious values can
Time fulfil the office of unveiling Truth': Panofsky *Studies in iconology*
p. 93 (see chap 3 on Time, and paintings there, especially Poussin *Il
ballo della vita humana*, Wallace Collection, repr in *JM : introductions*
in this series, and Bronzino *The exposure of luxury* National Gallery).
12 individual both (a) 'inseparable' (as *PL* IV 486) and also (b) greet
us each 'individually' with a kiss (contrast, for example, Buddhist
notions of *nirvana* – individuality dissolved).   **14 sincerely** completely.

Attired with stars, we shall for ever sit,
  Triumphing over Death, and Chance, and thee
  O Time.

22 **Chance** from the perspective of eternity chance doesn't exist.

At a solemn music

Edited by WINIFRED MAYNARD

Introduction

Milton did not record where he heard the music that occasioned
the writing of this poem, nor what music it was. Perhaps it was
some motets[1] or anthems sung by his father and friends at home,
or perhaps he had attended a choral service, for there were still
sung services in cathedrals and some college chapels, although
the Church of England discouraged the use of elaborate music in
worship. Such music could no doubt be a distraction to some
people, but it raised Milton's thoughts to the music of heaven,
and in this poem he invokes voice and verse, solemn song, so to
attune men to the praise of God offered in heaven that they may
offer answering praise on earth.[2]

Shape and style

The poem has only 28 lines, and its structure mirrors the thought,
just as vocal music then flowed with the sense of the words without being broken into regular bar-lengths. The opening idea
takes 24 lines to expound, and these form one sentence; the last
4 express the aspiration or prayer it leads to. Lines 1–5 invoke
voice and verse to make real to man's apprehension the heavenly
song; 6–16 evoke it to both eye and ear; 17–24 turn attention to the
response of earth; 25–8 are a prayer that earth may again join

---

[1] A motet is a piece of sacred music for several voices; like a madrigal,
it is polyphonic in texture, each voice having a melodious part, and all
combining harmoniously.

[2] See the chapter on music in *JM: introductions* in this series. To the
works on the power of music cited there add *Merchant of Venice* v i 55–89;
Wither's hymn *For a musician*; Benlowes *Poetic descent upon a private
music meeting*; Cowley *Davideis* 1 439–80; Wordsworth *On the power of
sound* (and, for light relief, his *Power of music*).

in the song of heaven. The long first sentence is clear in syntax and thought; but it also calls forth in the reader the sustained attentiveness of listening intently for something at the edge of the human range of perception.

Line-length and rhythm are as organic as sentence-length; with four exceptions, the lines have 10 syllables, but the opening lines show that we are not to expect an iambic pattern of stresses. Milton is thinking in terms of rhythms, not metre, just as vocal music was patterned by verbal phrases not metrical time, and the rhythms correspond to the sense. Lines 19–24 show this most strongly: in 19–21, the disruptive effects of sin are conveyed in strong accents juxtaposed without intervening weak ones,[1] over the line-ends: 'disproportioned síń/Járred against nature's chime, and with hársh díń/Bróke the fair music . . .'. There is no doubt that Milton intended these jolts: they are missing from his first two drafts of the poem, in the Trinity Manuscript, and he struggled with the passage until these vividly enactive rhythms emerged.[2] At 21–4 the phrasing lengthens and flows over the line-ends to mirror the smoothness and concord of a universe in unison with God, and the final alexandrine leaves the song continuing on.

Rhyme is also handled flexibly and purposively; after the opening 4 lines which rhyme alternately, couplet rhyme is used, except that lines 9 and 16 rhyme with each other and not with

[1] This is the essence of what Hopkins meant by 'sprung rhythm', which is based on stress alone: each foot must have one stress, but may or may not have other syllables, so two or more stresses may come in succession. Most English poetry combines or 'counterpoints' this varying speech-rhythm stress with an underlying regular metre. For Hopkins, Milton is the great exponent of this combination: 'the choruses of *Samson agonistes* are in my judgement counterpointed throughout; that is, each line (or nearly so) has two different coexisting scansions. But when you reach that point the secondary or "mounted rhythm", which is necessarily a sprung rhythm, overpowers the original or conventional one and then this last becomes superfluous and may be got rid of; by taking that last step you reach simple sprung rhythm. Milton must have known this but had reasons for not taking it.' (Letter to R. W. Dixon, 5 October 1878.) What might Milton's reasons have been?

[2] His first version was

> By leaving out those harsh chromatic jars
> Of sin that all our music mars.

Another was

> By leaving out those harsh ill sounding jars
> Of clamourous sin that all our music mars.

adjacent lines: the effect of this variation is that the 'sound-picture' completed at 16 is followed by a pause that fills with music as the rhyme of 'Singing everlastingly' takes up 9's 'solemn jubilee'. Such subtle organization of poetic effects reminds one of the poem's stimulus, for it parallels the musical texture of a motet, fluid, complex, and finely co-ordinated.[1]

Responding harmonies

The poet asks that man may receive, through earthly music, an impression, an image, of the heavenly music. But what kind of heavenly music? Is it the music of the spheres, which antedates Christianity, or the song of angelic hosts praising God in a Christian heaven? It is both. The idea of a correspondence between the nine spheres and the nine orders of angels holds them in poise. In Dante's *Paradiso*, canto XXVIII, Beatrice explains it to the poet. Thomas Heywood also explains it in book v of his *Hierarchy of the blessed angels* (1635), and sums up:

> The Primum Mobilë doth first begin
> To chime unto the holy Seraphim.
> The Cherubim doth make concordance even
> With the eighth sphere, namely the starry heaven;
> The Thrones, with Saturn; the like modulations
> Hath Jupiter with the high Dominations;
> The Virtues have with Mars a consonance sweet;
> The Potestates, with Sol in symptores meet;
> The Principates with Venus best agree;
> The Archangels with the planet Mercury,
> The Angels with the moon, which melody
> Hosanna sings to him that sits on high.[2]

Milton does not expound the correspondence, he *uses* it, so that both levels work together in the poem, their overtones interacting to infinity. There are cues attuning us to sphere-music throughout the poem, from the opening mention of sirens and spheres to the diapason that reminds us of the account of sphere-music in which earth has the same tone as the celestial sphere,

[1] M undoubtedly had in mind the Italian *canzone* form, as used by Petrarch, but for the *canzone* a stanza pattern is made and repeated. Milton uses his pattern only once, so his poem is really in madrigal form.

[2] The circles of angels relate inversely to those of space: the first angelic sphere, of seraphim, corresponds to the *primum mobile*, the ninth sphere: the innermost ring of angels is most divine because closest to the Godhead.

an octave below. But we cannot give an adequate account of the poem in terms of sphere-music only. The spheres made their music, in most accounts, involuntarily: the tones were the sound of each sphere's turning, the aural consequence of its performance of its role in the universal pattern. The song of *Music* is consciously offered praise, as seraphim and cherubim and the spirits of the righteous with voices and instruments worship the Most High. It is the 'Holy, holy, holy' of *Isaiah* vi 3 and the 'Alleluia!' of *Revelation* xix 1–6. The great vision, aspiration, and prayer of the poem is that the power of solemn music may make so real to man's uplifted understanding the worship of heaven that he may be drawn to make his response too, until he is finally united to God. The ending admits two meanings, that at our individual deaths we are united with God, and that at the end of the world mankind will be united with God. So the prayer may be both that each of us as individuals may live a life that makes music to God, and that human society may be drawn to live in accord with the will of God.

The tone of the poem assures us that this is a noble hope, and it is not dashed like the seemingly similar desire in *Nativity*, stanzas XIII–XV, to which Fate says no. What is the difference? The time-point in each poem is important: in *Nativity* the desire to hear the sphere-music is aroused by hearing the angelic song at the time of Christ's birth, that is, before his redeeming work has been done. In *Music* the time-point is the present: the way is open for man to live in tune with God.

At a solemn music

BLEST PAIR OF SIRENS, pledges of heaven's joy,
　　Sphere-born harmonious sisters, Voice, and Verse,
　　Wed your divine sounds, and mixed power employ
Dead things with inbreathed sense able to pierce,
And to our high-raised phantasy present,　　　　　　5

1 **sirens** singing goddesses borne on or born of the spheres. **pledges** children, and promises: earthly song gives promise of the union of heaven. 3–4 **employ** use that combined power which can pierce even sin-deadened souls: as rocks and trees were moved by the music of Orpheus. 5 **phantasy** imagination, perceptive faculty. Sir John Davies in his philosophical poem *Nosce te ipsum* 1599 has the senses as windows through

63

That undisturbèd song of pure concent,
Ay sung before the sapphire-coloured throne
To him that sits thereon
With saintly shout, and solemn jubilee,
Where the bright seraphim in burning row   10
Their loud uplifted angel trumpets blow,
And the cherubic host in thousand choirs
Touch their immortal harps of golden wires,
With those just spirits that wear victorious palms,
Hymns devout and holy psalms   15
Singing everlastingly;
That we on earth with undiscording voice
May rightly answer that melodious noise;
As once we did, till disproportioned sin
Jarred against nature's chime, and with harsh din   20
Broke the fair music that all creatures made
To their great Lord, whose love their motion swayed
In perfect diapáson, whilst they stood
In first obedience, and their state of good.
O may we soon again renew that song,   25
And keep in tune with heaven, till God ere long
To his celestial consort us unite,
To live with him, and sing in endless morn of light.

which the forms of things reach the brain, 'Where Phantasy, near handmaid to the mind, Sits and beholds and doth discern them all'. **present**
make known.   **6 concent** concord.   **7 Ay sung** forever sung with
holy shout and joyful sound, to God. **throne** as in Ezekiel's vision *Ez*. i, x.
10–11 these lines enforce sharp articulation like the tonguing of a trumpet.
Cf *PL* VIII 564 of the Son's return to heaven after creation: 'the bright
pomp ascended jubilant'.   **14 just spirits** 'the spirits of just men made
perfect' *Hebrews* xii.   **16** the line's shortness leads us to draw it out and
pause as if listening.   **18 answer** respond to, match. **noise** sound.
19 disproportioned musical, mathematical and aesthetic nexuses
combine: sin is discordant, disordered, deformed.   **20 chime** concord.
22 swayed God's love ordered the emotions of Adam and Eve in the
same way as it moved the outermost sphere, the *primum mobile*, and
hence the whole world.   **23 diapáson** concord of tones, especially at
the octave.   **24 obedience** before 'man's first disobedience' *PL* I 1,
which put the earth out of tune.   **27 consort** a number of instruments
or voices making music together. Also overtones from spouse, and
especially the church as bride of Christ.

L'allegro & Il penseroso

Edited by LORNA SAGE

Introduction

Opening exorcisms

These are reversed, left-handed invocations (compare the
'heavenly Muse' of *Nativity*) – ritual exorcisms to get rid of the
hindering or opposing deity, before invoking the 'goddesses'
Milton wants to celebrate. It is as important to respond to the
stagey, over-done manner of these lines marked off by their
metre as it is to work out the mythological references – the
point is that they're abusive. The 'horrid shapes' and the bastard
'brood of folly' are the same sort of hopelessly two-dimensional
creatures as Comus's rout later, and Milton probably was thinking about the conventions of masques and pageants. Simple
masques often started with an anti-masque, a ritualized parade
and defeat of a crowd of clownish-sinister vices, before going on
to explore their real subject, some personified virtue. Ben Jonson's
Pleasure reconciled to virtue (performed 1618), which Milton knew,
begins like that; Jonson's masque is relevant in other ways too,
because it sets out as though it is going to dramatize a choice
(between the primrose path of pleasure and the stony, uphill
struggle for virtue) and ends by arguing that the real choice (more
civilized, more intelligently moral) is *not to choose*, but to have it
both ways. Milton may be doing the same sort of thing: he
exorcises damaging, pathological melancholy and trivializing,
stupid mirth so that he can explore the creative possibilities of
both kinds of experience without choosing – yet.

None of Milton's many poetic sources tried to do anything
so interesting: they were mainly poems by different poets, not
distinct moods conjured up by the *same* imagination. See, for
example, Marlowe's *Come live with me and be my love*, with the
replies by Sir Walter Raleigh and Donne (*The bait*). J. B. Leish-

man *'L'allegro* and *Il penseroso* in their relation to 17c poetry' in *Milton* ed. A. Rudrum (Modern judgements series 1968) quotes and analyses sources and parallels. Closer to Milton in feeling are the two songs with which Shakespeare ended *Love's labour's lost* (which is about the wrongheadedness of immature choices): they are sung by Spring and Winter (in that order) and it's very clear that they do not, and cannot, refute or cancel each other. The power of Milton's twin poems lies in the fact that they get rid of the crude either/or state of mind at the very beginning. 'They are two noble efforts of the imagination' said Dr Johnson in his *Life of Milton* (worth looking up: Johnson liked these poems better than Milton's grander works).

Perhaps, therefore, the best way to translate the Italian titles would be 'the cheerful man' and 'the pensive man' – moods crystallized for a moment into types – rather than anything more rigid. The general areas of sensibility had been pretty well mapped already: melancholy, for example, had long been a fashionable posture (Jaques in Shakespeare's *As you like it*) and a whole generation's experience had been summed up (with an immense, scholarly background) in Robert Burton's *Anatomy of melancholy* 1621. On this see L. Babb *The Elizabethan malady* Michigan 1951 and (for images and theories of melancholy) Erwin Panofsky *Albrecht Dürer* Princeton 1943. Cheerfulness needed less theoretical justification: Shakespeare's early comedies, pastoral lyrics, marriage songs like Spenser's *Epithalamion* provide the background. Milton is appropriating a wealth of experience and making it his own. The metre of the 'exorcisms' was probably adapted from Italian, the octosyllabic couplets of the main body of each poem are English; the combination of the two is Milton's idea. Formally and thematically he consolidates, sophisticates – and innovates. For contrasting, detailed explications see C. Brooks and J. E. Hardy ed. *Poems of Mr John Milton* New York 1951 and D. C. Allen *The harmonious vision* Baltimore 1954.

The two goddesses

Mirth has too many parents, Melancholy too few; for both of them Milton bent mythological tradition so that our attention is focussed on ideas of conception. Mirth is associated twice over with the gods of the cycle of nature – Venus and Bacchus, and then (perhaps because the love-goddess and the wine-god are too experienced, too 'heavy'?) the west wind and the dawn. Zephyr

66

'breathes the spring', that is he inspires (literally) nature to create new life (see Zephyr in Botticelli's *Primavera*), and in his casual, generous, promiscuous way, he fathers Mirth. Saturn, Melancholy's father, is her grandfather too, and her mother Vesta is also her sister; her conception is deliberate and solemn. Whereas Mirth's family tree has many roots and many branches, Melancholy's narrows down through inbreeding and incest to arrive at unity and intensity. Milton seems to be exploring two different versions of creativity. (Pagan myth enables him to do this freely – compare the treatment of incest in Satan, Sin and Death in *PL* II.) Mirth is to do with multiplicity and variety and (because of nature) with growth; Melancholy with inwardness, solitary perfection and stasis (she is born wise). Either of them is a possible mistress for Milton's imagination, a possible muse: compare, in a quite different key, Keats's comic, lusty variation on the theme –

> Welcome Joy and welcome Sorrow
>   Lethe's weed and Hermes' feather
> Come today and come tomorrow
>   I do love you both together . . .
> Muses bright and muses pale,
> Bare your faces of the veil;
> Let me see, and let me write
> Of the day and of the night –
> Both together: let me slake
> All my thirst for sweet heart-ache . . .

The greed for experience ('Both together') suggests a kind of poetic promiscuity alien to Milton. But is it? His terms and his tone are much more controlled, but some of the same feelings – urgency, ambition, deliberate self-indulgence, curiosity, diffused sexuality – seem to lie behind it. And around this time, when he left Cambridge, and settled in the country at Horton (1632), he was consciously exploring his poetic identity and wooing the muses. In his last academic exercise he talks about the necessity of postponing the life of action and immersing himself in imaginative possibilities –

This I believe to be the meaning of Hesiod's holy sleep and Endymion's nightly meetings with the moon: this was the significance of Prometheus' withdrawal, under the guidance of Mercury, to the lofty solitude of the Caucasus, where at last he became the wisest of gods and men, so that his advice was sought by Jupiter himself concerning the marriage of Thetis. I can myself call to witness the woods and rivers and the beloved village elms, under whose shade I enjoyed (if I may tell the secrets of goddesses) such sweet intercourse with the Muses, as I still remember with delight. There I too, amid rural scenes and woodland solitudes, felt I had enjoyed a season of growth in a life of seclusion.

> Trans. Phyllis Tillyard *M's private correspondence and academic exercises* Cambridge 1932

The need to possess and to be possessed by the forces of nature and culture outside yourself was acknowledged by the classical doctrine that the young poet should write pastoral (like Virgil). After Milton's self-dedication in *Nativity* (at 21) and his failure with *The passion*, he seems to have deliberately slowed down, and allowed the chequered, various life around him to fill his imagination. It is an impulse that comes without classical rules: Milton at 23 naturally expressed his desire in terms of goddesses; compare this entry in the journal of Gerard Manley Hopkins:

July 28. 1867 I am three and twenty. – Bright extremely, though a shower or more fell; distances all fine blues; the sky working blue-silver; the clouds, which far off were in chains, were there covered in a blue light and shaded with blue shadow, and in the afternoon indeed shewed silver lips only and then were indistinguishable from blue sky below that; sunset bright – an edge of gold shewing amidst wet sandy gold; afterwards glowing ranks. – the timbered side of Frognal – Mr. Claypen's that was, Oak Hill, etc – from the fields towards Mr. Joseph Hoare's looked finer than I had ever seen it before: the foliage was so vivid with the breaks and the packing; the poplars there are there looked like velvet, shewing all dark except an edge of bright sprays along the top.

> *Journals and papers* ed. H. House and G. Storey Oxford University Press 1959

See J. S. Diekhoff *M on himself* Oxford 1939.

Their companions

Blake's illustrations show Mirth's followers skipping and floating, while Melancholy forms the still centre of a symmetrical tableau. Some of the goddesses' companions (especially Liberty and Contemplation) are spiritual beings, some are hardly more than figures of speech, and some, like 'Laughter holding both his sides', hover delightfully between the two. This semi-allegorical habit has a long history: Thomas Warton, in his footnote to smiles that live in dimples, says 'The radical thought might be traced backward to Horace, and from Horace to Euripides . . .' (*Poems upon several occasions* ed. Warton 2nd ed. 1791). See C. S. Lewis *The allegory of love* Oxford 1938; R. Tuve *Images and themes in five poems by M* Oxford 1957.

Each poem selects what its own particular sensibility needs to feed on: the lark/the nightingale, dawn/dusk, folk tales/philosophic myths, comedy in the theatre/tragedy in the study . . . These elaborate cross-references are not mechanically done (they don't, for example, always happen in the same place in each poem); searching for them is a good way to begin concentrated work on the poems. Some more detailed examples – beds of violets/secret shades; trip it as you go/keep thy wonted state; the hounds and horn/the curfew; sun begins his state/moon . . . near her highest noon; ploughman . . . whistles/bellman's . . . charm; Towers, and battlements/high lonely tower; cynosure [Ursa Minor]/outwatch the Bear; learned sock/buskin; tales/sage and solemn tunes; dream (129)/dream (147). And, on a larger scale, each poem explores a day, with l'allegro beginning in the morning, and il penseroso in the evening. You need, though, to explore the similarities as well as the contrasts – dawn and dusk, for example, are both thresholds between two worlds. The pattern is repeated *within* each poem: l'allegro (57) is 'not unseen', il penseroso (65) is 'unseen', but the lamp in his lonely tower is 'seen' (86). Even the placing of words shows this addiction to symmetry:

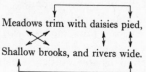

Here you get two kinds of symmetry, reversal and repetition, and each is done twice over (in the relations of the two halves of each line: in the relations of the lines to each other).

The landscape is perceived as pattern on a larger scale too: *L'allegro* is not just a series of scenes, but the portrait of a community – orderly, hierarchical, articulate; in *Il penseroso* nature is like a garden with 'walks' and 'groves' (133) and the living community is replaced with the community of the mighty dead, philosophers, artists, saints. It is as though these scenes bear the imprint of all the ways people have ordered them in the past; when Milton looks at a 'landscape' he thinks of paintings, and when he wants to describe the play of light and shade, he borrows the word 'chequered' from Shakespeare. This way of seeing rests on certain assumptions – for example (a) that 'reality' is the sum of what people (especially aritsts, but ordinary people too) have seen and imagined over generations (expressing itself in folk culture, in ceremonies like marriage, as well as self-conscious art); (b) that the way to perceive properly, ie humanly, is to fill your mind with expectations and patterns, *not* (as a later empiricist would say) to try to get rid of them. Many artists have shared this sense that what we see is the result of the imaginative efforts of previous generations – and not just those artists who thought of themselves as imitative. The painter Constable, setting out to see nature anew, found it filled with 'quotations' – 'I fancy I see Gainsborough in every hedge and hollow tree'. See E. H. Gombrich *Art and illusion* 1957 especially chapter 9 'The analysis of vision in art'. There are problems: for example, Milton makes nature and people all seem to meet the artist half-way. Very little *work* gets done, or at least we're not made aware of it. In an anti-pastoral mood, Hardy pointed out in *Tess of the D'Urbervilles* that milkmaids sing (tunelessly, without enthusiasm) in order to calm the cows down, and to make them easier to milk.

Certainly it's important to be *aware* of what the patterns in one's head do to the world one perceives. Milton demonstrates his own awareness by making his two observers 'see' quite differently: during the 18th century, however, the 'penseroso' way of seeing gradually took over in poetry and painting, and became the cult of the 'picturesque' and the 'sublime' (see 'M in literary history' in the *JM: introductions* volume in this series). That perhaps has made people more suspicious of Milton than he deserves. As a starting-point for thinking about different patterns of perception, consider this ironic speech by one of the characters in Jane Austen's *Sense and sensibility* 1811:

Remember I have no knowledge of the picturesque, and I shall offend you by my ignorance and want of taste if we come to particulars. I shall call hills steep which ought to be bold; surfaces strange and un-couth which ought to be irregular and rugged; and distant objects out of sight which ought to be indistinct through the soft medium of a hazy atmosphere. You must be satisfied with such admiration as I can honestly give: the hills are steep, the woods seem full of fine timber, and the valley looks comfortable and snug, with rich meadows and several neat farm-houses scattered here and there . . .

And see illustrations to these poems by Blake and Samuel Palmer.

Music

Sound patterns are even more important than visual ones, and intertwined with them –

> As may with sweetness, through mine ear,
> Dissolve me into ecstasies,
> And bring all heaven before mine eyes.
>
> *Penseroso* 164

Music lends wings to words, transforming them into a subtler medium so that they penetrate the soul; it is associated with Neo-Platonic doctrines about the (lost) harmony of the universe; it 'tunes' men's souls again so that they can experience, in brief moments of ecstasy, the spiritual splendour they forfeited when Adam fell. There were also more directly physiological explanations of how it worked. This is the Florentine Platonist Marsilio Ficino (1433–99) describing how the artist can re-form the quality of his listener's life:

Since song and sound come from the thoughts of the mind, from the impulse of the imagination, and from the passion of the heart and, together with the broken and formed air, move the air-like spirit of the listener, which is the bond of Soul and Body, it easily moves the imagination, affects the heart, and penetrates the inmost sanctuaries of the mind.

> Trans. P. O. Kristeller in *The philosophy of Marsilio Ficino*
> Harper and Row New York 1943

Music excites Milton because it is at once so powerful and so intimate, a 'language' without content, all form. The music l'allegro and il penseroso hear (different for each of them) seems as close as if it were being played inside their heads; they are no longer, for this timeless moment, perceiving patterns, they are being patterned themselves. (Compare the experience often described by mystics, in which the categories of 'subject' and 'object' lose all meaning.) There are many 17th-century poems which mimic the effects of music, for example Crashaw's *Music's duel*; but try looking up something less obvious, like *Ovid's banquet of sense* by George Chapman, which tries to trace the links between spirit and sense in literal detail. Milton's *Nativity*, *At a solemn music*, and *Arcades* 61–78 are relevant too, though it is worth noticing that they are all more theoretical and dogmatic about music and more suspicious of the senses. Il penseroso is attending a service in a solid and beautiful church, not straining

71

his ears for the music of the spheres. See S. Spaeth *M's knowledge of music* Princeton 1913 and, for the more elaborate theories, Frances A. Yates *The French academies of the 16c* 1947 (espec. chap 3) and John Hollander *The untuning of the sky* Princeton 1961. Listen to Handel's *L'allegro, il penseroso ed il moderato* 1740 and his setting of Dryden's baroque *Ode for St Cecilia's day.*

Choosing

There are ways of stating oppositions which make choice seem impossible or irrelevant:

Some old magical writer, I forget who, says if you wish to be melancholy hold in your left hand an image of the Moon made out of silver, and if you wish to be happy hold in your right hand an image of the Sun made out of gold.   W. B. Yeats *The philosophy of Shelley's poetry* 1900

The thought of having such power, the beauty of the possibility, quite takes away the desire finally to choose. Milton has done something similar in these two poems. He is experimenting with his sensibility, trying out in imagination (which means you don't have to decide, there's more room in the imagination than in the world) different images of what it means to be an artist. It means feeling that you belong to a secret order, almost a priesthood, that you are intense and solitary; it means being infinitely receptive to the creativity in the culture surrounding you, and wanting to participate in it. Both of these versions were obviously 'true' for Milton, in the sense that he experienced them both, weighed and handled them in his imagination. The result is that he portrays them in patterns rather than doctrines, in shades of light and dark, not right and wrong.

L'allegro

H ENCE loathèd Melancholy
Of Cerberus, and blackest Midnight born,
In Stygian cave forlorn

1 **Hence . . .** a (poetic) exorcism.   **Melancholy** here a savage, sick, destructive state of mind.   2 **Cerberus** many-headed watchdog of classical hell; the usual husband of Night is Erebus; M's mythologizing here impressionistic.   3 **Stygian** by river Styx, one of four rivers of classical hell = hellish.

'Mongst horrid shapes, and shrieks, and sights
  unholy,
Find out some uncouth cell,   5
  Where brooding Darkness spreads his jealous
    wings,
And the night-raven sings;
  There under ebon shades, and low-browed
    rocks,
As ragged as thy locks,
  In dark Cimmerian desert ever dwell.   10
But come thou goddess fair and free,
In heaven yclept Euphrósynë,
And by men, heart-easing Mirth,
Whom lovely Venus at a birth
With two sister Graces more   15
To ivy-crownèd Bacchus bore;
Or whether (as some sager sing)
The frolic wind that breathes the spring,
Zephyr with Aurora playing,
As he met her once a-Maying,   20
There on beds of violets blue,
And fresh-blown roses washed in dew,
Filled her with thee a daughter fair,
So buxom, blithe, and debonair.

5 **uncouth** far from civilization.   6 **brooding** bird-metaphor, also
modern sense? Cf dove=holy spirit *PL* I 20.   8 **low-browed**
over-hanging; landscape suggests threatening giant.   9 **ragged**
interchangeable with 'rugged' in 17c, fits rocks or locks.   10 **Cimmerian desert** desolate place at the end of the known world in Homer
Odyssey XI.   11 **But come . . .** invocation, change from difficult
alternating 6- and 10-syllable lines to flexible octosyllabics.   12 **yclept**
called; poetic archaism from Spenser, calls attention to itself to distinguish language of heaven from ours. Euphrosyne is Greek, Mirth
Anglo-Saxon. Mythological parentage, though unusual, explains itself.
17 **Or whether . . .** alternative family tree (see Introduction); both
poems have many alternative constructions eg *L'all* 47–8, 50, 89, 133 –
but not on the either/or model.   18 **breathes** used Latinately (*spirat*),
means impregnates and inspires.   19 **Zephyr . . . Aurora** west wind,
dawn; **playing** children's games and (here) love-play, rhyme connects
with Maying and fertility rites. Cf Herrick *Corinna's going a-Maying*
1648.   24 pliant, happy, graceful; a frequent formula.

Haste thee nymph, and bring with thee   25
Jest and youthful Jollity.
Quips and cranks, and wanton wiles,
Nods, and becks, and wreathèd smiles,
Such as hang on Hébë's cheek,
And love to live in dimple sleek;   30
Sport that wrinkled Care derides,
And Laughter holding both his sides.
Come, and trip it as you go
On the light fantastic toe,
And in thy right hand lead with thee,   35
The mountain nymph, sweet Liberty;
And if I give thee honour due,
Mirth, admit me of thy crew
To live with her, and live with thee,
In unreprovèd pleasures free;   40
To hear the lark begin his flight,
And singing startle the dull night,
From his watch-tower in the skies,
Till the dappled dawn doth rise;
Then to come in spite of sorrow,   45
And at my window bid good morrow,
Through the sweet-briar, or the vine,
Or the twisted eglantine.
While the cock with lively din,
Scatters the rear of darkness thin,   50
And to the stack, or the barn door,

26 Jest ... semi-personified attendants crowd into the verse: **Quips** and **cranks** are verbal gymnastics; **wanton wiles** could have evil connotations, but here innocently exuberant like the sex. **29 Hébë** eternally youthful cup-bearer to the gods. **31** syntax works both ways. Accidental? **33 Come ... go** as in a country dance; rhythm dances too. **35 right hand** Liberty has pride of place. **36 mountain nymph** because religious liberty, protestantism, flourishes in Swiss mountains? **38 crew** company, but usually bad company. Cf *PL* I 51. **40 unreprovèd** without blame, but has to remind himself? **free** repeated rhyme links back with Liberty, makes a natural break though sentence continues. **45 to come** parallels 'to live' (39) and 'to hear' (41). **in spite of** to spite (probably). **50 rear ... thin** the stragglers (of the army) of darkness.

Stoutly struts his dames before
Oft listening how the hounds and horn
Cheerly rouse the slumbering morn,
From the side of some hoar hill,   55
Through the high wood echoing shrill.
Sometime walking not unseen
By hedgerow elms, on hillocks green,
Right against the eastern gate,
Where the great sun begins his state,   60
Robed in flames, and amber light,
The clouds in thousand liveries dight,
While the ploughman near at hand,
Whistles o'er the furrowed land,
And the milkmaid singeth blithe,   65
And the mower whets his scythe,
And every shepherd tells his tale
Under the hawthorn in the dale.
Straight mine eye hath caught new pleasures
Whilst the landscape round it measures,   70
Russet lawns, and fallows grey,
Where the nibbling flocks do stray,
Mountains on whose barren breast
The labouring clouds do often rest:
Meadows trim with daisies pied,   75
Shallow brooks, and rivers wide.
Towers, and battlements it sees
Bosomed high in tufted trees,

---

52 his dames before quiet joke against strutting cock: before comes
after.   **57 not unseen** negative construction keeps him slightly aloof,
cf *Il pen* 65.   **60 his state** sun as king, starting on stately progress,
metaphor continued in robes and uniformed cloud-attendants.   **62
dight** richly clothed; rhyme repeated *Il pen* 159–60, but with dim, religious light.   **67 tells his tale** tells stories and counts his sheep (keeps a
tally). Work and play merge in pastoral.   **69 Straight . . .** decisive
change of rhythm, and feminine rhyme (third so far).   **70 measures**
surveys and composes the scene, as though for a painting.   **71 lawns
. . . fallows** pastures, ploughlands.   **73–4 barren . . . labouring**
sterile, pregnant: variety and symmetry of nature much stressed 71–6.
78 bosomed cf breast/rest rhyme 73–4.

Where perhaps some beauty lies,
The cynosure of neighbouring eyes.   80
Hard by, a cottage chimney smokes,
From betwixt two aged oaks,
Where Corydon and Thyrsis met,
Are at their savoury dinner set
Of herbs, and other country messes,   85
Which the neat-handed Phillis dresses;
And then in haste her bower she leaves,
With Thestylis to bind the sheaves;
Or if the earlier season lead
To the tanned haycock in the mead,   90
Sometimes with secure delight
The upland hamlets will invite,
When the merry bells ring round,
And the jocund rebecks sound
To many a youth, and many a maid,   95
Dancing in the chequered shade;
And young and old come forth to play
On a sunshine holiday,
Till the livelong daylight fail,
Then to the spicy nut-brown ale,   100
With stories told of many a feat,
How Faëry Mab the junkets eat,

79 lies dwells, perhaps languishes? **80 cynosure** focus, because Ursa Minor (*cynosura* in Latin) is the Pole Star by which sailors steer. **83 Corydon . . .** conventional names in literary pastoral. **85 messes** dishes. **86 dresses** prepares. **89 Or if . . .** M moves through from dawn to dusk, but his day comprises many days. Cf Wallace Stevens *Credences of summer* 'One day enriches a year . . . The more than casual blue/Contains the year and other years and hymns / And people, without souvenir'. **91 secure** free from care. **94 rebecks** simple fiddles. **98 sunshine holiday** holy day still; Christian feast days had often strategically supplanted those of pagan deities like the sun. **101 stories . . .** M's country people have their own culture, though it had begun to be appropriated by poets and dramatists (eg fairy lore in Shakespeare's *Midsummer night's dream*). **Mab** queen of fairies punished slatterns, cf Robert Graves's poem *Lollocks*; **the friar's lantern** (Jack O'Lantern, Will O' the Wisp) led late travellers astray; the **goblin** (Robin Goodfellow, Puck) was a mischievous joker, but worked for wages. Fairy people here not dainty or miniaturized but full size, a part of the community. Cf Edward Thomas's poem *Lob*. **102 junkets** dairy food.

She was pinched, and pulled she said,
And by the friar's lantern led
Tells how the drudging goblin sweat, 105
To earn his cream-bowl duly set,
When in one night, ere glimpse of morn,
His shadowy flail hath threshed the corn
That ten day-labourers could not end,
Then lies him down the lubber fiend, 110
And stretched out all the chimney's length,
Basks at the fire his hairy strength;
And crop-full out of doors he flings,
Ere the first cock his matin rings.
Thus done the tales, to bed they creep, 115
By whispering winds soon lulled asleep.
Towered cities please us then,
And the busy hum of men,
Where throngs of knights and barons bold,
In weeds of peace high triumphs hold, 120
With store of ladies, whose bright eyes
Rain influence, and judge the prize
Of wit, or arms, while both contend
To win her grace, whom all commend.
There let Hymen oft appear 125
In saffron robe, with taper clear,
And pomp, and feast, and revelry,
With mask, and antique pageantry,
Such sights as youthful poets dream

103 she unnamed dairymaid, Mab's victim. **108 shadowy** invisible or dark. **109 That ten ...** either: that ten men could not have threshed, or: that ten couldn't carry away next day. **110 lubber fiend** oafish spirit. **113 crop-full** with a full stomach; bird or animal metaphor, makes him natural? **114 matin rings** announces morning service; metaphor reminds us cock-crow drove away spirits. **120 weeds of peace** civilian clothes; if the knights wore armour it would be light and decorative, their battles were courtly games. In 1620s and 1630s the court was unheroic, played at war and negotiated peace. **122 Rain influence** casual poetic shorthand. Eyes=stars which exert influence over men's destinies; perhaps pun on rain/reign too. **125 Hymen** classical marriage-god, presides over the ceremony with his yellow robe and torch. **129 Such sights** the masques and pageants, or the whole, slightly unreal courtly scene?

77

On summer eves by haunted stream.   130
Then to the well-trod stage anon,
If Jonson's learnèd sock be on,
Or sweetest Shakespeare fancy's child,
Warble his native wood-notes wild,
And ever against eating cares,   135
Lap me in soft Lydian airs,
Married to immortal verse
Such as the meeting soul may pierce
In notes, with many a winding bout
Of linkèd sweetness long drawn out,   140
With wanton heed, and giddy cunning,
The melting voice through mazes running;
Untwisting all the chains that tie
The hidden soul of harmony.
That Orpheus' self may heave his head   145
From golden slumber on a bed
Of heaped Elysian flowers, and hear
Such strains as would have won the ear
Of Pluto, to have quite set free
His half-regained Eurýdicë.   150
These delights, if thou canst give,
Mirth with thee, I mean to live.

132–3 Shakespeare died 1616, Jonson 1637 (so was still alive when
M wrote this); they appear as writers of comedy (sock = classical
comic actor's footwear) neatly type-cast to fit with the poem's symmetrical patterning.   **136 Lydian airs** mimed in following lines:
sensuous, complex, gentle music (eg madrigals in 17c).   **138 meeting**
going halfway to meet (the music).   **139 bout** movement turning back
on itself.   **143 Untwisting . . .** the twists and turns of the music
'untwist' harmony's chains, give the **soul** of music a body to live in.
145 Orpheus mythic Greek bard whose music civilized men and even
trees and beasts; story of his love for Eurydice told in Ovid (*Metamorphoses* x) – his music won her back from Pluto, king of the dead, but
on condition he did not turn to look at her as they left the underworld.
147 Elysian in Elysium, classical paradise described in *Comus* 988–1002.
148 won the ear conventional phrase for getting favour of great man,
here given newly literal meaning.   **150 half-regained** M haunted by
the theme of the lost woman, cf Persephone *PL* iv 268–72.   **151–2**
closing formula reminiscent of Marlowe's 'Come live with me . . .';
asks for choice, but when M closes *Il pen* with a variation on these words
he is, formally at least, binding the two poems together.

Il penseroso

HENCE vain deluding Joys,
    The brood of Folly without father bred,
    How little you bestead,
Or fill the fixèd mind with all your toys;
Dwell in some idle brain,   5
    And fancies fond with gaudy shapes possess,
As thick and numberless
    As the gay motes that people the sunbeams,
Or likest hovering dreams
    The fickle pensioners of Morpheus' train.   10
But hail thou goddess, sage and holy,
Hail divinest Melancholy,
Whose saintly visage is too bright
To hit the sense of human sight;
And therefore to our weaker view,   15
O'erlaid with black staid wisdom's hue.
Black, but such as in esteem,
Prince Memnon's sister might beseem,
Or that starred Ethiop queen that strove

2 brood multiple offspring; 'without father' means that they're bastards, or that they're unnatural. Play on 'brood' and 'bred', and cf *L'all* 6. Negative melancholy was imagined as one heavy, obsessive figure; negative mirth is a swarm of disorderly insect-like creatures. **3 bestead** be of use. **4 toys** trivialities. **6 fancies ... possess** fill foolish wits with bright meaningless images. **10 pensioners** retainers, paid therefore fickle, who serve a great man, here Morpheus god of dreams. **11 But hail ...** invocation, more solemn that in *L'all*, repeated in next line. **14 hit the sense** suit, or penetrate, the physical sense. Our senses are dazzled by Melancholy's brightness, so that to us she will look dark. **16 O'erlaid ...** because her blackness is not real; she may have dark skin and hair, or be wearing a black veil (like Spenser's Una *Fairy queen* 1) – it doesn't matter because her blackness is a kind of veil anyway. Black is **wisdom's hue** because scholars develop a grey complexion, and because they toil and study at night for enlightenment. **17–18 such ... beseem** worthy of as much praise as would be fitting to give Prince Memnon's sister. He was a handsome Ethiopian prince in Homer. **19 starred Ethiop queen** Cassiopea, translated into stars for her rash boast 20–1.

To set her beauty's praise above   20
The sea-nymphs, and their powers offended.
Yet thou art higher far descended,
Thee bright-haired Vesta long of yore,
To solitary Saturn bore;
His daughter she (in Saturn's reign,   25
Such mixture was not held a stain)
Oft in glimmering bowers, and glades
He met her, and in secret shades
Of woody Ida's inmost grove,
Whilst yet there was no fear of Jove.   30
Come pensive nun, devout and pure,
Sober, steadfast, and demure,
All in a robe of darkest grain,
Flowing with majestic train,
And sable stole of cypress lawn,   35
Over thy decent shoulders drawn.
Come, but keep thy wonted state,
With even step, and musing gait,
And looks commercing with the skies,
Thy rapt soul sitting in thine eyes: 40
There held in holy passion still,
Forget thyself to marble, till

22 higher . . . descended punning on family tree and descent from
heaven, making us see usual rules don't apply, cf *L'all* 17.   **23 Vesta**
virgin goddess of the hearth, it's her chastity M stresses.   **24 Saturn**
ruler of classical golden age, supplanted by his son Jupiter (30); as
a planet he caused melancholy or saturnine temperament in those born
under his influence. He has two very different aspects: the primitive,
beneficent deity, and the savage god who devoured his children to keep
his throne.   **26 Such mixture** such intercourse, incest; M here (cf
blackness=brightness paradox) makes the taboo=the supernatural,
incest=purity (cf Christian mystery of immaculate conception). This
parentage, like Mirth's, M's own invention.   **31 nun** priestess.   **32**
formula cf *L'all* 24.   **33 grain** colour.   **35 cypress lawn** black linen,
but in common usage cypress meant black linen, lawn white linen, so M
still insists on dark/light contrast.   **37 wonted state** accustomed
stateliness; note stress, in rhythm and sense, on regularity and discipline.
39 commercing communing.   **40 rapt** entranced, possessed.   **41**
still unmoving and always (she is outside time).   **42 Forget thyself . . .**
her body vacant, waiting like a statue for her soul's return; cf M's sonnet
to Shakespeare. Submerged puns on marble/marvel and (in idea) on
astonishment.

With a sad leaden downward cast,
Thou fix them on the earth as fast.
And join with thee calm Peace, and Quiet,   45
Spare Fast, that oft with gods doth diet,
And hears the Muses in a ring,
Ay round about Jove's altar sing.
And add to these retired Leisure,
That in trim gardens takes his pleasure;   50
But first, and chiefest, with thee bring,
Him that yon soars on golden wing,
Guiding the fiery-wheelèd throne,
The cherub Contemplatiön,
And the mute Silence hist along,   55
'Less Philomel will deign a song,
In her sweetest, saddest plight,
Smoothing the rugged brow of night,
While Cynthia checks her dragon yoke,
Gently o'er the accustomed oak;   60
Sweet bird that shunn'st the noise of folly,
Most musical, most melancholy!
Thee chauntress oft the woods among,
I woo to hear thy even-song;
And missing thee, I walk unseen   65
On the dry smooth-shaven green,
To behold the wandering moon,
Riding near her highest noon,

43 sad, leaden solemn, heavy as lead (metal associated with Saturn).
44 as fast as tightly.   **46 diet** eat plainly. Cf Lady in *Comus* 764–
79; taming your body sets your soul free to hear the Muses
(47).   **48 Ay** forever.   **54 cherub Contemplatiön** not a baby-
angel, but powerful member of the heavenly hierarchy as his 'fiery-
wheelèd throne' (*Ezekiel* x) signifies. Contemplation parallels Liberty
(*L'all* 36) and seems to represent inward intensity *v* extrovert variety,
conscious purity *v* unthinking innocence, but no *easy* contrast.   **55
hist** urge in a whisper. Cf 'haste' *L'all* 25.   **56 Philomel . . .** nightingale, name = lover of song in Greek; **deign** condescend (to sing).   **58
Smoothing . . .** Cf effect of Lady's song in *Comus* 250.   **59 Cynthia**
one name of moon goddess (Diana, Hecate); **checks . . .** guides the
dragon-drawn chariot of the moon.   **64 even-song** evening service.
Cf the cock's matins *L'all* 114.   **67 wandering moon** feminine, hesi-
tant, lost – cf princely, confident sun *L'all* 60–2. These lines haunted

Like one that had been led astray
Through the heaven's wide pathless way;   70
And oft, as if her head she bowed,
Stooping through a fleecy cloud.
Oft on a plat of rising ground,
I hear the far-off curfew sound,
Over some wide-watered shore,   75
Swinging slow with sullen roar;
Or if the air will not permit,
Some still removèd place will fit,
Where glowing embers through the room
Teach light to counterfeit a gloom,   80
Far from all resort of mirth,
Save the cricket on the hearth,
Or the bellman's drowsy charm,
To bless the doors from nightly harm:
Or let my lamp at midnight hour,   85
Be seen in some high lonely tower,
Where I may oft outwatch the Bear,
With thrice great Hermes, or unsphere
The spirit of Plato to unfold
What worlds, or what vast regions hold   90

Shelley, see his fragment *Art thou pale for weariness* which in turn
haunted Stephen in Joyce's *Portrait of the artist as a young man.*   **74
curfew** evening bell which he hears across an estuary (?) so that it takes
on sound of water's ebb and flow 76.   **77 air** weather.   **78 still
removèd** quiet and remote, but perhaps 'still'=also.   **81 resort of
mirth** visitation by revellers. Cf 'in spite of sorrow' *L'all* 45.   **83
bellman's . . . charm** nightwatchman's blessing as he calls the hours.
85 midnight when worlds of men and spirits most open to each other.
87 outwatch the Bear stay up all night. For imagery of stars and towers
cf *L'all* 77–80.   **88 thrice great Hermes** Hermes Trismegistus, mythical half-divine Egyptian priest; Hermetic writings (probably written by
Alexandrian authors AD 200–300) combined ideas from Plato, the Bible
and many other sources, into magical theories of cosmic harmony.
This lore was revived in the renaissance, and excited not only artists,
but scientists like Galileo and Kepler, since it promised to restore
man's sovereignty over the natural world. **unsphere** call down from
the star his soul inhabits – one of Plato's many contradictory ways
of imaging immortality, so makes sense to call him down to ask
about it.

The immortal mind that hath forsook
Her mansion in this fleshly nook:
And of those daemons that are found
In fire, air, flood, or under ground,
Whose power hath a true consent   95
With planet, or with element.
Sometime let gorgeous Tragedy
In sceptred pall come sweeping by,
Presenting Thebes, or Pelops' line,
Or the tale of Troy divine.   100
Or what (though rare) of later age,
Ennoblèd hath the buskined stage.
But, O sad virgin, that thy power
Might raise Musaeus from his bower,
Or bid the soul of Orpheus sing   105
Such notes as warbled to the string,
Drew iron tears down Pluto's cheek,
And made hell grant what love did seek.
Or call up him that left half-told
The story of Cambuscan bold,   110
Of Camball, and of Algarsife,
And who had Canacë to wife,
That owned the virtuous ring and glass,
And of the wondrous horse of brass,
On which the Tartar king did ride;   115

92 **mansion ... nook** two ways of seeing soul's relation to body: 'mansion'
spacious and habitable, 'nook' cramping; cf *Comus* 1–7.   93 **daemons**
spirits controlling different aspects of nature, who can in turn be controlled.   95 **consent** sympathetic link that can be used for magical
operations.   97 **Tragedy** . . . imagined as spiritual presence. M refers
to themes of plays by Greek tragedians.   98 **sceptred pall** regal robes.
101 (though rare) M allows very little room for native Elizabethan and
Jacobean tragedy; Greek tragedy fits better because il penseroso lives in
his head and his books?   102 **buskined** tragic; ie where actors wear
the buskin. Cf *L'all* 132.   104 **raise Musaeus** conjure up spirit of
Musaeus, mythical poet like Orpheus, who here links back with *L'all*
145–50 (though M careful not to make symmetry too exact).   **109 him
that left half-told** Chaucer, who left his *Squire's tale* unfinished.
It was continued by Spenser (*Fairy queen* IV). M piecing together
a tradition leading to himself?   113 **virtuous** having magical
powers.

And if aught else, great bards beside,
In sage and solemn tunes have sung,
Of tourneys and of trophies hung;
Of forests, and enchantments drear,
Where more is meant than meets the ear.   120
Thus Night oft see me in thy pale career,
Till civil-suited Morn appear,
Not tricked and frounced as she was wont,
With the Attic boy to hunt,
But kerchieft in a comely cloud,   125
While rocking winds are piping loud,
Or ushered with a shower still,
When the gust hath blown his fill,
Ending on the rustling leaves,
With minute drops from off the eaves.   130
And when the sun begins to fling
His flaring beams, me goddess bring
To archèd walks of twilight groves,
And shadows brown that Sylvan loves
Of pine, or monumental oak,   135
Where the rude axe with heavèd stroke,
Was never heard the nymphs to daunt,
Or fright them from their hallowed haunt.
There in close covert by some brook,
Where no profaner eye may look,   140
Hide me from day's garish eye,
While the bee with honied thigh,
That at her flowery work doth sing,
And the waters murmuring

116 **great bards** Spenser and other allegorical romancers; 'bard' more
grand and priestly than 'poet'.   120 **Where more** . . . allegorical writing, where powerful political, religious, moral meanings lie hidden. Cf
collective, ritual, open art in *L'all*.   123 **tricked and frounced**
dressed up, her hair curled; colloquial words sound vulgar.   124
Attic boy Cephalus, Greek lover of Morn (Aurora).   127 **ushered** . . .
still led in by a gentle shower.   130 **minute drops** falling one a minute
and tiny; this line discreetly punctuates the poem too.   134 **Sylvan**
wood-god like Pan.   140 **eye** fear of spies acted out in 'i'/eye sounds
140–2.

With such consort as they keep,   145
Entice the dewy-feathered Sleep;
And let some strange mysterious dream,
Wave at his wings in airy stream,
Of lively portraiture displayed,
Softly on my eyelids laid.   150
And as I wake, sweet music breathe
Above, about, or underneath,
Sent by some spirit to mortals good,
Or the unseen genius of the wood.
But let my due feet never fail,   155
To walk the studious cloister's pale,
And love the high embowèd roof,
With antique pillars massy proof,
And storied windows richly dight,
Casting a dim religious light.   160
There let the pealing organ blow,
To the full-voiced choir below,
In service high, and anthems clear,
As may with sweetness, through mine ear,
Dissolve me into ecstasies,   165
And bring all heaven before mine eyes.
And may at last my weary age
Find out the peaceful hermitage,
The hairy gown and mossy cell,
Where I may sit and rightly spell   170
Of every star that heaven doth show,

---

145 consort harmony.   **147 Wave at his wings** ... hover or float;
dream/stream rhyme recalls *L'all* 129–30.   **153 mortals good** only the
pure can hear this music. Cf 47–8.   **154 genius** see *Arcades*, and Thyrsis
in *Comus*.   **155 due feet** disciplined steps, cf 'musing gait' 38.   **156 pale**
limit.   **158 massy proof** phrase as solid and impenetrable as what it talks
about; hard to fit it into the grammar.   **159 storied windows** stained
glass picturing Biblical scenes, making light in next line 'dim'.   **161–3**
blow ... below ... high acting out musical effect. Cf *Nativity* XIII.
165 Dissolve ... undo, separate soul from body (cf 'dissolution'
=death).   **169 hairy gown** ... traditional garb of the ascetic, also puts
him back in the natural landscape.   **170 spell** read in the book of
nature, find out her secrets.

And every herb that sips the dew;
Till old experience do attain
To something like prophetic strain.
These pleasures Melancholy give,   175
And I with thee will choose to live.

173 **old experience** long study; he has retreated from vision (166) to slow accumulation of knowledge.   175 **These pleasures . . .** places poem back inside frame.

Arcades & Comus

Edited by PETER MENDES

Introduction to Arcades and Comus

Occasions

Arcades was performed c. 1630–3 at Harefield in Middlesex, great house of the Countess of Derby. The masque culminated in the countess having her grandchildren presented to her as participants. Among them would be Lady Alice Egerton, Lord (John) Brackley (these are 'courtesy' titles) and Thomas Egerton, the children of Sir John Egerton, who lived nearby at Ashridge, Hertfordshire. He was a son of the countess's first husband; and married one of her daughters by her first marriage: so he was both the countess's stepson and her son-in-law. He had been made Earl of Bridgewater and in 1631 he was appointed Lord President of Wales. It was to celebrate his installation in that office at his official seat of Ludlow Castle, Shropshire, that *Comus* was commissioned, and performed there on 29 September 1634.

The Countess of Harewood, about 70 at the time of *Arcades*, had long been a patron of poets, including Spenser. Her second husband, Sir Thomas Egerton, had employed Donne as secretary. *Othello* was performed at Harefield (12 miles from Horton, Bucks, where Milton was to study later). But the connection between Milton and the Egerton family was probably effected by Henry Lawes. He was the children's music tutor; he had written for Carew's masque, *Coelum Britannicum*, which they had also taken part in; he set the *Comus* songs, designed and managed the production, and took the parts of Attendant Spirit and Thyrsis. See Appendix on the music; and Milton's sonnet to him.

In 1631 another son-in-law of the countess was executed, along with two of his servants, for sadism (causing his wife to be raped, debauching another woman) and for homosexuality with his servants. We do not know whether *Arcades* came before or after

87

this scandal but it seems very likely that *Comus* was intended partly as a ritual of purification. The cuts made for the acting version reduce the sexual content of speeches by the Lady and Comus.

Masque

A masque was a 17th-century mixture of opera and dancing, commissioned and produced to celebrate a courtly occasion such as a wedding, visit, installation. It was scripted, acted and sung like opera, into which the form later merged; but unlike opera it always ended with dancing in which the audience would join. In the earlier masques, these dances had been the centre of the entertainment but later the literary and mythological elements, which had provided an allegorical frame for the dances, were made (especially by Ben Jonson) much more important.

Masque originated in the medieval pre-Lenten revels, or carnival. *Carne vale* = farewell to the flesh, the last spree before the abstinence of Lent; it was a ritual dance which usually mimed the battle between self-restraint (Lent) and sensual release as symbolized by the Lord of Misrule (cf the contrast between Falstaff and the nobility in *Henry IV*). By the time of the Tudors, carnival revels had become ritualized and sophisticated into courtly masquerade balls. At the Tudor court, courtiers would disguise themselves ('masquerade'), pair off with the laides in a formal dance, and then invite the spectators to participate. At the court of James I these evolved into formal and costly ceremonials, lavishly staged at great expense (up to £30,000) to celebrate court occasions. Ben Jonson's masque *Hymenaei* celebrated the marriage of the Earl of Essex's son to the daughter of the Earl of Suffolk in 1606; his *Masque of blackness* was a Twelfth Night festival in honour of Queen Anne in 1605; it cost £3,000. The masque reached its pinnacle of popularity and achievement in James's reign, when the talents of Ben Jonson as poet-dramatist, and Inigo Jones as architect, and musicians such as Lawes, combined to produce the mixture of sumptuous neo-classic stage sets and finely functional scenarios which became the classic examples of the form.

At the courts of James I and Charles I masques became more intricately structured within dramatic and allegorical plots, and more spectacular.

Like much Elizabethan drama, the more sophisticated masques

of the great years of Jonson–Jones collaborations owed much to the medieval morality plays – with an important difference. Whereas the allegorical structure in the morality plays was Christian (characters representing Christian virtues and vices are usually named after them), masques provided James I and Charles I with a perfect vehicle for symbolizing the divine right of the Stuart king. The final dances represent the earthly order under the king (Queen Henrietta-Maria often figuring pre-eminently in them). This in turn mirrored the cosmic order of the universe and the music of the spheres. The antimasque, representing forces of anarchy, rebellion and disorder, was ultimately either reconciled to the ordered whole, or banished. To a king worried about the shakiness of his position, a series of masques would provide a potent, if somewhat expensive, means of wish-fulfilling fantasy – both for himself and his court. But it was a precarious image of security, for masque was essentially a secondary form of art, in that it could last only as long as the performance; at the end, the forces of disorder – transience and change – threaten once again. The masque writers took the renaissance habit of allegorizing the gods and stories of classical mythology. As these allegorical elements became more predominant, the Elizabethan masque began to exhibit a kind of plot, introduced by a Presenter, who would explain, in a prologue, the 'meaning' of what was to follow. The courtly dancers, representing (masquing as) classical gods and goddesses (which, in turn, were icons or symbols for virtues and vices), would finally assume in their culminating dance a symbolic contrast (*not* a dramatic conflict), in which those virtues and vices would be reconciled and harmonized. The title of one of Ben Jonson's most famous masques makes this explicit: *Pleasure reconciled to virtue.*

Another new element was the antimasque – an interlude of morris-dancing (usually by a professional troupe) whose crude bouncing rhythms would release anarchic vitality, temporarily shattering the calm and ceremonial dancing of the masquers. The antimasquers usually appeared dressed as rustics, thus prompting the symbolic equation disorderly rout = rustic, ordered harmony = court. For Milton in *Comus* this equation becomes more complex, for he uses two antimasques, one anarchic (Comus's revels), one in which order and degree prevail (the shepherds' dance which precedes the culminatory dances).

Prologue. Symbolic action introduced by the Presenter who also sets the scene. In his opening speech he would also hint at the meaning symbolized by the plot.

Antimasque. A comparatively noisy and disordered dance (the Elder Brother describes Comus's rout as a 'barbarous dissonance'). Performed by professional morris-dancers dressed as rustics.

Masque procession and plot. The musical disorder implied by the antimasque is allegorically acted out as a contrast to courtly order. This usually offered the audience an arrangement of masquers dressed as classical god and goddesses and representing contrasting virtues and vices. Then the masquers approach the person or persons being celebrated (the procession).

Epiphany and apotheosis. A god or (more usually) goddess resolves the contrasting virtues and vices by harmonizing it, usually in a song. This moment of sudden illumination (the epiphany) is succeeded by the apotheosis – the visible manifestation of that harmony implied by the song. This manifestation of harmonious order is the masquers' final dance, in which the whole audience, in strict order of degree, eventually join. This could last an hour or more.

Epilogue. The Presenter reappears, after the dances end, and again points the meaning implied by this complex of verse, music, spectacle and dance.

Introduction to Arcades

As it stands the plot of *Arcades* is skeletal: some shepherds and shepherdesses, lured by the fame of the countess, have come from Arcadia to seek her. The Genius of the Wood, like the Attendant Spirit in *Comus*, acts as impresario, and guides the arcadians to the countess. The action takes place outdoors. They come on her seated in her chair of state in front of the entrance of Harefield House. The Genius's speech about the music of the spheres gives the piece its ideological framework. He tells how he listens to the music of the spheres after tending the woods and gardens of Harefield, and how only a song which could imitate that divine harmony could do justice to the grace and nobility of the countess

(44–80). This hints at two 'meanings' to the action, both centring on a compliment to the countess: (1) her presence in England makes it a more perfect Arcadia than the original; and (2) a suggested parallel between the arcadians seeking the divine countess, and the search of the wise men for the infant Christ.

Arcades is firmly bound to, and limited by, its occasion. Milton's praise of the aristocracy is confident and pure: nature is seen as the material for civilized man to control and perfect, the golden age of pastoral is seen as a living possibility. Two years later, in *Comus*, Milton's exploration into nature and civilization was to produce a work in which the compliments and celebrations were more difficult to achieve.

Arcades

[*Members of the family, in pastoral dress, move towards the seat of state, with this song.*]

1st song

LOOK NYMPHS, and shepherds look,
    What sudden blaze of majesty
    Is that which we from hence descry
Too divine to be mistook:
    This, this is she   5
To whom our vows and wishes bend,
Here our solemn search hath end.

Fame that her high worth to raise,
Seemed erst so lavish and profuse,
We may justly now accuse   10
Of detraction from her praise,

Title Arcadès were the hunters and shepherds who lived in Arcadia, the traditional country of classical and renaissance pastoral – it is actually southern Greece, mountainous and secluded. The Arcadians had been there so long they were said to have lived before the moon. They were very musical. Their god was Pan. **3 descry** observe, see. **6 vows** prayers. **8 Fame** reputation, rumour. She was in fact renowned for her beauty. **9 erst** previously, until now.

Less than half we find expressed,
Envy bid conceal the rest.

Mark what radiant state she spreads,
In circle round her shining throne,   15
Shooting her beams like silver threads,
This, this is she alone,
    Sitting like a goddess bright,
    In the centre of her light.

Might she the wise Latona be,   20
Or the towerèd Cybelè,
Mother of a hundred gods;
Juno dares not give her odds;
    Who had thought this clime had held
    A deity so unparalleled?   25

*As they come forward, the Genius of the Wood appears, and
turning toward them, speaks.*

    Genius. Stay gentle swains, for though in this disguise,
I see bright honour sparkle through your eyes,
Of famous Arcady ye are, and sprung
Of that renownèd flood, so often sung,
Divine Alpheüs, who by secret sluice,   30
Stole under seas to meet his Arethuse;
And ye the breathing roses of the wood,
Fair silver-buskined nymphs as great and good,
I know this quest of yours, and free intent
Was all in honour and devotion meant   35

16 threads possibly stripes inlaid on the canopy of the throne·
20 Latona mother of Apollo, god of the sun, and of Diana, goddess
of the moon. Supposed to have been born in Britain.   **21 Cybelè**
'mother of 100 gods' who wore a towered crown, and was admired for
her wisdom. The countess had 18 grandchildren.   **23 Juno** queen of
the gods. **give her odds** compete.   **26 Genius** the Romans believed
that places and persons each had a separate 'genius' to watch over them.
gentle swains noble shepherds. He can see nobility in the boys' faces,
in spite of disguise.   **30 Alpheüs** river which flowed through Arcadia;
see *Lyc* 85.   **32 roses** the girls.   **33 buskined** Diana and her nymphs
wore boots as they were huntresses; masquers often wore silver boots.
34 free intent noble purpose.

To the great mistress of yon princely shrine,
Whom with low reverence I adore as mine,
And with all helpful service will comply
To further this night's glad solemnity;
And lead ye where ye may more near behold   40
What shallow-searching fame hath left untold;
Which I full oft amidst these shades alone
Have sat to wonder at, and gaze upon:
For know by lot from Jove I am the power
Of this fair wood, and live in oaken bower,   45
To nurse the saplings tall, and curl the grove
With ringlets quaint, and wanton windings wove.
And all my plants I save from nightly ill,
Of noisome winds, and blasting vapours chill.
And from the boughs brush off the evil dew,   50
And heal the harms of thwarting thunder blue,
Or what the cross dire-looking planet smites,
Or hurtful worm with cankered venom bites.
When evening grey doth rise, I fetch my round
Over the mount, and all this hallowed ground,   55
And early ere the odorous breath of morn
Awakes the slumbering leaves, or tasselled horn
Shakes the high thicket, haste I all about,
Number my ranks, and visit every sprout
With puissant words, and murmurs made to bless.   60
But else in deep of night when drowsiness
Hath locked up mortal sense, then listen I
To the celestial sirens' harmony,

39 solemnity celebration, festival.   **47 wanton** loose.   **52 cross**
slanting. **planet** Saturn.   **60 puissant** having magical powers. **mur-**
murs spells.   **63 harmony** in a part of the *Republic* called the Myth
of Er (x 616) Plato envisions the structure of the universe, and of
human existence linked to it, like this. There is a colossal stroke of light,
like a cosmic rainbow. From the top of it hangs a spindle (a spindle is a
spinning instrument: it is shaft with a cup called a whorl at one end,
and a barb called a hook at the other). The spindle hangs by its hook.
Its base lies in the lap of Anangke, Necessity, as she sits below. The
whorl contains other whorls, to accommodate all the circles of the stars
and planets. Each circle has a siren standing on it. As the spindle spins,
the whorls revolve and the sirens sing, emitting the music of the spheres.

That sit upon the nine enfolded spheres,
And sing to those that hold the vital shears, 65
And turn the adamantine spindle round,
On which the fate of gods and men is wound.
Such sweet compulsion doth in music lie,
To lull the daughters of Necessity,
And keep unsteady Nature to her law, 70
And the low world in measured motion draw
After the heavenly tune, which none can hear
Of human mould with gross unpurgèd ear;
And yet such music worthiest were to blaze
The peerless height of her immortal praise, 75
Whose lustre leads us, and for her most fit,
If my inferior hand or voice could hit
Inimitable sounds, yet as we go,
Whate'er the skill of lesser gods can show,
I will assay, her worth to celebrate, 80
And so attend ye toward her glittering state;
Where ye may all that are of noble stem
Approach, and kiss her sacred vesture's hem.

2nd song

O'er the smooth enamelled green
Where no print of step hath been, 85
   Follow me as I sing,
   And touch the warbled string.
Under the shady roof
Of branching elm star-proof.
   Follow me, 90

The three Fates, who are the daughters of Necessity, sing to the sirens'
songs. Lachesis, whose task is to assign each man his lot, sings of things
past; Clotho, who spins the thread of each man's life, sings of things
present; Atropos, who slits the threads, of things to come. **71 measured** rhythmical. **73** The Genius can hear the music of the spheres,
which to the 'gross' ears of ordinary mortals is inaudible. The idea that
sin caused this 'grossness' was a Christian addition to the Platonic
myth. **74 blaze** proclaim. **77 hit** equal. **82 stem** family. **84
enamelled** smooth, but also bright. There would probably have been a
dance of the nymphs and shepherds between the songs.

I will bring you where she sits
Clad in splendour as befits
    Her deity.
Such a rural queen
All Arcadia hath not seen.   95

3rd song

Nymphs and shepherds dance no more
    By sandy Ladon's lilied banks,
        On old Lycaeus or Cyllénè hoar,
            Trip no more in twilight ranks,
            Though Erymanth your loss deplore,   100
            A better soil shall give ye thanks.
From the stony Maenalus,
Bring your flocks, and live with us,
Here ye shall have greater grace,
To serve the Lady of this place.   105
    Though Syrinx your Pan's mistress were,
    Yet Syrinx well might wait on her.
        Such a rural queen
        All Arcadia hath not seen.

Introduction to Comus

Masque and drama

A study of *Comus*, even with an imaginative effort to see it as it
happened in its original performance, leaves us with the impression that the dances fulfil no more than a secondary function.
Instead of being central, they seem almost formal additions,
peripheral to the masque's true centre – the clash of will and

96 dance stop dancing in Arcadia; dance here instead.   **97 Ladon** another
Arcadian river.   **98 Lycaeus . . . Cyllénè . . . Erymanth[us] . . .**
Maenalus mountains in Arcadia.   **106 Syrinx** an Arcadian nymph,
chaste as Diana and often mistaken for her. Pan chased her; to escape,
she turned into reeds, from which he made pan pipes (=syrinx). It is
not clear what the compliment means but she was treated as a symbol of
immortality through death and art.

idea in the Comus / Lady debate scene. The pivot of this masque is untypically a clash, not a symbolic reconciliation in the final dances. Literary and dramatic elements threaten to fracture the allegorical structure of song, dance and visual effect. Since one of the basic demands of drama (as opposed to allegory) is precisely that it represent a dialectic clash of wills, in which argument and action can *change* the protagonists, we can see in what a curious position this places *Comus*. For though its overall structure remains allegorical (we're never really in doubt as to what will happen to the Lady, the Attendant Spirit is always nearby), in its most powerful scene we are presented with more than a token contrast of vice and virtue: we are involved in a debate which prompts the disturbing questions posed by a play.

Yet to Milton it was always a *Mask presented at Ludlow Castle* – the title in all editions printed in Milton's lifetime: it was the 18th-century editors who shortened the title to *Comus*. Let us identify the purely masque elements in *Comus*:

Prologue. The Attendant Spirit's opening speech, which sets the scene and the mythological scheme in which the plot will take place, and makes the connection between the action and the event which it celebrates.

Antimasque. Comus's rout.

Epiphany. Sabrina's song and its magical effect (the freeing of the Lady from the bonds of a darker kind of magic).

Masque procession. There is none. At the point where one might be expected (ie after the country dancing when the scene shifts to Ludlow Town and the President's Castle and the children enter with the Attendant Spirit) the Bridgewater Manuscript makes it clear that they enter 'towards the end of these sports'.

Presentation. The children are presented to their father by the Attendant Spirit's song (966).

Apotheosis. The final dance, preceded by the second antimasque: the shepherds' dance. (Though this, unlike Comus's rout, emphasizes order and degree, since the rustics give way to the 'other trippings . . ./of lighter toes' of the main dancers.)

Epilogue. The Attendant Spirit concludes by indicating the meaning of the whole complex of spectacle, music, dance and verse.

The elements are certainly there; Milton does provide the occasion with an elaborate compliment and a fitting celebration. He also makes sure to remind the audience, via the Attendant Spirit, of the occasion by bringing it into the script:

> . . . all this tract that fronts the falling sun
> A noble peer of mickle trust, and power
> Has in his charge . . .
> Where his fair offspring nursed in princely lore,
> Are coming to attend their father's state,
> And new-entrusted sceptre, but their way
> Lies through the perplexed paths of this drear wood.   30

But apart from the invocation to Sabrina, the goddess of the local river Severn, the next reference to the celebrations comes approximately 900 lines later, where the Spirit promises to lead the children to

> . . . your father's residence,
> Where this night are met in state
> Many a friend . . .
> And our sudden coming there
> Will double all their mirth and cheer.   946

In terms also of stage machinery and lavish scenery, compared with the extravagance of a Jonson–Jones production, *Comus* is noticeably frugal. The one mechanical device necessary was a trap-door and pulley to allow Sabrina to rise and descend, and the scenery probably comprised two painted backcloths (the 'wild wood' and the Ludlow town and castle) which could be drawn aside to disclose an inner stage representing the interior of Comus's 'stately palace'.

The collaboration between Ben Jonson and Inigo Jones finally terminated in a famous quarrel over their relative importance in the creation of a court masque. Jones maintained that the spectacle was primary; briefly, Jonson's argument ran: the spectacle merely appeals to the senses and is transitory, the poetry appeals to the mind and lasts. In *Comus*, Milton avoids the problem by virtually including the spectacle in the poetry. The wild wood is present there, in the poetry. The landscape in which it all happens is really situated in Milton's own mind, where he attempts to resolve the clash within himself between Milton the puritan and Milton the humanist poet. *Comus* takes up a dilemma central to all his work: to what extent is nature and its pleasures dangerous? Can aesthetic pleasure be reconciled with ethical virtue?

sex and marriage with the chastity and self-negation fitting us
'. . . to climb/Higher than the sphery chime'?

The answers to these questions won't be provided in this introduction: but let us now look at the complexities of the work in
more detail (and in roughly chronological order) with them in
mind.

Prologue

In his opening speech the Attendant Spirit's lavish poetry creates
the visual scene; but he also hints at his role in the moral scheme
of the work:

> Yet some there be that by due steps aspire
> To lay their just hands on that golden key
> That opes the palace of eternity:
> To such my errand is . . .   12–15

In his outline we are presented with two contrasting worlds: the
regions of mild and serene air (4) and 'the smoke and stir of this
dim spot Which men call earth', already suggesting one of the
crucial questions posed by the work. Are we to take the Attendant
Spirit's description of the natural world also as a moral evalua-
tion? Is earth (this dim, dark spot) morally antagonistic to the
regions of mild and serene air which the Spirit will associate,
in the epilogue, with classical Arcadia and Christian Heaven?
His attitude towards nature seems severe: in order for 'some' to
lay 'just hands' on the 'golden key' (virtue) before death comes,
it appears that external aid may be necessary (external to nature –
the Spirit doesn't belong to the 'dim, dark spot'). A hostile moral
slant is given to man as a natural being: his body is seen as 'a
sin-worn mould', giving off 'rank vapours'. This severity is, of
course, Christian: it accepts the corruption due to the fall; and
the need for help.

The speech is also gesturing to the stage set and scenery,
inviting the audience to participate in the artificiality of the
masque conventions. In terms of stage production, the Spirit
'descends' from above the stage (the pulley system), into the
'wild wood'. A rough cosmology is sketched, symbolized by the
spatial architecture of the stage set, with heaven above, earth
(and hell?) at stage level. The Ptolemaic system saw earth as
centre of the cosmos, with the planets circling it; so the Attendant
Spirit could enlist his original audience's acceptance of the stage

as a microcosm of earth and its universe: 'all the world's a stage'. Cf the more recent dramatic attempts to make the stage = world equation realistically viable: the drawing rooms of Ibsen and Chekhov, Pinter's attics and basements, the decaying room surrounded by external devastation of Beckett's *Endgame*.

Hierarchy and plot

It was a renaissance assumption that creation was ordered in a hierarchical pattern, the great chain of being. The system descends from God and his angels, down through man at its centre, to lower beasts, vegetables, inanimate matter. Two worlds were posited; the heavenly (inhabited by God and angels), and the earthly or natural (the domain of man and beast). Upright man spanned the dividing line – his mind and soul aspiring upwards to the angels, his lower sensual nature drawing him downwards to bestial pleasure.

Within this structure the plot attempts to resolve itself. On the simple narrative level it is pure fairy-tale: innocent child falls into clutches of evil magician, and is rescued by the powers of good. White magic (haemony, the harmonious power of Sabrina's song) can overcome black magic (the power of Comus's wand). She is delivered to her parents and all ends happily; in masque terms, the final dance can take place.

Yet complexities begin to arise when we see the plot in the philosophical context sketched above, for the action takes place primarily in the natural world: the 'dim spot/Which men call earth'. As far as *Comus* goes, this means the 'wild wood' with Comus's palace, and Ludlow with the President's castle. The children's voyage (of life?) to father and civilized court entails their finding a way through the 'paths of this drear wood', where Comus holds sway. It is a moral, as well as a physical, journey. In the 'wild wood' of life (adolescence?) heaven sends us trials to prove our worth. As the Spirit sings, when presenting the children to their father:

> Heaven hath timely tried their youth,
> Their faith, their patience and their truth,
> And sent them here through hard assays
> With a crown of deathless praise,
> To triumph in victorious dance . . .   969–73

As Milton was to write ten years later in *Areopagitica*, 'what purifies us is trial, and trial is by what is contrary'. Of course, the great works of his maturity all centre on scenes of trial: Adam and Eve's in *PL*, Christ's in *Paradise regained*, Samson's in *Samson agonistes*. And since the great poet can always imaginatively identify with the 'possible other case' (in Henry James's words), the trial is an interior one, dramatically externalized in his art. So the drama which takes place in the wild wood is to be seen from more than one standpoint. Milton allows Comus a strong poetic case, for Comus expresses an aspect of Milton's own personality. We are introduced to Comus and his wild wood by the antimasque.

Antimasque

After the panoramic view offered by the Attendant Spirit's speech, we close up on the dramatically noisy entry of Comus and his 'rout of monsters'. A stage direction in the Trinity manuscript says 'They come on in a wilde and antic fashion', and according to the printed direction 'making a riotous and unruly noise'.

The pagan god of excess was called Dionysus by the Greeks and Bacchus by the Romans. From his union with Circe, the enchantress of Homer's *Odyssey* whose embrace turned men to swine, Comus was born. His domain in this work is strictly pagan – the world of nature. Apart from vague intimations of 'some superior power' (800) supporting the Lady, he is incapable of apprehending any other world but his own, any other morality than his own (the Lady's insistence on the virtue of chastity and self-restraint is, in his scheme of things, meaningless). His morality is founded on the 'virtue' of sensual pleasure. As Comus enters with his disciples 'headed like sundry sorts of wild beasts', the implication is there: the drama is to centre on a clash of values. On the one hand the abundant anarchy of nature (the instinctive life of the senses is no more than an imitation of how nature works); and on the other, the order which comes from self-restraint, with its associated values of 'virtue', 'chastity', and 'virginity' the three pillars of the Lady's argument.

Their entrance also makes the point musically: the Trinity manuscript calls for 'a wilde, rude and wanton antic'. Conventional to antimasque, yes; but the later Comus-Lady debate gives it a more than conventional force. The dramatic impact is one of uncontrolled energy, springing from spontaneous impulse. The whole work offers itself to Freudian terminology, with the dark wild wood as the landscape of Milton's subconscious, anarchic and sexually vital (the musical *Hair* sees the world as Comus does); and Ludlow and its castle, ceremonially ordered and civilized, as the restraining super-ego which can only build by re-channelling or sublimating that sexual energy into civilized 'virtuous' endeavour: the cost of civilization is repression.

In terms of the masque convention, it is the reconciliation of these contraries (order / anarchy, Chastity/licentiousness, harmony/dissonance, light/darkness) that we look for in the final dance: we do not find it. For all that the 'wild wood' represents, and the force of Comus's poetry, is rejected, repressed. The final apotheosis, according to the Attendant Spirit, is a 'victorious dance/O'er sensual folly, and intemperance' (974).

Antimasque in this work is not token disorder finally incorporated into a larger order; it is a threatening force to be defeated before the civilized rituals can begin.

Between their entrance and the 'wilde rude and wanton antic', Comus exhorts his followers to

> Midnight shout, and revelry,
> Tipsy dance, and jollity. 103–4

The poetry following the Spirit's stately blank verse races along, miming the energy and movement of the revellers; it is an incitement to dance. And Comus, seeing their dance as a mimic celebration of the way the universe works, gives us a taste of his poetic power; and stakes his own claim to the music of the spheres:

> We that are of purer fire,
> Imitate the starry choir,
> Who in their nightly watchful spheres,
> Lead in swift round the months and years. 111–14

This is the imaginative world of *A midsummer night's dream*: it seems severe to describe it as a 'barbarous dissonance', as the Attendant Spirit does (549). Of course, this is not the whole story: Comus moves on to sex and witchcraft:

> Come let us our rites begin,
> 'Tis only daylight that makes sin . . .
> Hail, goddess of nocturnal sport
> Dark veiled Cotytto . . . 125–9

At the Black Mass the female witches offer themselves sexually to the 'priest' yet here we feel Milton is reminding us that this is, after all, the antimasque, and therefore morally suspect. But in showing his poetic virtuosity, he gives Comus a verbal power which later weakens the moral point about defeating 'sensuous folly and intemperance'.

Pastoral drama

From this point to the final presentation and dances, Milton uses another renaissance convention: the plot thickens as masque merges into pastoral drama. Again, genre is used for Milton's own purposes. We already have pastoral setting and language: the Lady speaks of

> . . . the loose unlettered hinds,
> When for their teeming flocks, and granges full,
> In wanton dance they praise the bounteous Pan . . .   173–5

The Attendant Spirit enters the action 'habited like a shepherd' (Thyrsis: 488); the Comus-Lady scene will take the form of a debate about the uses of nature; the wild wood offered as a variation on Arcadia. But it is an Arcadia turned upside down and seen as morally hostile. The paradox emerges in the Lady's ambivalence about country life: compare the attitude expressed in her speech quoted above, with her reaction to Comus in 'harmless villager' disguise:

> Shepherd I take thy word,
> And trust thy honest offered courtesy,
> Which oft is sooner found in lowly sheds
> With smoky rafters, than in tapestry halls
> And courts of princes, where it first was named,
> And yet is most pretended . . .   320–5

The countryside is seen on the one hand as hopelessly primitive and 'wanton' (the Pan rituals of primitive societies were essentially fertility rites – hence 'bounteous'); yet the pastoral commonplace of innocent countryside versus decadent court is also used. We remind ourselves that the puritan Milton, faced in 1634 with the extremes of the Cavalier-Roundhead argument and impending civil war, had very much in mind the hated moral laxity of the Stuart court. Years later he was to apostrophize the innocent bower of Adam and Eve thus:

> Here Love his golden shafts employs, here lights
> His constant lamp, and waves his purple wings,
> Reigns here and revels; not in the bought smile

Of harlots, loveless, joyless, unendeared,
Casual fruition, nor in court amours,
Mixed dance, or wanton masque, or midnight ball . . .

PL IV 763

The Lady's ambivalent attitude towards 'natural' life is peculiar to, and inherent in, pastoral itself. What is pastoral, and how does it work?

We all have dream pictures of an ideal world. W. H. Auden divides these into two types: Edens and New Jerusalems. Eden derives from the past, New Jerusalem is the possible future. Marx's ideal world, for example, is a New Jerusalem – a Utopia history is moving towards. For Freud the ideal world is past – the Eden of the womb. For the renaissance, the dream of an ideal world was backward looking: back to the civilizations of Greece and Rome. The renaissance poets therefore accept the literary Eden of the classics: the myth of the golden age. This, for Ovid, was the earliest of the 'ages' of the world, which progressively declined through the silver and bronze, to the iron age. Effectively, the golden age was a time of harmony between man and nature, all strife absent, food and drink available through nature's bounty, the climate eternal spring, 'work' unnecessary, the only occupations the tending of sheep and poetic discussions about love's sweet pain: an escapist literary dream-world (the great classical exponents of the genre were all city men – Theocritus in sophisticated Alexandria writing about the shepherds of his native Sicily, Virgil dreaming of pastures and eternal spring in the harsh realities of Augustan Rome). It is the kind of escape which successive ages call on literature to provide: the remote Gothic castle, the exotic and passionate experiences of the Byronic hero, the clearcut distinction between good and bad of the worlds of the Western and James Bond, the nostalgic heroisms of Tolkien's dreamworld. Pastoral was the renaissance escapist dream and its imaginary landscape was called Arcadia – in reality a harsh rocky area of Greece, but in pastoral the ideal landscape.

Some of the classical pastorals took the form of dialogue poems; the renaissance writers provided a plot and turned them into dramas. They become more sophisticated, centrally organized around a passion-reason debate. The three pastoral dramas most available to Milton were Tasso's *Aminta* (first performed in 1573), Guarini's *Il pastor fido* (*The faithful shepherd* 1585) and Fletcher's *The faithful shepherdess* (1608), and all centred on such debates though making different points. Tasso presents a pure golden age naturalism: love if you will; if it pleases, it is permitted; natural instinct is right. Nature in *Il pastor fido* is fallen; the debate is between Chastity and Lust, the message implied: 'Love, if it's lawful'. Similarly, Fletcher argues, 'Love, if it's lawful', but adds, 'it's better to be a virgin'.

Comus offers a naturalist argument. Milton, while fully sensible of its attractions (the beauty of Comus's poetry), morally rejects it. To Comus the wild wood is of 'prosperous growth' (269); it is 'drear', 'ominous' and 'a dungeon' to everyone else. This is no Arcadia. Nature is hostile, the implications of pastoral are questioned. In the wood, the Lady is an alien – she falls immediately for Comus's disguise, Echo does *not* reply to her plea for help (as it conventionally did in pastoral), and she is *physically* helpless in Comus's palace.

History will give a partial explanation of M's hostility to nature. By the 1630s, the puritan fear of the tyranny of the flesh, and materialism, cast a cold moral eye on nature; so the pastoral commonplace about innocent nature becomes ambiguous. Agricultural festivities carry undertones of lustful promiscuity (hence the 'loose unlettered hinds . . . In wanton dance'); Hamlet can use the phrase 'country matters' as a sexual pun.

The political unease and fear of impending civil war also call into question any naturalist arguments about freedom and liberty – what is needed is rather authority and restraint. The feeling, later given succinct expression by the political philosopher, Thomas Hobbes, that human life (and nature) is, without the restraining authority of the state, essentially destructive ('nasty, solitary, brutish and short'), is very much in the air.

This is all hard for us to take today; we are much more likely to cast a cold eye on the destructive effects of a technological 'civilization' – the bomb, pollution, Marcuse's one-dimensional man, mass media thought-control. Dr Strangelove has become more sinister than Comus. But we have the romantics behind us: Rousseau tells us that we are born innocent and corrupted by society; Locke's attitude to politics is laissez-faire and anti-authoritarian; Blake and Wordsworth see London as hell (see Blake's *London* and book VII of *The prelude*); Freud theorizes that civilization has made neurotics of us; Lady Chatterley has to return to the wood to find sexual fulfilment.

So for Milton, nature is enticingly 'bounteous', but morally dangerous: Comus and his wild wood threaten to make beasts of us. But *at the same time*, he also despairs of the decadence of

Charles's stately court. Stalemate for the pastoral debate: the Spirit, attempting an answer in his epilogue, leaves nature ('this dim spot Which men call Earth') below and soars back to his 'heavenly mansion' above 'in regions mild of calm and serene air', with the advice: you too can follow if you can deny the 'natural' in yourselves.

Chastity

Five years previously we find Milton writing to his friend Charles Diodati in the Latin *Elegia VI*, praising Diodati's 'light-footed' verses: 'But why complain that banquet and bottle frighten poetry away? Song loves Bacchus, and Bacchus loves songs' (14). All this, he continues, is fine for a love poet;

> But the poet who writes about wars, and about a heaven ruled
> over by a Jove who has outgrown his boyhood, about heroes who
> stick to their duty and princes who are half gods . . . let
> this poet live frugally . . . In addition, his youth must be
> chaste and free from crime, his morals strict and his hand
> unstained . . . For the poet is sacred to the gods: he is
> their priest; his innermost heart and his mouth are both full
> of Jove.

Already Milton saw himself (while he wrote *Nativity*) as courting divine wisdom and inspiration through a life of negation and restraint. In the climactic passage of *Il penseroso* (pre-figuring the Spirit's epilogue and written half-way between *Elegia VI* and *Comus*), the verse spirals upwards, lifting the poet's soul away from his 'sin-worn mould':

> Or let my lamp at midnight hour,
> Be seen in some high lonely tower,
> Where I may oft outwatch the Bear,
> With thrice great Hermes, or unsphere
> The spirit of Plato to unfold
> What worlds, or what vast regions hold
> The immortal mind that hath forsook
> Her mansion in this fleshly nook . . .   85–92

Lady Alice

As well as speaking morally for Milton, the Lady is also Lady Alice Egerton. For Bridgewater and his audience, Milton stylizes her adolescent problems, faced as she must be with 'the blind mazes' of life (181). She enters (169) in darkness and her fear of the dark wood is childlike as well as 'puritan':

> A thousand fantasies
> Begin to throng into my memory
> Of calling shapes, and beckoning shadows dire,
> And airy tongues that syllable men's names
> On sands, and shores, and desert wildernesses.   204

Though fearful of the darkness of the 'tangled wood' she is also hopeful that it may turn out to be benignly pastoral and offer 'such cooling fruit As the kind hospitable woods provide' (186). But the dignity of her innocence is balanced by its naïveté: she is duped by Comus in 'gentle villager' disguise ('magic dust') and his 'well-placed words of glozing courtesy' (161). She falls for the pastoral myth in lines 322–7; the pastoral standpoint hovers uncertainly for a moment between 'honest offered' and 'glozing'. With Comus sounding very much like Puck in *A midsummer night's dream* –

> I know each lane and every alley green
> Dingle, or bushy dell, of this wild wood,
> And every bosky bourn from side to side   312

– the wild wood *is* made to seem benignly pastoral: Milton *does* allow Comus a poetically persuasive case (to what extent is Comus 'glozing' in these descriptive passages: 294–301, 311–18?). Aesthetically, Milton is committed to nature's poetic potential; yet the moral strictures are already there: the Lady's song, instead of bringing Echo's answer, attracts her would-be seducer. Pastoral is a deception.

Light and dark

Yet in the midst of darkness, and 'with dangers compassed round', Milton gives the Lady a security which we may find irritatingly complacent:

> These thoughts may startle well, but not astound
> The virtuous mind, that ever walks attended
> By a strong siding champion conscience . . .   211

And she has an inner light which, though ineffective to help her physically out of the dark wood, will keep her soul intact. Then (212–19) a light-dark opposition emerges: nature (the wild wood) is dark and inhospitable, the Lady is physically helpless

106

(she can't see); yet she can see within herself, and above to the heavenly regions: 'white-handed hope Thou hovering angel . . . and . . . chastity I see ye visibly'. Dark nature seems to be split from the 'heavenly regions Of calm and serene air', the body ('this sin-worn mould') from the mind and soul: the dualism implied in the Attendant Spirit's opening speech is here being extended.

An early Christian sect, the Manichees, believed that all matter was evil; it was the province of the devil, and was to be shunned. The whole moral universe was divided into black (nature, the body) and white (heaven, the soul); there was no possible commerce between them. Moral and religious salvation took the form of a flight from the physical world of nature and the body. With the recurrent imagery of light and dark arising from the action in the wild wood, Milton seems close to the Manichaean implication that the visible world itself (nature itself, not just its pastoral image) is a deception, a lie. Of course, the substantial beauty of the nature poetry prevents the work from becoming mystically vague and other-worldly, but since this poetry supports Comus's position (Nature is reality; live according to its laws), this leaves the Lady, and the Attendant Spirit in his epilogue, dangerously close to the Manichaean doctrine.

Divine philosophy

We mustn't read too much dramatic significance into the Brothers' debate (330–488). The occasion demanded the participation of the two boys and Milton allows them an impressive education. Milton was also using the occasion to expound his own views on education: this is what well-educated boys sound like. In his *Tractate on education* (1644) he asserts: 'I will point to you the right path of a noble and virtuous education; laborious indeed at the first ascent, but else so smooth, so green, so full of good prospect, that the harp of Orpheus was not more charming.' The Younger Brother shows himself a good pupil by responding to his elder's defence of chastity with the exclamation: 'How charming is divine philosophy' (475).

Yet some dramatic points do emerge. The Elder Brother's philosophical fluency is unmatched by experience and gives him, in countering his young brother's fears for their sister's safety, a priggish doctrinaire complacency (of course, his worth hasn't yet been Miltonically proved by 'trial'; but it is curious that

Milton should imply that indoctrination will save you when you are eventually 'tried' – after all, Raphael's indoctrination of Adam and Eve did not, in effect, make much difference to the outcome of their 'trial', and the Elder Brother, for all his adolescent bravado, does fail to capture Comus's wand). And he is not wholly right in his confident assertions of his sister's imperviousness to fears (365–71), for we have already seen her quite shaken by 'A thousand fantasies' and we know that she is in danger. But the Platonism which informs this section of the work has a further importance.

Plato and music

The Elder Brother's speech on chastity (452–74) has a significance which reverberates through the whole work, and gives ideological sanction to the Lady's position. The ideas derive from Plato, and we must now examine them.

The great chain of being, the dualistic world (spiritual and natural, light and dark), the distrust of sensual knowledge and pleasure – all are the mixed Christian-Platonic doctrines of the Florentine Neo-Platonists. Their psychology said that man has three basic faculties: the mind or soul, reason, and the sensual appetites. These in turn correspond to the hierarchical structure of the universe: God, the ideal world of Forms, and nature. Socrates tells of a voyage to the world of Forms, where the structure of the world is revealed, with the motions of the eight planets in their spheres. On each circle sits a Siren, each one singing a single note, and together creating the 'music of the spheres' (*Arcades* 62–73). This concept of harmony is for Plato, as for Milton, a metaphor relevant to human psychology: the individual is in a state of harmony when all his faculties keep to their hierarchical positions, hence creating a state of psychological equilibrium (ie the sensual appetites do not usurp the superior status of reason or soul). This musical metaphor also blends neatly with the Christian history of the Fall. Before the Fall, man could hear the music of the spheres, but the apple so disturbed the order of our faculties that we became deaf to the divine harmony. That is, we were deaf to it in our *natural* state: the Elder Brother is saying (452–7) that those chosen few who are so strengthened by their love of chastity that they can withstand their natural instincts, and can progressively sublimate their body into spirit or soul, eventually regain their ability to hear the 'sphery chime'. Milton is providing a philosophical structure to support the Lady's coming trial; and that structure puts Comus firmly in his place as the speech continues:

> but when lust
> By unchaste looks, loose gestures, and foul talk,
> But most by lewd and lavish act of sin,
> Lets in defilement to the inward parts,
> The soul grows clotted by contagión,
> Embodies, and imbrutes, till she quite lose
> The divine property of her first being.   462–8

When the Younger Brother describes this doctrine as 'musical as is Apollo's lute' (477) it is the Neo-Platonic cosmic harmony that Milton is appealing to and celebrating. The masque 'imitates' it and its message is based on it. Comus may have a poetic case, but it can find no philosophical support in this scheme.

Song and poetry

We have already heard the evidence of the Lady's own harmony: her song (229–42) reveals her inner quality; it opposes the 'barbarous dissonance' of Comus's rout. The song is also an appeal to Echo to answer (where are my brothers?), to allow her to reunite with them. But the song also calls for another reunion: by her answer Echo, 'daughter of the sphere' (240), would create a musical counterpoint with the song to connect it with the music of the spheres. The poetic line lengthens to invite the synthesis: 'And give resounding grace to all heaven's harmonies' (242). (The Bridgewater Ms reads 'And hold a counterpoint to all heaven's harmonies'.) The harmonizing answer doesn't come, as it did in earlier masques such as Browne's *Inner Temple masque*. Ironically the song does call forth a ravishing poetic response; but from Comus:

> Can any mortal mixture of earth's mould
> Breathe such divine enchanting ravishment?

He then makes the holy-harmony connection for Milton:

> Sure something holy lodges in that breast,
> And with these raptures moves the vocal air
> To testify his hidden residence . . .   245–7

This Shakespearean intensity undermines any attempt to fix Comus at this point as a glozing seducer. The poetry speaks of a genuine response (at the simple level he's praising Lady Alice's singing, but also soliloquizing as a dramatic character here) to a *kind* of poetry that is new to him: comparing it with his previous musical criterion (his mother Circe and the Sirens three, 'as they sung, would take the prisoned soul, And lap it in Elysium' 255), he concludes:

> Yet they in pleasing slumber lulled the sense,
> And in sweet madness robbed it of itself,
> But such a sacred, and home-felt delight,
> Such sober certainty of waking bliss,
> I never heard till now . . .   259–63

Here Milton is using Comus to distinguish two kinds of song (and poetry), and implying that they are connected with different stages in the moral hierarchy.

Again the appeal is to Plato: Socrates would have poetry banished from his ideal republic because he sees its effect on people in Comus's terms: by 'lulling' the 'sense' (Comus is punning on 'sense' – it means rational sense as well as 'the senses'), poetry puts reason (and self-control) to sleep ('pleasing slumber'), thus driving the audience into a 'sweet madness'. This would ultimately undermine the social macrocosm: poetry is dangerous and must be banished. This argument is still used by opponents of freedom of expression in the arts. Milton is intending us to see Comus's kind of poetry, and its connected kind of music, as dangerous in this sense; but, he implies, there is a higher kind of music, which springs from and celebrates reason and soul, and which can lift us away from seductive nature up towards the 'sphery chime'. Comus, on hearing the Lady's song, acknowledges its superior power (261–3).

There are two ways of taking his statement, 'I'll speak to her And she shall be my queen' (263). She commands a music beyond his powers; she would make a valuable addition to his collection of beast-humans. The acquisitive seducer panting after the purity of a well-bred virgin – this is certainly implied by Milton. But, to reiterate, Comus's poetic response *feels* genuine, and we may see his offer also as genuine (like Satan's offer to Adam and Eve: he is so struck by their beauty that he wants them on his side: 'Hell shall unfold To entertain you two, her widest gates, And send forth all her kings' *PL* IV 381). What happens to the Lady later in Comus's palace obviously encourages the acquisitive seducer view, but at this point it is difficult to deny Comus some sympathy.

Two kinds of poetry, then. Milton's Platonic hierarchy insists that the Lady's be granted a higher status: we are prepared for her moral victory. Yet it is a mark of Milton's greatness that the debate is more complex than that. Can a morality which after all appeals to a realm above and beyond nature justify itself poetically?

Magic

With the entrance of Thyrsis, the pastoral game resumes; the rhymed couplets (494) emphasize convention; but this section fulfils an important function. With Comus now offstage, Milton attempts to balance the view of nature. The Spirit sums it up: the nature presented so far has been the 'hideous wood' (519), controlled by Comus, whose purpose is to corrupt man's divine potential with bestial pleasure, symbolized by his 'pleasure's poison' which

> The visage quite transforms of him that drinks,
> And the inglorious likeness of a beast
> Fixes instead, unmoulding reason's mintage
> Charactered in the face . . .
>
> 526–9

Another response to the Lady's song is offered:

> a soft and solemn-breathing sound
> Rose like a stream of rich distilled perfumes,
> And stole upon the air . . .
>
> 554–6

The Younger Brother extends the contrast, making the sinister connection: wild wood – darkness – hell:

> O night and shades,
> How are ye joined with hell in triple knot
> Against the unarmed weakness of one virgin
> Alone, and helpless!
>
> 579–82

The Elder Brother emphasizes the Lady's security according to the hierarchy underlying the action:

> Virtue may be assailed, but never hurt,
> Surprised by unjust force, but not enthralled . . .
>
> 588–9

He goes on to implicate Comus in the self-defeating logic of sin:

> But evil on itself shall back recoil,
> And mix no more with goodness, when at last
> Gathered like scum, and settled to itself
> It shall be in eternal restless change
> Self-fed, and self-consumed . . .
>
> 592–6

a compelling portrait of the hell of pride and egotism, the incapacity to love anything or anyone beyond oneself ('settled to itself'); the poetry foreshadows Satan's great self-consuming soliloquies in *PL* IV.

The persuasive power of the poetry is capped by a splendid rhetorical gesture: young Egerton points to above the painted scenery from where the Attendant Spirit had been lowered at the beginning of the performance ('regions of calm and serene air') and says:

> If this fail
> The pillared firmament is rottenness,
> And earth's base built on stubble.   596–8

If all I've said is not true, then (a) the whole Christian-Platonic hierarchical structure is a sham; and (b) the whole stage set is about to collapse.

The scene makes another important point: the Spirit tells the Elder Brother to put up his sword,

> Far other arms, and other weapons must
> Be those that quell the might of hellish charms . . .   611

To counter the 'virtue' of Comus's magic dust and wand, the Spirit has 'a virtuous plant', haemony. There has been much discussion of what haemony allegorically represents. Obviously temperance; beyond this Coleridge's suggestion that it derives from the Greek words for 'blood' and 'wine' seems most persuasive, with its allegorical connections with the Last Supper and the crucifixion: salvation through sacrifice. However, it seems to me possible to take it at the simplest level: to offset bad magic you need good magic. What does Comus's magic dust *represent*, anyway? As the Thyrsis disguise presents a good shepherd to balance Comus's evil disguise, so we are shown that nature can provide white magic – haemony – to do battle against the powers of darkness. Also Thyrsis and his Orphic powers,

> Who with his soft pipe, and smooth-dittied song,
> Well knows to still the wild winds when they roar,
> And hush the waving woods,   86

can create a 'platonic' order from an unruly nature. And thirdly, with the magical redeeming power of Sabrina (water), Milton is trying to balance the view of nature. The wild wood contains good shepherds and antidote herbs and cool liquors, as well as Comus with his magic dust and bestial poison.

But the questions are still begged: the good shepherd disguise is just as much a sham as Comus's – more so, since the disguised Attendant Spirit is not a natural being (nor was Comus originally; but he finds it congenial); and haemony doesn't grow in this wild wood: 'in another country, as he said, Bore a bright golden flower, but not in this soil' (631). The masque's allegorical scheme forces Milton to try and have nature both ways: as dangerous and darkly sensual, *and* as a source of healing and life. The paradox is central to Milton as humanist poet and puritan and it is the source of the work's richness.

The debate : nature

Allegorically the Comus–Lady debate represents vice versus virtue. In masque terms, this would be a schematic contrast which would reach its culmination in the final dances, where pleasure would be reconciled to virtue. Superficially, it can work at this level (and probably did for its original audience). But Milton is attempting to work out his own problems, as well as writing the script for an evening's celebrations. And it is this debate, rather than the dances, which formed the organizing centre and dramatic climax of the work. For the meaning of Milton's masque, as opposed to its conventional purpose, centres, as his three great works were later to do, on the moment of trial. As he was to say ten years later in *Areopagitica*:

What wisdom can there be to choose, what continence to forbear without the knowledge of evil?... I cannot praise a fugitive and cloistered virtue, unexercised and unbreathed, that never sallies out and sees her adversary . . . that which purifies us is trial, and trial is by what is contrary. The virtue therefore which is but a youngling in the contemplation of evil, and knows not the utmost that vice promises to her followers, and rejects it, is but a blank virtue, not a pure; her whiteness is but an excremental whiteness . . .

This could be Milton's summing up of what he had tried to show in his masque. But in the artistic rendering of what is essentially a moral trial, Milton's imaginative involvement with the 'contrary' standpoint (Comus) tends to raise questions in an open-minded response to the work's intended message.

Milton's awareness of this fact is shown in the ways by which he limits Comus's argument from nature. Following the passage from *Areopagitica* quoted above, Milton continues:

Which was the reason why our sage and serious poet Spenser, whom I dare to be known to think a better teacher than Scotus or Aquinas, describing true temperance under the person of Guyon, brings him in with his palmer (shepherd) through the bower of earthly bliss that he might see and know, and yet abstain.

Spenser, in *The fairy queen*, presents two images of nature: one is vicious and enticingly sinful, the Bower of Bliss, commitment to which turns men into beasts; the other is innocent and erotically fulfilling, the Garden of Adonis, which Spenser describes in images of the golden age. For Spenser, therefore, nature can be used for evil *and* for good. Now Milton's masque also makes an appeal to the Garden of Adonis, when the Attendant Spirit's epilogue spirals upward imaginatively to embrace it. But Milton's Garden of Adonis exists exclusively above and beyond 'the smoke and stir of this dim spot'. For Spenser, it is subject to the laws of nature and to the ravages of time, and yet defeats time by the eternal renewal of the seasons: 'eterne in mutability, And by succession made perpetual' (III vi 47) (cf the healing view of nature in *Winter's tale*). But the implication of the Attendant Spirit's epilogue is that the Garden of erotic fulfilment (Adonis) exists *above* a nature subject to time and seasonal change. By this scheme, Comus can only represent nature as a Bower of Bliss: bestial, fallen, artificial; the Lady must reject it to show herself worthy of attaining the paradise above. Her rejection therefore involves a repudiation of nature itself. Her elder brother says.

> He that has light within his own clear breast
> May sit in the centre, and enjoy bright day . . .   381

The 'bright day' to which the Lady has access is not of this world; the 'light' within her breast corresponds with, and aspires to, the Attendant Spirit's domain:

> those happy climes that lie,
> Where day never shuts his eye,
> Up in the broad fields of the sky.   978

But this 'meaning' is only given full sanction when the debate is seen retrospectively from the epilogue. Let us look more closely at the debate itself.

Poetry versus morals

The first point to make is that Comus is more poetically persuasive than the Lady. His speeches show a sensibility open to the abundant delights of natural experience (they seem to re-create those delights in language), whereas the Lady's moral position can only allow her to draw on philosophical abstraction and, at most, strident assertion. Comus, arguing for concrete pleasures, can freely indulge his facility for the sensuously particular image; the Lady can only negate him with concepts ('the sage and serious doctrine of virginity') which she acknowledges he can't understand.

But Comus is no innocent pastoral figure. He does represent a primitive and spontaneous natural energy (the antimasque), but Milton is at pains in the debate to present him also as a sophisticated libertine: his 'stately palace, set out with all manner of deliciousness' might suggest a Cavalier poet from Charles I's court. It is a brilliant stroke to juxtapose the extreme sophistication of the 'stately palace' with the natural primitivism of the 'wild wood' since Milton can thereby connect the decadence of court life with the kind of naturalist philosophy that leads to it: Comus is made to use the conventional arguments common to the seduction poems of the Cavalier poets (eg Carew, Herrick, Lovelace).

> If you let slip time, like a neglected rose
> It withers on the stalk with languished head ...   742

is much more beautifully expressed than Herrick's

> Gather ye rosebuds while ye may
> Old Time is yet a'flying ...

but the idea is the same.

In Comus's brilliant second speech, the movement is typically a surge of all-embracing vitality, immediately curbed and restrained by an undermining note of self-centred acquisitiveness:

> Wherefore did nature pour her bounties forth,
> With such a full and unwithdrawing hand,
> Covering the earth with odours, fruits, and flocks,
> Thronging the seas with spawn innumerable,
> But all to please, and sate the curious taste?   709

The first four lines seem to offer the abundance and erotic fulfilment of the Garden of Adonis; the fifth line limits it to the selfish egotism of the Bower of Bliss. We are reminded of the Elder Brother's logic of sin,

> settled to itself
> It shall be in eternal restless change
> Self-fed, and self-consumed   596

Again, we may feel, Comus is right in his beautiful lines against 'virginity':

> Beauty is nature's coin, must not be hoarded,
> But must be current, and the good thereof
> Consists in mutual and partaken bliss,
> Unsavoury in the enjoyment of itself.   738

Out of context, yes, we accept; but at this moment Milton has too much working against Comus. We reluctantly qualify this as 'glozing courtesy' – he wants her precisely to 'hoard' her along with the rest of his harem; the 'mutual and partaken bliss' is merely a line in seduction. Comus's poetic virtuosity is amoral.

We accept this reluctantly because the Lady, though supported by the controlling Platonic framework, is so poetically impoverished. The 'sober certainty of waking bliss' which so struck Comus on hearing her song is here lacking:

> I had not thought to have unlocked my lips
> In this unhallowed air . . .
> I hate when vice can bolt her arguments,
> And virtue has no tongue to check her pride . . .   755

The 'sober certainty' is there, but 'waking bliss' seems way off the mark – in fact she exhibits in statements like these, her own kind of 'pride' and egotism (Wilson Knight sees her here as a virgin hysterically frozen by her fear of sexual experience). She of course does have a point in her speech on the democratic implications of temperance:

> If every just man that now pines with want
> Had but a moderate and beseeming share
> Of that which lewdly-pampered luxury
> Now heaps on some few with vast excess,
> Nature's full blessings would be well-dispensed
> In unsuperfluous even proportion . . .   767

A generous and sympathetically humane statement but embarrassingly ironic – for she has already shown hauteur toward the peasants ('loose, unlettered kinds'); and it must have given the Bridgewater audience a slightly uneasy moment during the masque, itself an example of 'vast excess'.

· No one wins the debate because they are arguing at different levels of the Platonic hierarchy: Milton makes this clear in the Lady's opening speech:

> Thou canst not touch the freedom of my mind
> With all thy charms, although this corporal rind
> Thou hast immanacled, while heaven sees good.   662

But for the intervention of heaven in the shape of the Attendant Spirit, this impasse could not have been broken. For Comus's ultimate appeal is to nature's fertility, the Lady's to a world of higher status. For all his glozing motives, Comus's values are basically aesthetic, and his criterion is pleasure. The Lady is a Platonist and knows that pleasure is of the senses, and must thus be kept in its subservient place by reason and the 'soul', lest they be 'in sweet madness robbed' of themselves by the sensual music. She must hear his poetry as false:

> Enjoy your dear wit, and gay rhetoric
> That hath so well been taught her dazzling fence,
> Thou art not fit to hear thyself convinced . . .   791

But her argument is directed to and sanctioned by the soul, which Comus hasn't got: 'Thou hast nor eat, nor soul to apprehend' (783). Milton tries to tilt the stalemate in favour of the Lady; he allows her some powerful rhetoric of her own:

> Thou art not fit to hear thyself convinced.
> Yet should I try, the uncontrollèd worth
> Of this pure cause would kindle my rapt spirits
> To such a flame of sacred vehemence,
> That dumb things would be moved to sympathize . . .   791

Comus could throw the 'gay rhetoric' taunt back at her here, but Milton, in a passage added between the Trinity Manuscript and the first published version, has him trembling with fear 'of some superior power', and sweating over it: 'a cold shuddering dew Dips me all o'er'. For she doesn't bring about this threatened cataclysmic victory (Samson *does* pull down the corrupt temple), and the implications are that she can't – she's been shown throughout to be physically powerless in the wild wood.

Just as Comus has 'no ear' for her 'serious doctrine', so her dismissal of his superb second speech (egotistic, but it is the all-embracing renaissance egotism of Marlowe's Faustus and Tamburlaine) as 'false rules pranked in reason's garb' surely misses the point. In Comus's world of values there are no rules to prove truth or falsity – truth is the pleasure of the immediate moment. Poetry balances morality: they are both necessary.

The stately palace and Ludlow Castle

When the scene shifts to Ludlow Castle (956–7), we are presented with another kind of civilization. Comus's stately palace suggests a society based on libertine naturalism in which Comus can only hold power by enslaving his subjects in the 'sensual sty' (a possible allusion to Charles I's court here). Without the alternative image of a 'good' civilization (Ludlow), the message would be unambiguous: nature is completely fallen; the world is no more than the sum of wild wood and stately palace. But at Ludlow the jigs and rural dance of the swains offer another kind of antimasque to balance the earlier 'rout'. Comus's revels represent a natural life-force subject to no higher authority; the spirit which informs their rites is the same which controls 'the starry choir' and the tides (115). But the swains at Ludlow know and accept their lowly status and formally retreat at the Spirit's command ('Back, shepherds, back, enough your play') to make way for the 'Other trippings to be trod Of lighter toes . . .' as the Egerton family join in the concluding masque dances. This offers a way out of the Manichaean identification of this world (nature) with the flesh and the devil, suggested by the action in the wild wood and stately palace. With the reuniting of the children and parents, the allegorical drama fades, and we are brought back to the reality of the occasion. What we have been watching has been the trial and testing of education (nurture) and innate nobility (gentility) of the Egerton children. The dances at the end celebrate two things: historically, the installation of the new lord president; and, dramatically, the suitability of the Egerton family to hold high and important office.

But just as the epilogue points once more to allegory, so we are left with the symbolic implications of Ludlow. An ordered, ceremonious, hierarchical civilization is possible in this world, but noble birth in itself is not enough to achieve it; trial and temptation 'o'er sensual folly and intemperance' are necessary states in the evolution toward that ideal society. So the wild wood, rather than being a symbol for life itself, represents a crucial stage in life. For Dante, this stage was middle age; for Milton, it is adolescence. The action has shown the noble nature of the Egerton children, but it has also completed their formal education (nurture) by submitting it to practical trial: 'what purifies us is trial, and trial is by what is contrary'.

Epilogue

The evolution from adolescence to a civilized maturity, then, involves a purifying process. Nature may be fallen, but it can be redeemed by nurture – a 'good' civilization is possible on earth. This would seem to be what the final dance is celebrating. But with the epilogue, earlier complexities and contradictions re-appear. The vision of paradise he offers does not seem to be of this world: it exists in 'the broad fields of the sky' (978) and 'far above' (1003). It is described in images of erotic love – Venus and Adonis, Cupid and Psyche – which are classical, mythological. In the *Fairy queen*, both the Bower of Bliss (evil erotic love) and the Garden of Adonis (good erotic love) exist in *this* world; in *Comus* the suggestion is that only Comus's kind of love – sensual, libertine, fallen – can exist here and now: the Garden of Adonis exists only in heaven. The Lady's stand on the 'sage and serious doctrine of virginity' becomes relevant once again.

The problem can be brought into focus by comparing the Lady with another noble girl lost in rude nature. Perdita, in *The winter's tale*, also undergoes a nurturing process, but it is one which can accommodate the vitality of 'great creating nature', and so culminate in a marriage ending. The tone and substance of the Lady's arguments are difficult to square with any re-conciliation between erotic pleasure and Christian virtue. In *Comus*, the Shakespearean vision of 'great creating nature' has become the 'wild wood' of anarchic confusion, and Comus is its personified spirit. The purifying nurture of the Lady entails a rejection, not an accommodation of nature. Hence the final words of the Attendant Spirit: 'Or if virtue feeble were Heaven itself would stoop to her.'

Even a virtue which has proved itself (ie no longer 'fugitive and cloistered') is no guarantee of strength in *this* world. This world is not the point. At the end, Milton the puritan seems to have triumphed over Milton the classical humanist.

Milton's quarrel with himself

W. B. Yeats has written, 'Out of our quarrels with ourselves we make poetry.' The pivot of Milton's three great works, the moment towards which their separate actions tend, is typically a trial or temptation. Eve, Christ and Samson are all tried; one to fall, one to stand triumphantly, one to endure tragically. In each case we feel the clash to be genuine: we feel Milton to be equally involved on both sides of the debate. We feel that Milton knows the secure repose which comes of obedience to restraint and authority, but also the wilful energy which comes of rebellion. In

Comus, Milton the puritan (at Cambridge he was called 'the lady of Christ's') is tempted and tried by Milton the renaissance poet. For the former, nature's fecund abundance is fallen and basically evil, for the latter it is the expression of God's bounty. The puritan hero's inclination is to retreat from the subtle seductions of nature, where the expression of love centres on the sexual act (the dangers of pastoral), into a cocoon of chastity, only to emerge (when the natural world is transcended) into the select world of heavenly grace ('higher than the sphery chime'). Contrarily, the natural world is the element in which the renaissance poet defines himself – he participates in it and, if a true poet, subdues it to his will: 'still the wild winds when they roar And hush the waving woods'.

All this should not lead to the facile equation poet = Comus, puritan = Lady, which would entail the kind of allegorical simplification that I've been questioning in *Comus*. But it does suggest that these conflicting impulses in Milton mark the contrary poles within which the work moves and lives. In the *Marriage of heaven and hell* Blake says, 'Without contraries is no progression.' Virtue cannot be defined without its contrary, vice; in a poetic work which seeks to show the achievement of virtue, one contrary is as necessary as the other. The Lady, without Comus, would exhibit a 'blank' virtue; the Puritan who would negate the 'simple, sensuous and passionate' side of himself to achieve purity, would exhibit an 'excremental whiteness'.

Text

There are two handwritten versions. The first, known as the Trinity Ms, is in the library of Trinity College, Cambridge. It is in Milton's own handwriting and represents the earlier version; but its numerous corrections were probably added after the other Ms was written out. This second version, known as the Bridgewater Ms, is a shortened text, probably an acting script. There were three editions of *Comus* in Milton's lifetime: separately in 1637, and in the collected volumes of 1645 and 1673. The present text is based on 1673 but its orthography and some of the stage directions have been modernized; some of the more interesting lines and directions cut from the printed texts are cited in the notes.

A masque

presented at Ludlow Castle *1634* on Michaelmas night, before
the right honourable *John*, *Earl of Bridgewater*, *Viscount
Brackley*, *Lord President of Wales*, and one of His Majesty's
most honourable *Privy Council*

Eheu quid volui misero mihi! floribus austrum Perditus . . .

[O what have I done to myself? I have loosed the sirocco onto my
flowers . . .]

The Attendant Spirit, afterwards disguised as Thyrsis, a shepherd
(Henry Lawes). [In the Bridgewater Ms the Spirit is called 'the
Daemon'. In classical mythology, daemons live in a limbo on the
moon awaiting the separation of mind from soul, after which the mind
returns to the sun. They return to earth at times to protect good from
evil.]

Comus, son of Bacchus and Circe, enchanter of the wild wood. [Greek
κῶμος = revelry and is associated with 'hairy'. A character has been
made of Comus by classical and renaissance writers; he has tended to
be either a graceful rose-crowned dancer, or (as in Jonson's *Pleasure
reconciled to virtue*) 'the god of cheer' and 'the bouncing belly'.
Either way he drinks wine.]

The Lady (Lady Alice Egerton)
Elder Brother (Lord Brackley)
Younger Brother (Thomas Egerton)
Sabrina, nymph of the River Severn
Rout of monsters enchanted by Comus [the antimasque, in animal masks]
Water nymphs attendant on Sabrina
Country dancers [the 'good' antimasque = of shepherds]
Courtly dancers [the 'masquers', including the three principals]

Scene 1   A wild wood. The Attendant Spirit descends.

Spirit.   Before the starry threshold of Jove's court
My mansion is, where those immortal shapes
Of bright aërial spirits live ensphered
In regions mild of calm and sérene air,
Above the smoke and stir of this dim spot,   5
Which men call earth, and, with low-thoughted care

2 mansion dwelling-place.   **3 ensphered** in one of the celestial
spheres, probably the outermost, which in the Ptolemaic cosmos would
be nearest to heaven.

Confined, and pestered in this pinfold here,
Strive to keep up a frail, and feverish being
Unmindful of the crown that virtue gives
After this mortal change, to her true servants   10
Amongst the énthron'd gods on sainted seats.
Yet some there be that by due steps aspire
To lay their just hands on that golden key
That opes the palace of eternity:
To such my errand is, and but for such,   15
I would not soil these pure ambrosial weeds,
With the rank vapours of this sin-worn mould.
    But to my task. Neptune besides the sway
Of every salt flood, and each ebbing stream,
Took in by lot 'twixt high, and nether Jove,   20
Imperial rule of all the sea-girt isles
That like to rich, and various gems inlay
The unadorned bosom of the deep,
Which he to grace his tributary gods
By course commits to several government,   25
And gives them leave to wear their sapphire crowns,
And wield their little tridents, but this isle
The greatest, and the best of all the main
He quarters to his blue-haired deities,
And all this tract that fronts the falling sun   30
A noble peer of mickle trust, and power
Has in his charge, with tempered awe to guide
An old, and haughty nation proud in arms:

7 **pestered** herded like cattle in a pen.   10 **change** death; also the
constant mutability of life.   16 **ambrosial** ambrosia was the food
of paradise so his robes are heavenly.   17 **sin-worn** worn out by sin
and worn by sin (as clothes). Note the dualistic implications, earth and
body being associated with dim corruption, air and spirit with bright
purity; also between those whose thoughts tend towards this type, and
the few who aspire.   20 **high, and nether Jove** Zeus, god of the
heavens; Hades, god of the underworld.   24 **tributary** those who
pay tribute.   25 **By course** in due order. **several** distributed
among individuals.   27 **this isle** Britain.   29 **quarters** allots. **blue-
haired** sea gods often wore blue hair in masques; hence also sapphire
crowns 26.   30 **tract** Wales.   31 **peer** the Earl of Bridgewater.
mickle great.   32 **tempered** avoiding extremes. **guide** govern.

Where his fair offspring nursed in princely lore,
Are coming to attend their father's state,   35
And new-entrusted sceptre, but their way
Lies through the pérplexed paths of this drear wood,
The nodding horror of whose shady brows
Threats the forlorn and wandering passenger.
And here their tender age might suffer peril,   40
But that by quick command from sovran Jove
I was despatched for their defence, and guard;
And listen why, for I will tell you now
What never yet was heard in tale or song
From old, or modern bard in hall, or bower.   45
    Bacchus, that first from out the purple grape,
Crushed the sweet poison of misusèd wine
After the Tuscan mariners transformed,
Coasting the Tyrrhene shore, as the winds listed,
On Circè's island fell (who knows not Circe   50
The daughter of the sun? Whose charmed cup
Whoever tasted, lost his upright shape,
And downward fell into a grovelling swine),
This nymph that gazed upon his clustering locks,
With ivy berries wreathed, and his blithe youth,   55
Had by him, ere he parted thence, a son
Much like his father, but his mother more,
Whom therefore she brought up and Comus named,
Who ripe, and frolic of his full-grown age,
Roving the Celtic, and Iberian fields,   60
At last betakes him to this ominous wood,

35 **state** the earl's official acceptance of his chair of state.   37 **pér-plexed** tangled, confusing. **wood** traditional image for the temptations of life; cf the opening of Dante's *Inferno*: 'In the middle of life's road, I found myself in a dark wood, where the straight road became confused.' 39 **passenger** wayfarer.   44 **never yet was heard** Comus's ancestry is M's invention.   48 **After . . . transformed** referring to an incident in Ovid's *Metamorphoses* in which some Tuscan sailors were transformed into dolphins by Bacchus.   49 **Tyrrhene** the sea between Italy and Corsica. **listed** chose.   50 **Circè** sorceress who changed men into swine by enticing them to drink from her enchanted cup. She tempted Odysseus to her island. **fell** landed.   58 **brought up** Comus's upbringing is set against the children's.   60 **fields** France and Spain.

And in thick shelter of black shades embowered,
Excels his mother at her mighty art,
Offering to every weary traveller,
His orient liquor in a crystal glass,   65
To quench the drought of Phoebus, which as they taste
(For most do taste through fond intemperate thirst)
Soon as the potion works, their human countenance,
The express resemblance of the gods, is changed
Into some brutish form of wolf, or bear,   70
Or ounce, or tiger, hog, or bearded goat,
All other parts remaining as they were,
And they, so perfect is their misery,
Not once perceive their foul disfigurement,
But boast themselves more comely than before   75
And all their friends, and native home forget
To roll with pleasure in a sensual sty.

   Therefore when any favoured of high Jove,
Chances to pass through this adventurous glade,
Swift as the sparkle of a glancing star,   80
I shoot from heaven to give him safe convóy,
As now I do: but first I must put off
These my sky-robes spun out of Iris' woof,
And take the weeds and likeness of a swain,
That to the service of this house belongs,   85
Who with his soft pipe, and smooth-dittied song,
Well knows to still the wild winds when they roar,
And hush the waving woods, nor of less faith,

63 **art** magic. 'Art' here carries sinister undertones of artificial and false.
65 **orient** shining. 66 **Phoebus** the sun. 67 **fond** foolish. 69 **express**
clearly stamped. 72 **parts** in the *Odyssey*, the whole body was changed
by Circe but it is easier for actors to wear animal masks over the head.
It is anyway sufficient for M's purpose: the head is the seat of reason.
83 **sky-robes . . .** robes spun from the rainbow. Neo-Platonic daemons
were able to assume any bodily shape and also, like air and water, to take
on various colours. 84 **the weeds and likeness of a swain** clothes
and appearance of a shepherd. When he reappears he will have changed
his rainbow robes for pastoral costume. 86 Milton is praising the musical capabilities of Lawes by comparing him to Orpheus, whose music
could control nature. He is also indirectly praising his own control of
language. 88 **nor of less faith** no less loyal than he is musical.

And in this office of his mountain watch,
Likeliest, and nearest to the present aid   90
Of this occasion. But I hear the tread
Of hateful steps, I must be viewless now.

*Comus enters with a charming-rod in one hand, his glass in the
other, with him a rout of monsters, headed like sundry sorts of
wild beasts, but otherwise like men and women, their apparel
glistering, they come in making a riotous and unruly noise, with
torches in their hands.*

Comus. The star that bids the shepherd fold,
Now the top of heaven doth hold,
And the gilded car of day,   95
His glowing axle doth allay
In the steep Atlantic stream,
And the slope sun his upward beam
Shoots against the dusky pole,
Pacing toward the other goal   100
Of his chamber in the east.
Meanwhile, welcome joy, and feast,
Midnight shout, and revelry,
Tipsy dance, and jollity.
Braid your locks with rosy twine   105
Dropping odours, dropping wine.
Rigour now is gone to bed,
And Advice with scrupulous head,
Strict Age, and sour Severity,
With their grave saws in slumber lie.   110
   We that are of purer fire

92 viewless invisible. Trinity Ms 'they come on in a wild and antic
fashion. Intrant Komatores'. This represents, with the dance which
follows, the first antimasque. The country dances at Ludlow are the
second. **93 star** Hesperus, the evening star. **95–7 gilded** Ovid in the
Metamorphoses describes the sun's chariot as having an axle made of gold.
allay cool, as in tempering metal. **steep** flowing fast. Greek science saw
the sea as a river which surrounded the earth. **98 slope** sloping.
99 dusky pole topmost part of the sky which darkens as the sun sinks,
leaving a last 'upward beam' of light. **105 rosy twine** wreaths of
roses. **110 saws** maxims. **111 fire** Comus claims that being more
spirited = more spiritual. The idea of the cosmos being essentially a

Imitate the starry choir,
Who in their nightly watchful spheres,
Lead in swift round the months and years.
The sounds, and seas with all their finny drove   115
Now to the moon in wavering morris move,
And on the tawny sands and shelves,
Trip the pert fairies and the dapper elves;
By dimpled brook, and fountain-brim,
The wood-nymphs decked with daisies trim,   120
Their merry wakes and pastimes keep:
What hath night to do with sleep?
Night hath better sweets to prove,
Venus now wakes, and wakens Love.
Come let us our rites begin,   125
'Tis only daylight that makes sin
Which these dun shades will ne'er report.
Hail goddess of nocturnal sport
Dark-veiled Cotytto, to whom the secret flame
Of midnight torches burns; mysterious dame   130
That ne'er art called, but when the dragon womb
Of Stygian darkness spits her thickest gloom,
And makes one blot of all the air,
Stay thy cloudy ebon chair,
Wherein thou rid'st with Hecat', and befriend   135
Us thy vowed priests, till utmost end
Of all thy dues be done, and none left out,
Ere the blabbing eastern scout,
The nice morn on the Indian steep
From her cabined loophole peep,   140
And to the tell-tale sun descry

universal dance was Platonic. It was popularized by Sir John Davies's
poem *Orchestra* 1596.   **112 choir** the harmonious movement of the
stars each in its own sphere, which creates the music of the spheres (the
'sphery chime' of 1020) cf *PL* iii 579–61.   **115 sounds** straits.   **116
morris** morris (Moorish) dance, commonly performed on May Day and
Whitsuntide in 16th- and 17th-century England. The puritans tried to
suppress it.   **121 wakes** revels.   **129 Cotytto** a Thracian goddess,
whose sensual rites were held secretly at night.   **134 Stay** halt.   **135
Hecat'** Hecate, goddess of witchcraft.   **139 nice** modest, squeamish.

Our concealed solemnity.
Come, knit hands, and beat the ground,
In a light fantastic round.

Dance

Break off, break off, I feel the different pace,   145
Of some chaste footing near about this ground.
Run to your shrouds, within these brakes and trees,
Our number may affright: some virgin sure
(For so I can distinguish by mine art)
Benighted in these woods. Now to my charms,   150
And to my wily trains, I shall ere long
Be well stocked with as fair a herd as grazed
About my mother Circe. Thus I hurl
My dazzling spells into the spongy air,
Of power to cheat the eye with blear illusion,   155
And give it false presentments, lest the place
And my quaint habits breed astonishment,
And put the damsel to suspicious flight,
Which must not be, for that's against my course;
I under fair pretence of friendly ends,   160
And well-placed words of glozing courtesy
Baited with reasons not unplausible
Wind me into the easy-hearted man,
And hug him into snares. When once her eye
Hath met the virtue of this magic dust,   165
I shall appear some harmless villager
And hearken, if I may her business hear.
But here she comes, I fairly step aside.

142 solemnity celebration.   **144 round** country dance in which the
dancers form a circle by holding hands.   **145 Break off** the rollicking
rhythm of the octosyllabics, as well as the revelling dance, breaks off here.
The 'different pace' of the pentameter takes over as Comus's convention
of speaking. He uses no other from now on.   **147 shrouds** shelters,
hiding places.   **151 trains** tricks, traps.   **154 dazzling** implies
brightness and illusion. Comus would throw some kind of glittering
powder into the air at this point.   **156 presentments** appearances;
hence, hallucinations.   **161 glozing** flattering, deceitful.   **165 virtue**
power, effectiveness. Comus's 'virtue' of deceit *v* the Lady's moral and
religious 'virtue'.

The Lady enters.

Lady. This way the noise was, if mine ear be true,
My best guide now, methought it was the sound   170
Of riot, and ill-managed merriment,
Such as the jocund flute, or gamesome pipe
Stirs up among the loose unlettered hinds,
When for their teeming flocks, and granges full,
In wanton dance they praise the bounteous Pan,   175
And thank the gods amiss. I should be loth
To meet the rudeness, and swilled insolence
Of such late wassailers; yet O where else
Shall I inform my unacquainted feet
In the blind mazes of this tangled wood?   180
My brothers when they saw me wearied out
With this long way, resolving here to lodge
Under the spreading favour of these pines,
Stepped as they said to the next thicket-side
To bring me berries, or such cooling fruit   185
As the kind hospitable woods provide.
They left me then, when the grey-hooded even
Like a sad votarist in palmer's weed
Rose from the hindmost wheels of Phoebus' wain.
But where they are, and why they came not back,   190
Is now the labour of my thoughts, 'tis likeliest
They had engaged their wandering steps too far,
And envious darkness, ere they could return,
Had stole them from me, else O thievish night

169 **if mine ear be true** cf 996 'List mortals, if your ears be true'. 170 **best guide** now that she can't see in the darkness. Hearing was second to sight in the renaissance hierarchy of the senses. 171 **ill-managed** ill-regulated, dissonant, disorderly. 173 **loose . . . hinds** dissolute peasants. 174 **flocks, and granges** spring, and autumn; meat, and corn. 175 **Pan** god of nature's profusion, and of wantonness. 177 **swilled** drunken. 178 **wassailers** revellers. 188 **sad** serious. **votarist** pilgrim, in a grey gown. A palmer was one who had made the pilgrimage to the Holy Land. 192 **engaged** risked. 193 **darkness** is personifying night and darkness as being hostile to, and distinguished from, nature and her stars. The Lady is confused about nature in this speech – the wild wood is both threatening and benign.

128

Why shouldst thou, but for some felonious end,   195
In thy dark lantern thus close up the stars,
That nature hung in heaven, and filled their lamps
With everlasting oil, to give due light
To the misled and lonely traveller?
This is the place, as well as I may guess,   200
Whence even now the tumult of loud mirth
Was rife, and perfect in my listening ear,
Yet nought but single darkness do I find.
What might this be? A thousand fantasies
Begin to throng into my memory   205
Of calling shapes, and beckoning shadows dire,
And airy tongues, that syllable men's names
On sands, and shores, and desert wildernesses.
These thoughts may startle well, but not astound
The virtuous mind, that ever walks attended   210
By a strong siding champion conscience. . .
O welcome pure-eyed faith, white-handed hope,
Thou hovering angel girt with golden wings,
And thou unblemished form of chastity,
I see ye visibly, and now believe   215
That he, the Supreme Good, to whom all things ill
Are but as slavish officers of vengeance,
Would send a glistering guardian if need were
To keep my life and honour unassailed.
Was I deceived, or did a sable cloud   220
Turn forth her silver lining on the night?
I did not err, there does a sable cloud
Turn forth her silver lining on the night,
And casts a gleam over this tufted grove.
I cannot hallo to my brothers, but   225
Such noise as I can make to be heard farthest
I'll venture, for my new-enlivened spirits
Prompt me; and they perhaps are not far off.

202 perfect distinct.   **211 siding** conscience is at her side as a
protector.   **214 chastity** M substitutes chastity for charity in the
trio with faith and hope.

(Sings)

Sweet Echo, sweetest nymph that liv'st unseen
  Within thy airy shell   230
 By slow Meänder's margent green,
And in the violet-embroidered vale
 Where the love-lorn nightingale
Nightly to thee her sad song mourneth well.
Canst thou not tell me of a gentle pair   235
  That likest thy Narcissus are?
   O if thou have
  Hid them in some flowery cave,
   Tell me but where
  Sweet queen of parley, daughter of the sphere.   240
 So mayst thou be translated to the skies,
And give resounding grace to all heaven's harmonies.
Comus. Can any mortal mixture of earth's mould
Breathe such divine enchanting ravishment?
Sure something holy lodges in that breast,   245
And with these raptures moves the vocal air
To testify his hidden residence;
How sweetly did they float upon the wings
Of silence, through the empty-vaulted night
At every fall smoothing the raven down   250
Of darkness till it smiled: I have oft heard
My mother Circe with the Sirens three,
Amidst the flowery-kirtled Naiades
Culling their potent herbs, and baleful drugs,
Who as they sung, would take the prisoned soul,   255

229 Echo pined away with desire for the unwilling Narcissus, until she became no more than a voice. He was punished by falling in love with his own reflection in the water, and was finally transformed into a flower. **230 shell** vault of the sky. **231 margent** bank. **240 parley** speech. **241 translated** elevated. **247 his** refers to the 'something holy'. **residence** the Lady's soul. **248 they** ie the musical 'raptures' of 246. **250 fall** musical cadence. **252 Sirens** the two Sirens in the *Odyssey* have no connection with Circe. They lived on an island off Sicily, near the rock of Scylla, and lured sailors to their destruction by their songs. Milton links them with Circe, whose songs could also enchant. **253 Naiades** river nymphs who wait on Circe. **255 take** enrapture.

And lap it in Elysium, Scylla wept,
And chid her barking waves into attention,
And fell Charybdis murmured soft applause:
Yet they in pleasing slumber lulled the sense,
And in sweet madness robbed it of itself,   260
But such a sacred, and home-felt delight,
Such sober certainty of waking bliss
I never heard till now. I'll speak to her
And she shall be my queen. Hail foreign wonder
Whom certain these rough shades did never breed   265
Unless the goddess that in rural shrine
Dwellest here with Pan, or Sylvan, by blest song
Forbidding every bleak unkindly fog
To touch the prosperous growth of this tall wood.
Lady. Nay, gentle shepherd, ill is lost that praise   270
That is addressed to unattending ears,
Not any boast of skill, but extreme shift
How to regain my severed company
Compelled me to awake the courteous Echo
To give me answer from her mossy couch.   275
Comus. What chance good lady hath bereft you thus?
Lady. Dim darkness, and this leafy labyrinth.
Comus. Could that divide you from near-ushering
    guides?
Lady. They left me weary on a grassy turf.
Comus. By falsehood, or discourtesy, or why?   280
Lady. To seek in the valley some cool friendly spring.
Comus. And left your fair side all unguarded lady?
Lady. They were but twain, and purposed quick return.
Comus. Perhaps forestalling night prevented them.
Lady. How easy my misfortune is to hit!   285
Comus. Imports their loss, beside the present need?

257 barking waves Scylla was a nymph transformed into a barking
monster by Circe. She lived on a rock between Italy and Sicily, opposite
Charybdis, who had been transformed into a whirlpool. To sailors, the
barking seemed to come from the waves.   **267 Sylvan** adjective from
Sylvanus, who was god of the woods.   **272 extreme shift** last resource.
285 hit guess at.   **286** does their loss mean anything to you, apart
from their value as guides?

Lady. No less than if I should my brothers lose.
Comus. Were they of manly prime, or youthful bloom?
Lady. As smooth as Hebe's their unrazored lips.
Comus. Two such I saw, what time the laboured ox   290
In his loose traces from the furrow came,
And the swinked hedger at his supper sat;
I saw them under a green mantling vine
That crawls along the side of yon small hill,
Plucking ripe clusters from the tender shoots,   295
Their port was more than human, as they stood;
I took it for a faëry vision
Of some gay creatures of the element
That in the colours of the rainbow live
And play in the plighted clouds. I was awe-struck,   300
And as I passed, I worshipped; if those you seek
It were a journey like the path to heaven,
To help you find them.
Lady.   Gentle villager
What readiest way would bring me to that place?
Comus. Due west it rises from this shrubby point.   305
Lady. To find out that, good shepherd, I suppose,
In such a scant allowance of star-light,
Would overtask the best land-pilot's art,
Without the sure guess of well-practised feet.
Comus. I know each lane, and every alley green   310
Dingle, or bushy dell of this wild wood,
And every bosky bourn from side to side
My daily walks and ancient neighbourhood,
And if your stray attendance be yet lodged,
Or shroud within these limits, I shall know   315
Ere morrow wake, or the low-roosted lark
From her thatched pallet rouse, if otherwise

289 Hebe goddess of youth. **292 swinked** worn out from work.
293 mantling covering, as with a mantle. **296 port** bearing. Milton is
complimenting the Egerton boys here, but to what extent is Comus dis-
sembling in 296–303? **300 plighted** folded, plaited. **311 Dingle**
glade, valley. **312 bosky bourn** stream edged with bushes. **314**
whether your lost companions have already found lodging, or are still
sheltering within the bounds of this wood . . . **317 pallet** bed of straw.

I can conduct you lady to a low
But loyal cottage, where you may be safe
Till further quest.   320
Lady.   Shepherd I take thy word,
And trust thy honest-offered courtesy,
Which oft is sooner found in lowly sheds
With smoky rafters, than in tapestry halls
And courts of princes, where it first was named,
And yet is most pretended: in a place   325
Less warranted than this, or less secure
I cannot be, that I should fear to change it,
Eye me blest Providence, and square my trial
To my proportioned strength. Shepherd lead on. . . .

                    Exit Comus and Lady.

                    Enter the two Brothers.

Eld. Bro. Unmuffle ye faint stars, and thou fair moon   330
That wontest to love the traveller's benison,
Stoop thy pale visage through an amber cloud,
And disinherit Chaos, that reigns here
In double night of darkness, and of shades;
Or if your influence be quite dammed up   335
With black usurping mists, some gentle taper
Though a rush-candle from the wicker hole
Of some clay habitation visit us
With thy long levelled rule of streaming light,
And thou shalt be our star of Arcady,   340
Or Tyrian Cynosure.
You. Bro.   Or if our eyes

321 courtesy the art of living in a civilized court. The Lady is criti-
cizing the present decadence of court life.   **328 square** adjust.
331 wontest are accustomed to. **benison** blessing.   **337 wicker hole**
window with wicker-work covering.   **339 rule** ray of light.   **340
Arcady** the Arcadian nymph Caliosto was turned into the Great Bear
(star of Arcady). Her son was turned into the Lesser Bear (Cynosure)
which guided the Tyrian sailors. The Elder Brother is asking for a ray of
light from a cottage to be their guide.

                              133

Be barred that happiness, might we but hear
The folded flocks penned in their wattled cotes,
Or sound of pastoral reed with oaten stops,
Or whistle from the lodge, or village cock   345
Count the night-watches to his feathery dames,
'Twould be some solace yet some little cheering
In this close dungeon of innumerous boughs.
But O that hapless virgin our lost sister
Where may she wander now, whither betake her   350
From the chill dew, amongst rude burs and thistles?
Perhaps some cold bank is her bolster now
Or 'gainst the rugged bark of some broad elm
Leans her unpillowed head fraught with sad fears,
What if in wild amazement, and affright,   355
Or while we speak within the direful grasp
Of savage hunger, or of savage heat?
Eld. Bro. Peace brother, be not over-exquisite
To cast the fashion of uncertain evils;
For grant they be so, while they rest unknown,   360
What need a man forestall his date of grief,
And run to meet what he would most avoid?
Of if they be but false alarms of fear,
How bitter is such self-delusión!
I do not think my sister so to seek,   365
Or so unprincipled in virtue's book,
And the sweet peace that goodness bosoms ever,
As that the single want of light and noise
(Not being in danger, as I trust she is not)
Could stir the constant mood of her calm thoughts,   370
And put them into misbecoming plight.
Virtue could see to do what virtue would
By her own radiant light, though sun and moon

343 **wattled cotes** sheepfolds fenced by hurdles.   344 **reed** shepherds' pipes or flutes.   349 **hapless** unfortunate.   356–64 omitted
in both Mss.   357 **heat** lust.   358 **over-exquisite** over-subtle, over-
careful.   359 **cast** forecast.   361 **forestall** delay.   365 **so to seek**
so much at a loss.   371 **misbecoming** unbecoming.   372–4 cf Jonson
Pleasure reconciled to virtue 'She, she it is in darkness shines / Tis

Were in the flat sea sunk. And wisdom's self
Oft seeks to sweet retired solitude,   375
Where with her best nurse, contemplation
She plumes her feathers, and lets grow her wings
That in the various bustle of resort
Were all to-ruffled, and sometimes impaired.
He that has light within his own clear breast   380
May sit in the centre, and enjoy bright day,
But he that hides a dark soul, and foul thoughts
Benighted walks under the midday sun;
Himself is his own dungeon.
You. Bro.   'Tis most true
That musing meditation most affects   385
The pensive secrecy of desert cell,
Far from the cheerful haunt of men, and herds,
And sits as safe as in a senate-house,
For who would rob a hermit of his weeds,
His few books, or his beads, or maple dish,   390
Or do his grey hairs any violence?
But beauty like the fair Hesperian tree
Laden with blooming gold, had need the guard
Of dragon-watch with unenchanted eye,
To save her blossoms, and defend her fruit   395
From the rash hand of bold incontinence.
You may as well spread out the unsunned heaps
Of miser's treasure by an outlaw's den,
And tell me it is safe, as bid me hope
Danger will wink on opportunity,   400
And let a single helpless maiden pass
Uninjured in this wild surrounding waste.

she that still herself refines / By her own light to every eye / More
seen, more known, when Vice stands by' 313–16. **375 seeks to**
resorts to. **377 plumes** preens. **378 resort** gathering of people.
381 centre of the earth. **392 Hesperian tree** the tree which bore
golden apples, and was guarded by the Hesperides (daughters of Hesperus) and a dragon. Here it is compared with the Lady's beauty; later
(981) it becomes part of the Spirit's picture of his arcadian paradise in
the sky. The tree was given as a wedding present to Hera when she
married Zeus, and it carries connotations of marriage.

Of night, or loneliness it recks me not,
I fear the dread events that dog them both,
Lest some ill-greeting touch attempt the person   405
Of our unowned sister.
Eld. Bro.   I do not, brother,
Infer, as if I thought my sister's state
Secure without all doubt, or controversy:
Yet where an equal poise of hope and fear
Does arbitrate the event, my nature is   410
That I incline to hope, rather than fear,
And gladly banish squint suspicion.
My sister is not so defenceless left
As you imagine, she has a hidden strength
Which you remember not.   415
You. Bro.   What hidden strength,
Unless the strength of heaven, if you mean that?
Eld. Bro. I mean that too, but yet a hidden strength
Which if heaven gave it, may be termed her own:
'Tis chastity, my brother, chastity:
She that has that, is clad in cómplete steel,   420
And like a quivered nymph with arrows keen
May trace huge forests, and unharboured heaths,
Infamous hills, and sandy perilous wilds,
Where through the sacred rays of chastity,
No savage fierce, bandit, or mountaineer   425
Will dare to soil her virgin purity.
Yea there, where very desolation dwells
By grots, and caverns shagged with horrid shades,
She may pass on with unblenched majesty,
Be it not done in pride, or in presumptión.   430
    Some say no evil thing that walks by night

403 **it recks me not** I care not.   404 **them both** ie night and loneliness.   406 **unowned** lost.   407 **Infer** conclude.   410 **arbitrate**
decide. **event** outcome.   412 **squint suspicion** suspicion personified
as having a squint.   418 **termed her own** ie not just heavenly, but
integral to her; hence a human quality, like integrity.   422 **trace**
cross, traverse. **unharboured** without shelter.   429 **unblenched** un-
dismayed.

In fog, or fire, by lake, or moorish fen,
Blue meagre hag, or stubborn unlaid ghost,
That breaks his magic chains at curfew time,
No goblin, or swart faëry of the mine,   435
Hath hurtful power o'er true virginity.
Do ye believe me yet, or shall I call
Antiquity from the old schools of Greece
To testify the arms of chastity?
Hence had the huntress Dian her dread bow   440
Fair silver-shafted queen for ever chaste,
Wherewith she tamed the brinded lioness
And spotted mountain pard, but set at nought
The frivolous bolt of Cupid, gods and men
Feared her stern frown, and she was queen of the   445
     woods.
What was that snaky-headed Gorgon shield
That wise Minerva wore, unconquered virgin,
Wherewith she freezed her foes to cóngealed stone,
But rigid looks of chaste austerity,
And noble grace that dashed brute violence   450
With sudden adoration, and blank awe.
   So dear to heaven is saintly chastity,
That when a soul is found sincerely so,
A thousand liveried angels lackey her,
Driving far off each thing of sin and guilt,   455
And in clear dream, and solemn vision
Tell her of things that no gross ear can hear;
Till oft converse with heavenly habitants
Begin to cast a beam on the outward shape,

432 moorish marshy.   **438 schools** of philosophy; probably meaning
Plato.   **439 testify** vouch for.   **440 Dian** ie Diana, the Roman
goddess of hunting, famous for her chastity. Often associated with the
moon.   **442 brinded** striped.   **443 pard** leopard.   **447 Minerva**
Roman goddess of wisdom – also of war. Her shield bore the head of the
Gorgon Medusa.   **450 dashed** abashed, overwhelmed.   **451 blank**
helpless with amazement.   **454 liveried** dressed in uniform. **lackey**
accompany as guards.   **458 oft converse** frequent conversation.   **455–
62** 'Those who are remarkable for having lived holy lives are released
from this earthly prison, and go to their pure home which is above, and

137

The unpolluted temple of the mind,   460
And turns it by degrees to the soul's essence,
Till all be made immortal: but when lust
By unchaste looks, loose gestures, and foul talk,
But most by lewd and lavish act of sin,
Lets in defilement to the inward parts,   465
The soul grows clotted by contagión,
Embodies, and imbrutes, till she quite lose
The divine property of her first being.
Such are those thick and gloomy shadows damp
Oft seen in charnel-vaults, and sepulchres   470
Lingering, and sitting by a new-made grave,
As loth to leave the body that it loved,
And linked itself by carnal sensuality
To a degenerate and degraded state.
You. Bro. How charming is divine philosophy!   475
Not harsh, and crabbed as dull fools suppose,
But musical as is Apollo's lute,
And a perpetual feast of nectared sweets,
Where no crude surfeit reigns.
Eld. Bro.   List, list, I hear
Some far-off hallo break the silent air.   480
You. Bro. Methought so too; what should it be?
Eld. Bro.   For certain
Either some one like us night-foundered here,
Or else some neighbour woodman, or at worst,
Some roving robber calling to his fellows.
You. Bro. Heaven keep my sister, again, again, and   485
        near,
Best draw, and stand upon our guard.

dwell in purer earth' Plato *Phaedo* 114; cf *PL* v 497–500. **464–74** Cf
Plato *Phaedo* 81: 'If when the soul departs from the body it is still
impure . . . such a soul is depressed and dragged down again to the visible
world, because she is afraid of the invisible and of the world below –
prowling about tombs and sepulchres, where . . . are seen ghostly appari-
tions and souls, which have not departed pure.' **467 Embodies,
and imbrutes** becomes made of matter, and bestial. **468 property** characteristics. **482 night-foundered** lost and sunk in
night.

Eld. Bro.   I'll hallo,
If he be friendly he comes well, if not,
Defence is a good cause, and heaven be for us.

Enter the Attendant Spirit habited like a shepherd.

That hallo I should know, what are you? speak;
Come not too near, you fall on iron stakes else.   490
Spir. What voice is that, my young Lord? speak again.
You. Bro. O brother, 'tis my father shepherd sure.
Eld. Bro. Thyrsis? Whose artful strains have oft delayed
The huddling brook to hear his madrigal,
And sweetened every musk-rose of the dale,   495
How camest thou here good swain? hath any ram
Slipped from the fold, or young kid lost his dam,
Or straggling wether the pent flock forsook?
How couldst thou find this dark sequestered nook?
Spir. O my loved master's heir, and his next joy,   500
I came not here on such a trivial toy
As a strayed ewe, or to pursue the stealth
Of pilfering wolf, not all the fleecy wealth
That doth enrich these downs, is worth a thought
To this my errand, and the care it brought.   505
But O my virgin Lady, where is she?
How chance she is not in your company?
Eld. Bro. To tell thee sadly shepherd, without blame,
Or our neglect, we lost her as we came.
Spir. Ay me unhappy then my fears are true.   510
Eld. Bro. What fears good Thyrsis? Prithee briefly shew.
Spir. I'll tell ye, 'tis not vain or fabulous,

488 The Spirit is now in pastoral disguise, and the pastoral note is taken up
in the artificial sound of the rhymed couplets 494–510. **494 huddling**
hastening, but huddled together as the water in front slows down to hear
the singing. **500 next** next to succeed him, also nearest to his heart.
501 toy trifle. **512 fabulous** fictitious (the adjective of 'fabled').
512–18 M is, in these lines, alluding to the renaissance habit of using
classical myths as allegories (fables) of Christian truths. So, in a sense,
he is offering a way of interpreting his masque (especially crucial passages
such as the Spirit's opening speech and epilogue).

139

(Though so esteemed by shallow ignorance)
What the sage poets taught by the heavenly Muse,
Storied of old in high immortal verse   515
Of dire chimeras and enchanted isles,
And rifted rocks whose entrance leads to hell,
For such there be, but unbelief is blind.
    Within the navel of this hideous wood,
Immured in cypress shades a sorcerer dwells   520
Of Bacchus, and of Circe born, great Comus,
Deep skilled in all his mother's witcheries,
And here to every thirsty wanderer,
By sly enticement gives his baneful cup,
With many murmurs mixed, whose pleasing poison   525
The visage quite transforms of him that drinks,
And the inglorious likeness of a beast
Fixes instead, unmoulding reason's mintage
Charactered in the face; this have I learnt
Tending my flocks hard by in the hilly crofts,   530
That brow this bottom glade, whence night by night
He and his monstrous rout are heard to howl
Like stabled wolves, or tigers at their prey,
Doing abhorrèd rites to Hecatè
In their obscurèd haunts of inmost bowers,   535
Yet have they many baits, and guileful spells
To inveigle and invite the unwary sense
Of them that pass unweeting by the way.
    This evening late by then the chewing flocks
Had taken their supper on the savoury herb   540
Of knot-grass dew-besprent, and were in fold,

514 sage poets Homer and Virgil, but probably also Spenser, whom Milton elsewhere refers to as 'sage and serious'. **516 chimeras** mythological monsters, part lion, part goat, part dragon. **519 navel** centre. **525-9** Example of the use of a 'fabulous' myth to represent a truth. The audience knows the animal heads of Comus's band are masks worn by actors, but they allegorize a Christian-Platonic message: submission to one's senses and passions undermines the divine quality of reason. The process 'imbrutes' 467. Cf lines 456-68. **529 Charactered** stamped with an image – as on a coin. **530 crofts** enclosed fields. **538 unweeting** unaware. **541 besprent** sprinkled.

I sat me down to watch upon a bank
With ivy canopied, and interwove
With flaunting honeysuckle, and began
Wrapt in a pleasing fit of melancholy   545
To meditate my rural minstrelsy,
Till fancy had her fill, but ere a close
The wonted roar was up amidst the woods,
And filled the air with barbarous dissonance
At which I ceased, and listened them a while,   550
Till an unusual stop of sudden silence
Gave respite to the drowsy frighted steeds
That draw the litter of close-curtained sleep;
At last a soft and solemn-breathing sound
Rose like a steam of rich distilled perfumes,   555
And stole upon the air, that even silence
Was took ere she was ware, and wished she might
Deny her nature, and be never more
Still to be so displaced. I was all ear,
And took in strains that might create a soul   560
Under the ribs of death, but O ere long
Too well I did perceive it was the voice
Of my most honoured Lady, your dear sister.
Amazed I stood, harrowed with grief and fear,
And O poor hapless nightingale thought I,   565
How sweet thou sing'st, how near the deadly snare!
Then down the lawns I ran with headlong haste
Through paths, and turnings often trod by day,
Till guided by mine ear I found the place
Where that damned wizard hid in sly disguise   570
(For so by certain signs I knew) had met
Already, ere my best speed could prevent,
The aidless innocent Lady, his wished prey,
Who gently asked if he had seen such two,
Supposing him some neighbour villager;   575

544 flaunting waving.   **546** To play my shepherd's pipes.   **547 ere
a close** before the end of a cadence.   **549 barbarous dissonance** the
sound of Comus's 'measure'.   **557 took** enraptured.

Longer I durst not stay, but soon I guessed
Ye were the two she meant, with that I sprung
Into swift flight, till I had found you here,
But further know I not.

You. Bro.   O night and shades,
How are ye joined with hell in triple knot   580
Against the unarmed weakness of one virgin
Alone, and helpless! Is this the confidence
You gave me brother?

Eld. Bro.   Yes, and keep it still,
Lean on it safely, not a period
Shall be unsaid for me: against the threats   585
Of malice or of sorcery, or that power
Which erring men call chance, this I hold firm,
Virtue may be assailed, but never hurt,
Surprised by unjust force, but not enthralled,
Yea even that which mischief meant most harm   590
Shall in the happy trial prove most glory.
But evil on itself shall back recoil,
And mix no more with goodness, when at last
Gathered like scum, and settled to itself
It shall be in eternal restless change   595
Self-fed, and self-consumed. If this fail,
The pillared firmament is rottenness,
And earth's base built on stubble. But come, let's on.
Against the opposing will and arm of heaven
May never this just sword be lifted up;   600
But for that damned magician, let him be girt
With all the grisly legións that troop
Under the sooty flag of Acheron:
Harpies and hydras, or all the monstrous forms

576 Longer I durst not stay he had the magic herb with him
when he found her; why did he not rescue her at that point? The
Elder Brother surely gives the reason in lines 587–91. The 'happy
trial' is necessary to prove the Lady's virtue.   **584 period** sentence.
597 The pillared firmament as *Job* xxvi 'The pillars of heaven';
possibly also the stage-setting at Ludlow.   **603 Acheron** hell and its
powers.   **604 Harpies and hydras** Harpies were birds with women's
faces. The Hydra was a nine-headed serpent killed by Hercules.

'Twixt Africa and Ind; I'll find him out,   605
And force him to restore his purchase back,
Or drag him by the curls, to a foul death,
Cursèd as his life.
Spir.   Alas good venturous youth,
I love thy courage yet, and bold emprise,
But here thy sword can do thee little stead,   610
Far other arms, and other weapons must
Be those that quell the might of hellish charms,
He with his bare wand can unthread thy joints,
And crumble all thy sinews.
Eld. Bro.   Why prithee shepherd
How durst thou then thyself approach so near   615
As to make this relation?
Spir.   Care and utmost shifts
How to secure the Lady from surprisal,
Brought to my mind a certain shepherd lad
Of small regard to see to, yet well skilled
In every virtuous plant and healing herb   620
That spreads her verdant leaf to the morning ray,
He loved me well, and oft would beg me sing,
Which when I did, he on the tender grass
Would sit, and hearken even to ecstasy,
And in requital ope his leathern scrip,   625
And show me simples of a thousand names
Telling their strange and vigorous faculties;
Amongst the rest a small unsightly root,
But of divine effect, he culled me out;
The leaf was darkish, and had prickles on it,   630
But in another country, as he said,
Bore a bright golden flower, but not in this soil:
Unknown, and like esteemed, and the dull swain
Treads on it daily with his clouted shoon,

606 **purchase** ill-gotten gain.   609 **bold emprise** chivalric enterprise.
618 **shepherd** M himself?   620 **virtuous** effective in healing.
625 **scrip** bag.   626 **simples** basic (unmixed) medicinal herbs.
634 **clouted** hob-nailed.

And yet more med'cinal is it than that moly   635
That Hermes once to wise Ulýsses gave;
He called it haemony, and gave it me,
And bade me keep it as of sovran use
'Gainst all enchantments, mildew blast, or damp
Or ghastly Furies' apparitión;   640
I pursed it up, but little reckoning made,
Till now that this extremity compelled,
But now I find it true; for by this means
I knew the foul enchanter though disguised,
Entered the very lime-twigs of his spells,   645
And yet came off: if you have this about you
(As I will give you when we go) you may
Boldly assault the necromancer's hall;
Where if he be, with dauntless hardihood,
And brandished blade rush on him, break his glass,   650
And shed the luscious liquor on the ground,
But seize his wand, though he and his cursed crew
Fierce sign of battle make, and menace high,
Or like the sons of Vulcan vomit smoke,
Yet will they soon retire, if he but shrink.   655
Eld. Bro. Thyrsis lead on apace, I'll follow thee,
And some good angel bear a shield before us.

Exit.

Scene 2. *Comus's palace.*

The scene changes to a stately palace, set out with all manner of deliciousness : soft music, tables spread with all dainties. Comus appears with his rabble, and the Lady set in an enchanted chair, to whom he offers his glass, which she puts by, and goes about to rise.

635 moly plant given to Ulysses to make him immune to Circe's spells.   **637 haemony** Haemonia was the classical land of magic herbs. It is also connected with the Greek words for blood and wine, this giving it a Christian symbolic force.   **645 lime-twigs** bird-snares: twigs coated with bird-lime. Continues the image of the lady as nightingale 565.   **657** Trinity Ms reads 'And good heaven cast his best regard upon us'. At this point we have the first of two changes of scene. The 'wild wood' backdrop and décor gives way to the 'Stately palace'.

Comus. Nay lady sit; if I but wave this wand,
Your nerves are all chained up in alabaster,
And you a statue, or as Daphne was   660
Root-bound, that fled Apollo,
Lady.   Fool do not boast,
Thou canst not touch the freedom of my mind
With all thy charms, although this corporal rind
Thou hast immanacled, while heaven sees good.
Comus. Why are you vexed Lady? why do you frown?   665
Here dwell no frowns, nor anger, from these gates
Sorrow flies far: see, here be all the pleasures
That fancy can beget on youthful thoughts,
When the fresh blood grows lively, and returns
Brisk as the April buds in primrose season.   670
And first behold this cordial julep here
That flames, and dances in his crystal bounds
With spirits of balm, and fragrant syrups mixed.
Not that nepenthes which the wife of Thone,
In Egypt gave to Jove-born Helena   675
Is of such power to stir up joy as this,
To life so friendly, or so cool to thirst.
Why should you be so cruel to yourself,
And to those dainty limbs which Nature lent
For gentle usage, and soft delicacy?   680
But you invert the covenants of her trust,
And harshly deal like an ill borrower
With that which you received on other terms,
Scorning the unexempt condition
By which all mortal frailty must subsist,   685
Refreshment after toil, ease after pain,

---

660 Daphne metamorphosed into a laurel-tree as she fled from
Apollo. Comus's point is presumably, that an escape from sex is an
escape from life (human life, at any rate). **662–4** The Manichean mind-
body duality is evident here. The 'corporal rind' (body) is reminiscent
of the 'sin-worn mould' of line 17. **670–704** A late insertion in Trinity
Ms. Comus's speech originally ran '. . . in primrose season. O foolishness
of men'. **671 julep** drink. **674 nepenthes** a pain-killing drug, given
by Thone's wife to Helen of Troy to drown her sorrows. **684 unexempt** from which none are exempted.

That have been tired all day without repast,
And timely rest have wanted, but fair virgin
This will restore all soon.
Lady.   'Twill not false traitor,
'Twill not restore the truth and honesty   690
That thou hast banished from thy tongue with lies,
Was this the cottage, and the safe abode
Thou told'st me of? What grim aspects are these,
These ugly-headed monsters? Mercy guard me!
Hence with thy brewed enchantments, foul deceiver,   695
Hast thou betrayed my credulous innocence
With vizored falsehood, and base forgery,
And wouldst thou seek again to trap me here
With liquorish baits fit to ensnare a brute?
Were it a draught for Juno when she banquets,   700
I would not taste thy treasonous offer; none
But such as are good men can give good things,
And that which is not good, is not delicious
To a well-governed and wise appetite.
Comus. O foolishness of men! that lend their ears   705
To those budge doctors of the Stoic fur,
And fetch their precepts from the Cynic tub,
Praising the lean and sallow abstinence.
Wherefore did nature pour her bounties forth,
With such a full and unwithdrawing hand,   710

697 vizored covered with a mask (vizor).   **699 liquorish** sweet,
but with overtones of lustful.   **702** The lady's definition of 'good'
would, of course, be quite different from that of Comus.   **706 budge**
pompous, solemn. **Stoic fur** the Stoic gown. For Seneca, the most famous
Roman Stoic philosopher, the body is the prison of the soul, and the
soul's true life only begins when it is freed from the body. Another
Stoic tenet was the renunciation of natural and worldly pleasures.   **707**
Cynic a Greek philosophical school which held that the pleasures of
life must be renounced in the interests of the development of the individual's will and self-control. **tub** Diogenes, the most famous of the
Cynics, was supposed to have opted to live in a barrel.   **709–54** The
main idea informing Comus's great speech (ie that the sheer creative
profusion of nature is in itself good and should be imitated by man) comes
from Lucretius, and was fairly commonplace in Elizabethan poetry,
notably in Shakespeare's *Venus and Adonis* and Spenser's description
of the Garden of Adonis in *The fairy queen* (see Appendix).

Covering the earth with odours, fruits, and flocks,
Thronging the seas with spawn innumerable,
But all to please, and sate the curious taste?
And set to work millions of spinning worms,
That in their green shops weave the smooth-haired silk   715
To deck her sons, and that no corner might
Be vacant of her plenty, in her own loins
She hutched the all-worshipped ore, and precious gems
To store her children with; if all the world
Should in a pet of temperance feed on pulse,   720
Drink the clear stream, and nothing wear but frieze,
The all-giver would be unthanked, would be
     unpraised,
Not half his riches known, and yet despised,
And we should serve him as a grudging master,
As a penurious niggard of his wealth,   725
And live like nature's bastards, not her sons,
Who would be quite surcharged with her own weight,
And strangled with her waste fertility;
The earth cumbered, and the winged air darked with
     plumes,
The herds would over-multitude their lords,   730
The sea o'erfraught would swell, and the unsought
     diamonds
Would so emblaze the forehead of the deep,
And so bestud with stars, that they below

715 shops workshops.   **718 hutched** stored in a hutch (copper).
The gems lie in the earth, not really the same as 'nature'.   **720
pet** fit. **pulse** beans, peas.   **721 frieze** coarse cloth, a hairshirt.
722 The all-giver nature.   **728 strangled** Comus is saying that by
repressing the force of nature within, the Lady commits a kind of suicide.
But from the standpoint of the Lady and the Elder Brother, it is Comus
who, by submitting himself to the anarchic profusion of nature, is
destroying himself. See 775–8 and 592–6: uncontrolled nature, like evil,
is seen as 'self-fed, self-consumed'.   **732 forehead** the deep is the
earth's centre; its forehead would then be that part of the crust nearest
the surface, where diamonds are found. To 'they below' (spirits in hell)
the diamonds above would seem like stars in the sky. It was an ancient
belief that precious stones reproduced themselves like animals.   **733
they below** gods and monsters of the sea.

Would grow inured to light, and come at last
To gaze upon the sun with shameless brows.   735
    List Lady be not coy, and be not cozened
With that same vaunted name virginity,
Beauty is nature's coin, must not be hoarded,
But must be current, and the good thereof
Consists in mutual and partaken bliss,   740
Unsavoury in the enjoyment of itself.
If you let slip time, like a neglected rose
It withers on the stalk with languished head.
Beauty is nature's brag, and must be shown
In courts, at feasts, and high solemnities   745
Where most may wonder at the workmanship;
It is for homely features to keep home,
They had their name thence; coarse complexions
And cheeks of sorry grain will serve to ply
The sampler, and to tease the housewife's wool.   750
What need a vermeil-tinctured lip for that
Love-darting eyes, or tresses like the morn?
There was another meaning in these gifts,
Think what, and be advised; you are but young yet.
Lady. I had not thought to have unlocked my lips   755
In this unhallowed air, but that this juggler
Would think to charm my judgement, as mine eyes
Obtruding false rules pranked in reason's garb.
I hate when vice can bolt her arguments,
And virtue has no tongue to check per pride: 760
Impostor do not charge most innocent nature,
As if she would her children should be riotous
With her abundance she, good cateress,
Means her provision only to the good

---

734 inured rendered less sensitive.   **736 cozened** duped, cheated.
744 brag display.   **749 sorry grain** poor colour.   **750 sampler** a
sample pattern of needlework. **tease** comb.   **751 vermeil-tinctured**
red-tinted.   **753 meaning in** purpose for.   **757–8** 'Would cheat my
reason with false rules made to sound plausible, just as he cheated my
eyes disguised as a good shepherd'. Pranked=dressed up gaudily.
759 bolt sift.

That live according to her sober laws,   765
And holy dictate of spare temperance:
If every just man that now pines with want
Had but a moderate and beseeming share
Of that which lewdly-pampered luxury
Now heaps upon some few with vast excess,   770
Nature's full blessings would be well-dispensed
In unsuperfluous even proportion,
And she no whit encumbered with her store,
And then the giver would be better thanked,
His praise due paid, for swinish gluttony   775
Never looks to heaven amidst his gorgeous feast,
But with besotted base ingratitude
Crams, and blasphemes his feeder. Shall I go on?
Or have I said enough? To him that dares
Arm his profane tongue with contemptuous words   780
Against the sun-clad power of chastity;
Fain would I something say, yet to what end?
Thou hast nor ear, nor soul to apprehend
The sublime notion, and high mystery
That must be uttered to unfold the sage   785
And serious doctrine of virginity,
And thou art worthy that thou shouldst not know
More happiness than this thy present lot.
Enjoy your dear wit, and gay rhetoric
That hath so well been taught her dazzling fence;   790
Thou art not fit to hear thyself convinced.
Yet should I try, the uncontrollèd worth
Of this pure cause would kindle my rapt spirits
To such a flame of sacred vehemence,

767-72 If nature's blessings were equally distributed, instead of being
heaped upon the wealthy few, then, as King Lear says: 'distribution
should undo excess And each man have enough'.   773 no whit encumbered she is answering Comus's point about nature being 'strangled
with her waste fertility'.   775-6 Of those who 'have no experience of
wisdom or virtue', Plato says in the *Republic*: 'With their eyes bent
earthwards and their heads bowed down over the table, they eat like
cattle grazing and copulating'.   790 fence art of fencing.   793 rapt
inspired.

That dumb things would be moved to sympathize,   795
And the brute earth would lend her nerves, and
    shake,
Till all thy magic structures reared so high,
Were shattered into heaps o'er thy false head.
Comus, aside. She fables not, I feel that I do fear
Her words set off by some superior power;   800
And though not mortal, yet a cold shuddering dew
Dips me all o'er, as when the wrath of Jove
Speaks thunder, and the chains of Érebus
To some of Saturn's crew. I must dissemble,
And try her yet more strongly. Come, no more,   805
This is mere moral babble, and direct
Against the canon laws of our foundation;
I must not suffer this, yet 'tis but the lees
And settlings of a melancholy blood;
But this will cure all straight, one sip of this   810
Will bathe the drooping spirits in delight
Beyond the bliss of dreams. Be wise, and taste. . .

*The Brothers rush in with swords drawn, wrest his glass out of
his hand, and break it against the ground ; his rout make sign of
resistance but are all driven in. The Attendant Spirit comes in.*

Spir. What, have you let the false enchanter scape ?
O ye mistook, ye should have snatched his wand
And bound him fast; without his rod reversed,   815
And backward mutters of dissevering power,
We cannot free the Lady that sits here

803 Érebus original darkness. Erebus was the son of Chaos, which pre-
dated the creation of the world.   **804 Saturn's crew** the Titans, who
with Saturn were chained underground after being defeated by Zeus.
808 lees sediment of wine. Comus here is giving a medical explanation
of the Lady's passion for chastity.   **812** Trinity Ms reads 'The brothers
rush in strike his glass down. The monster's shapes make as though they
would resist but are all driven in. Daemon enter with them'.   **815 his
rod reversed** Wilson Knight argues that the Lady's paralysis is symbolic
of hysterical frigidity, and anxiety about sex. 'The reversal of Comus'
rod is needed to unbend the spell: which suggests a redirection of the
same instinct. But the rod is lost; instinct sunk in repression.'

In stony fetters fixed, and motionless;
Yet stay, be not disturbed: now I bethink me,
Some other means I have which may be used,   820
Which once of Meliboeus old I learnt
The soothest shepherd that ever piped on plains.
    There is a gentle nymph not far from hence,
That with moist curb sways the smooth Severn stream,
Sabrina is her name, a virgin pure,   825
Whilom she was the daughter of Locrine,
That had the sceptre from his father Brute.
The guiltless damsel flying the mad pursuit
Of her enragèd stepdame Guendolen,
Commended her fair innocence to the flood   830
That stayed her flight with his cross-flowing course,
The water-nymphs that in the bottom played,
Held up their pearlèd wrists and took her in,
Bearing her straight to aged Nereus' hall,
Who piteous of her woes, reared her lank head,   835
And gave her to his daughters to imbathe
In nectared lavers strewed with asphodel,
And through the porch and inlet of each sense
Dropped in ambrosial oils till she revived,
And underwent a quick immortal change   840
Made goddess of the river; still she retains

821 Meliboeus a character in Virgil's *Eclogue* I; possibly Spenser, who tells the story of Sabrina in *Fairy queen* II x.   **823 a gentle nymph** the Sabrina story was originally told by Geoffrey of Monmouth in his chronicle of early British history, and M re-tells it in his *History of Britain*. The son of Brutus of Troy (Brute), Locrine inherited the throne of England. He was betrothed to Gwendolen of Cornwall, but loved Estrildis, by whom he had a daughter Sabrina. He divorced Gwendolen, who then killed him, and had Estrildis and Sabrina thrown into the river which then became known as the Severn. The myth's function here is to associate virginity (Sabrina is 'a virgin pure') with nature (the Severn) to balance the Lady's near-rejection of nature in her debate with Comus. Of the four natural elements, earth and fire seem to be on Comus's side, while air and water are 'good' (Sabrina, the 'liquid air' which the Spirit breathes in the 'broad fields of the sky' 980). See diagram in Appendix. **not far** the Severn is quite near Ludlow Castle.   **826 Whilom** formerly. **830** ie 'threw herself into the river'.   **833 pearlèd** with drops of water. **834 Nereus' hall** bottom of the sea.   **837 asphodel** immortal flower which grows on the Elysian fields in Homer's *Odyssey*.

Her maiden gentleness, and oft at eve
Visits the herds along the twilight meadows,
Helping all urchin blasts, and ill-luck signs
That the shrewd meddling elf delights to make,   845
Which she with precious vialed liquors heals.
For which the shepherds at their festivals
Carol her goodness loud in rustic lays,
And throw sweet garland wreaths into her stream
Of pansies, pinks, and gaudy daffodils.   850
And, as the old swain said, she can unlock
The clasping charm, and thaw the numbing spell,
If she be right invoked in warbled song,
For maidenhood she loves, and will be swift
To aid a virgin such as was herself   855
In hard-besetting need, this will I try,
And add the power of some adjuring verse.

(Sings)

Sabrina fair
   Listen where thou art sitting
Under the glassy, cool, translucent wave,   860
   In twisted braids of lilies knitting
The loose train of thy amber-dropping hair,
      Listen for dear honour's sake,
      Goddess of the silver lake,
         Listen and save.   865
Listen and appear to us

844 urchin blasts the infectious influence of evil spirits. **845 shrewd**
spiteful.   **846 vialed** contained in vials.   **851 old swain** Meliboeus
(Spenser). **she can unlock** Sabrina's magical powers are Milton's addition
to the myth.   **858–1022** From this point the verse aspires to the condition of music. Apart from the Spirit's three songs (one to Sabrina, one
to the 'Country Dancers', one to the Egertons) and Sabrina's one song, the
verses in octosyllabics are, according to the Bridgewater Ms, 'the verse to
sing, or not'; while the Trinity Ms directs the deliverer of the Epilogue:
'the Daemon sings, or says'.   **866** The list of classical water gods which
follows (each with its associated stock epithet) reinforces the appeal to
the 'good magic' of water – not only the Severn, but water itself (Oceanus,
Neptune).

In name of great Océanus,
By the earth-shaking Neptune's mace,
And Tethys' grave majestic pace,
By hoary Nereus' wrinkled look,   870
And the Carpathian wizard's hook,
By scaly Triton's winding shell,
And old soothsaying Glaucus' spell,
By Leucothea's lovely hands,
And her son that rules the strands,   875
By Thetis' tinsel-slippered feet,
And the songs of Sirens sweet,
By dead Parthenopè's dear tomb,
And fair Ligea's golden comb,
Wherewith she sits on diamond rocks   880
Sleeking her soft alluring locks,
By all the nymphs that nightly dance
Upon thy streams with wily glance,
Rise, rise, and heave thy rosy head
From thy coral-paven bed,   885
And bridle in thy headlong wave,
Till thou our summons answered have.

                              Listen and save.

Sabrina rises, attended by water-nymphs, and sings.

By the rushy-fringed bank,
Where grows the willow and the osier dank,   890

867 Océanus the Greeks believed the ocean was a great stream
which encircled the earth. 'Great Oceanus' was its personified god.
869 Tethys wife of Oceanus.   **870 Nereus** father of the Nereids
(sea nymphs).   **871 the Carpathian wizard** Proteus, the shepherd of
Neptune's seals, had the magical power to change his shape at will.
He lived in the Carpathian sea (according to Virgil).   **872 Triton** half-
man, half-fish, he was Neptune's herald (his trumpet was a conch-shell).
873 Glaucus a sea-god prophet.   **874 Leucothea** 'the white goddess'
– the name by which Ino, daughter of Cadmus, was worshipped by
after she jumped into the sea to escape her enraged husband.   **875 her
son** ie Melicerter, also drowned, and deified with his mother.   **876
Thetis** one of the Nereids. Homer calls her 'silver footed' in the *Iliad*.
878 Pathenopè one of the Sirens (the other two were Ligea and Lucosia).
886 bridle in restrain, hold in check.

My sliding chariot stays,
Thick set with agate, and the azurn sheen
Of turkis blue, and emerald green
    That in the channel strays,
Whilst from off the waters fleet   895
Thus I set my printless feet
O'er the cowslip's velvet head,
    That bends not as I tread,
Gentle swain at thy request
    I am here.   900
Spir. Goddess dear
We implore thy powerful hand
To undo the charmèd band
Of true virgin here distressed,
Through the force, and through the wile   905
Of unblessed enchanter vile.
Sabr. Shepherd 'tis my office best
To help ensnarèd chastity;
Brightest Lady look on me,
Thus I sprinkle on thy breast   910
Drops that from my fountain pure,
I have kept of precious cure;
Thrice upon thy finger's tip,
Thrice upon thy rubied lip,
Next this marble venomed seat   915
Smeared with gums of glutinous heat
I touch with chaste palms moist and cold,
Now the spell hath lost his hold;
And I must haste ere morning hour
To wait in Amphitritè's bower.   920

Sabrina descends, and the Lady rises out of her seat.

Spir. Virgin, daughter of Locrine,
Sprung of old Anchises' line

892 azurn azure.   **893 turkis** turquoise.   **916 glutinous** viscous.
920 Amphitritè Neptune's wife.   **922 Anchises' line** mythical Trojan
kings of Britain descended from Anchises (father of Aeneas, hero of
Virgil's *Aeneid*).

154

May thy brimmèd waves for this
Their full tribute never miss
From a thousand petty rills,   925
That tumble down the snowy hills;
Summer drouth, or singèd air
Never scorch thy tresses fair,
Nor wet October's torrent flood
Thy molten crystal fill with mud,   930
May thy billows roll ashore
The beryl, and the golden ore,
May thy lofty head be crowned
With many a tower and terrace round,
And here and there thy banks upon   935
With groves of myrrh, and cinnamon.
Come Lady while heaven lends us grace,
Let us fly this cursèd place,
Lest the sorcerer us entice
With some other new device.   940
Not a waste or needless sound
Till we come to holier ground,
I shall be your faithful guide
Through this gloomy covert wide,
And not many furlongs thence   945
Is your father's residence,
Where this night are met in state
Many a friend to gratulate
His wished presence, and beside
All the swains that there abide,   950
With jigs, and rural dance resort,
We shall catch them at their sport,
And our sudden coming there
Will double all their mirth and cheer;
Come let us haste, the stars grow high,   955
But night sits monarch yet in the mid sky.

956–7 Trinity Ms stage direction: 'Exeunt/The scene changes and then
is presented Ludlow town/and the president's castle then enter country
dancers and such/like gambols etc. After those sports the Daemon

Scene 3. *Ludlow.*

The scene changes, presenting Ludlow Town and the President's Castle ; then come in Country Dancers, after them the Attendant Spirit, with the two Brothers and the Lady.

Song

Spir. Back, shepherds, back, enough your play,
Till next sunshine holiday,
Here be without duck or nod
Other trippings to be trod   960
Of lighter toes, and such court guise
As Mercury did first devise
With the mincing Dryadès
On the lawns, and on the leas.

This second song presents them to their father and mother.

Noble Lord, and Lady bright,   965
I have brought ye new delight,
Here behold so goodly grown
Three fair branches of your own,
Heaven hath timely tried their youth,
Their faith, their patience, and their truth,   970
And sent them here through hard assays
With a crown of deathless praise,
To triumph in victorious dance
O'er sensual folly, and intemperance.

The dances ended, the Spirit epilogizes.

Spir. To the ocean now I fly,   975
And those happy climes that lie
Where day never shuts his eye,

with the 2 bro. and the Lady enter/the Daemon sings.'   **962 Mercury** herald of the gods, who had winged feet.   **971 assays** trials, temptations.   **976–8** Milton is identifying a region, as he describes it in two lines of the Trinity Ms (inserted between lines 978–9): 'Far beyond earth's end,/Where the welkin clear doth bend.' According to Plutarch, the Elysian plain ('the broad fields of the sky') was the part of the moon facing heaven.

Up in the broad fields of the sky:
There I suck the liquid air
All amidst the gardens fair   980
Of Hesperus, and his daughters three
That sing about the golden tree:
Along the crispèd shades and bowers
Revels the spruce and jocund Spring,
The graces, and the rosy-bosomed hours,   985
Thither all their bounties bring,
That there eternal summer dwells,
And west winds, with musky wing
About the cedarn alleys fling
Nard, and cassia's balmy smells.   990
Iris there with humid bow,
Waters the odorous banks that blow
Flowers of more mingled hue
Than her purflèd scarf can shew,
And drenches with Elysian dew   995
(List mortals if your ears be true)
Beds of hyacinth, and roses,
Where young Adonis oft reposes,

979 **liquid** flowing, pure (water), as opposed to the baseness of matter
(earth). See note to 823.   980 **the gardens fair** gardens of
the Hesperides (see note to 392).   983 **crispèd** ruffled by the
wind.   984 **spruce** dainty.   985 **graces** the three graces of classical
mythology were Euphrosyne (the light-hearted), Aglaia (the bright one)
and Thalia (the blossoming one).   **hours** goddesses of the seasons.
Seasonal change was seen as the Dance of the Hours.   990 **Nard, and
cassia** aromatic plants.   991 **Iris** the rainbow.   994 **purflèd** many
coloured, embroidered.   995–1010 These lines are not in either of the
two Ms versions but were added in 1637.   996 (**List mortals if your
ears be true**) he is about to speak truths which only the pure can understand, ie 'things that no gross ear can hear' 457. 'True' also brings in the
musical analogy of harmony with truth.   998 **Adonis** a youth loved by
Venus ('the Assyrian queen'), he was killed by a wound inflicted by a
boar and brought back to life on condition that he spend six months on
earth with Venus, and six months in hades. The myth became an allegory
for the summer-winter cycle of nature. In Spenser's *Fairy queen* the
Garden of Adonis symbolizes the creativity of nature, which finds
eternity in constant seasonal change – in contrast to the artificial nature
of the Bower of Bliss. The Spirit's paradise, however, is here seen to be
above, not in, the world of nature.

Waxing well of his deep wound
In slumber soft, and on the ground   1000
Sadly sits the Assyrian queen;
But far above in spangled sheen
Celestial Cupid her famed son advanced,
Holds his dear Psyche sweet entranced
After her wandering labours long,   1005
Till free consent the gods among
Make her his eternal bride,
And from her fair unspotted side
Two blissful twins are to be born,
Youth and Joy; so Jove hath sworn.   1010

   But now my task is smoothly done,
I can fly, or I can run
Quickly to the green earth's end,
Where the bowed welkin slow doth bend,
And from thence can soar as soon   1015
To the corners of the moon.

   Mortals that would follow me,
Love virtue, she alone is free,
She can teach ye how to climb
Higher than the sphery chime;   1020
Or if virtue feeble were,
Heaven itself would stoop to her.

1002–4 far above in Spenser's *Fairy queen* Cupid and Psyche live in
the earthly Garden of Adonis. Their daughter is Pleasure. Another
version (Apuleius's *Golden ass*) is that Jove brings Psyche to heaven
(having given her immortality), where she marries Cupid. Boccaccio
allegorizes the myth as a reconciliation of the soul (Psyche) with divine
reason and love or *agapè* (Cupid) – 'from this love is born Pleasure, which
is eternal bliss and joy'. M here seems to see their love as celestial, and
thus 'far above' the earthly love symbolized by Venus and Adonis.
1010 Youth and Joy M substitutes these for Pleasure, as the offspring
of the marriage. **1014 bowed welkin** the curve of the heavens. **1020
the sphery chime** the musical spheres.

Appendix to Comus

Structure

Character
in masque

super-natural	human	element	hierarchy of cosmos	place in masque
Spirit		air 'the liquid air' 979	X transcendental world of grace above nature	'regions mild of calm and serene air' 4; 'the broad fields of the sky' 978
	Earl	earth	A civilized nature produced by human effort to rise from B by enduring trial which tempts a descent to C	Ludlow Castle and town
Sabrina		water		River Severn; Ocean 975; Nereus's hall 834
			B unaltered nature of animal and plant life	the wild wood
Comus		earth and fire	C nature made sinful by artifice	Comus's stately palace; masks

Milton's moral purpose requires the distinctions to be maintained between levels and places; but the effect of the poetry given to Comus is to dissolve distinctions. Note how the supernatural characters all move across boundaries: Comus 'descended' from divine ancestry; the Spirit descends, Sabrina rises. Consider the location of the Lady in terms of boundaries. Consider some of the adjuncts of the characters, eg the association of the Spirit with rainbows, and with Cupid and Psyche, Venus and Adonis as contrasted with Comus's attendant deities; Comus and sticky 'heat', the Lady and coolness. The diagram is only a framework, not complete.

Masque

Inspect Inigo Jones's designs for stage-sets and costumes; you will find illustrations sections in Spencer's *Book of masques* and Nicholl's *Stuart masques* (see Book list).

Here is a list of some of the masques by Ben Jonson and Inigo Jones:

Hymenaei. Performed 5 January 1606 to celebrate the union of two great English families, Devereux (son of the Earl of Essex) and Howard (daughter of the lord chamberlain). In the preface to the printed text (see below) Jonson divides the masque-performance into 'soul' and 'body'; the soul being the text, which is 'impressing' and 'lasting'; and the body being the 'outward' show – the beautiful scenery and costumes, which are 'momentary' and 'merely taking'. We see the body with our senses; we apprehend the soul with our understanding. Here, Jonson is claiming the more important role in the production of a masque (and control over Inigo Jones).

It is a noble and just advantage that the things subjected to understanding have of those which are objected to sense, that the one sort are but momentary, and merely taking; the other impressing, and lasting: else the glory of all these solemnities had perished like a blaze, and gone out in the beholders' eyes, so short-lived are the bodies of all things, in comparison of their souls. And, though bodies oft-times have the ill luck to be sensually preferred, they find afterwards the good fortune (when souls live) to be utterly forgotten. This it is hath made the most royal princes and greatest persons (who are commonly the personators of these actions) not only studious of riches and magnificence in the outward celebration or show (which rightly becomes them) but curious after the most high and hearty inventions to furnish the inward parts (and those grounded upon antiquity, and solid learnings) which, though their voice be taught to sound to present occasions, their sense or doth or should always lay hold on more removed mysteries. And, howsoever some may squeamishly cry out that all endeavour of learning, and sharpness in these transitory devices, especially where it steps beyond their little or (let me not wrong 'em) no brain at all, is superfluous; I am contented, these fastidious stomachs should leave my full tables, and enjoy at home their clean empty trenchers, fittest for such airy tastes: where perhaps a few Italian

161

Tethys or a nymph, an ink and wash sketch by Inigo Jones for *Tethys' festival*, written by Samuel Daniel and danced by James I's queen, Anne of Denmark, and her ladies, on 5 June 1610 in honour of the creation of her son Henry as Prince of Wales. 'Now concerning their habits: first their head-tire was composed of shels and corrall, and from a great Muriake shell in forme of the crest of an helme, hung a thin wauing vaile. Their vpper garments had the bodies of sky-coloured taffetaes for lightnes, all embroidered with maritime invention: then had they a kinde of halfe skirts of cloth of siluer imbrordered with golde, all the ground work cut out for lightnes, which hung down ful, & cut in points: vnderneath that, came bases (of the same as their bodies) beneath their knee. The long skirt was wrought with lace, waued round like a Riuer, and on the banks sedge and Seaweedes, all of gold . . .'

herbs, picked up and made into a salad, may find sweeter acceptance than
all the most nourishing and sound meats of the world.

JONSON preface to *Hymenaei*

The masque of Oberon. Performed 5 June 1610 to celebrate Prince
Henry's inauguration as Prince of Wales.

The hue and cry after Cupid. On the marriage of Viscount Hadding-
ton to the Earl of Sussex's daughter. At court, Shrove Tuesday
night 1608 (Ash Wednesday, the first day of Lent, is the day
after Shrove Tuesday).

Love freed from ignorance and folly. Performed in honour of the
queen at court on 3 February 1611. The masque cost £600 to
mount; Ben and Inigo got £40 each for their script and designs
(cf the £20,000 cost of Shirley's *Triumph of peace* twenty years
later).

Pleasure reconciled to virtue. First performed on Twelfth Night
1618 for King James; here Comus makes his first appearance in a
masque.

*The scene was the mountain Atlas, who had his top ending in the figure of an
old man, his head and beard all hoary and frost, as if his shoulders were
covered with snow ; the rest wood and rock. A grove of ivy at his feet, out of
which, to a wild music of cymbals, flutes and tabors, was brought forth
Comus, the god of cheer or the belly, riding in triumph, his head crowned
with roses and other flowers, his hair curled: they that waited upon him
crowned with ivy, their javelins done about with it ; one of them going with
Hercules his bowl borne before him, while the rest presented him with this
hymn.*

. . . . . .

*After this, the whole grove vanished, and the whole music was discovered,
sitting at the foot of the mountain, with Pleasure and Virtue seated above
them. The choir invited Hercules to rest with this song.*

> Great friend, and servant of the good,
> Let cool a while thy heated blood,
> And from thy mighty labour cease.
> Lie down, lie down,
> And give thy troubled spirits peace,
> Whilst Virtue, for whose sake
> Thou dost this god-like travail take,
> May of the choicest herbage make
> (Here on this mountain bred)
> A crown, a crown
> For thy immortal head.

Here Hercules being laid down at their feet, the second anti-masque, which was of Pigmies, appeared.

> *1 Pigmy.*   Yes, peace.
> *3 Pigmy.* Triumph; we have him, boy.
> *4 Pigmy.* Sure, sure, he is sure.
> *1 Pigmy.* Come, let us dance for joy.

At the end of their dance, they thought to surprise him, when suddenly, being awaked by the music, he roused himself, and they all ran into holes.

Song

> Wake, Hercules, awake; but heave up thy black eye,
> 'Tis only asked from thee to look, and these will die,
> > Or fly.
> > Already they are fled,
> > Whom scorn had else left dead.

At which, Mercury descended from the hill, with a garland of poplar to crown him.

> *Mercury.* Rest still, thou active friend of virtue; these
> Should not disturb the peace of Hercules.
> Earth's worms, and honour's dwarfs, at too great odds
> Prove, or provoke, the issue of the gods.
> See here a crown the agèd hill hath sent thee,
> My grandsire Atlas, he that did present thee
> With the best sheep that in his fold were found,
> Or golden fruit on the Hesperian ground,
> For rescuing his fair daughters, then the prey
> Of a rude pirate, as thou cam'st this way;
> And taught thee all the learning of the sphere,
> And how, like him, thou might'st the heavens upbear,
> As that thy labour's virtuous recompense.
> He, though a mountain now, hath yet the sense
> Of thanking thee for more, thou being still
> Constant to goodness, guardian of the hill,
> Antaeus by thee suffocated here,
> And the voluptuous Comus, god of cheer,
> Beat from his grove, and that defac'd. But now
> The time's arrived that Atlas told thee of, how
> By unaltered law, and working of the stars,
> There should be a cessation of all jars
> 'Twixt Virtue and her noted opposite,
> Pleasure; that both should meet here, in the sight
> Of Hesperus, the glory of the west,
> The brightest star, that from his burning crest
> Lights all on this side the Atlantic seas,
> As far as to thy pillars, Hercules.
> See where he shines, Justice and Wisdom placed
> About his throne, and those with Honour graced,
> Beauty and Love. It is not with his brother
> Bearing the world, but ruling such another

Is his renown. Pleasure, for his delight,
Is reconciled to Virtue; and this night
Virtue brings forth twelve Princes have been bred
In this rough mountain, and near Atlas' head,
The hill of knowledge; one, and chief, of whom
Of the bright race of Hesperus is come,
Who shall in time the same that he is be,
And now is only a less light than he.
These now she trusts with Pleasure, and to these
She gives an entrance to the Hesperides,
Fair Beauty's garden; neither can she fear
They should grow soft, or wax effeminate here,
Since in her sight, and by her charge all's done,
Pleasure the servant, Virtue looking on.

*Here the whole choir of music called the twelve masquers forth from the lap
of the mountain . . . [with a song invoking Atlas to open. The 12 courtly
masquers descend, and dance; then there is a 2nd song; a 2nd dance;
3rd song; after which] . . . they danced with the ladies, and the whole revels
followed; which ended, Mercury called to him in this following speech;
which was after repeated in song by two trebles, two tenors, a bass, and the
whole chorus.*

The fourth Song

An eye of looking back were well,
Or any murmur that would tell
    Your thoughts, how you were sent,
        And went
    To walk with Pleasure, not to dwell.
These, these are hours by Virtue spared
Herself, she being her own reward,
        But she will have you know
          That though
Her sports be soft, her life is hard.
You must return unto the hill,
        And there advance
With labour, and inhabit still
        That height and crown,
From whence you ever may look down
        Upon triumphèd Chance.
She, she it is in darkness shines,
'Tis she that still herself refines
By her own light to every eye,
More seen, more known when Vice stands by;
And though a stranger here on earth,
In heaven she hath her right of birth;
        There, there is Virtue's seat.
      Strive to keep her your own;
        'Tis only she can make you great,
      Though place here make you known.

*After which, they danced their last dance, and returned into the scene, which
closed, and was a mountain again, as before.*

One might say of the two most famous masques of Charles I's court that their 'souls' were smothered by their overwhelming visual magnificence. One of these was James Shirley's *The triumph of peace*, financed by the Inns of Court to show support for Charles, after he had been attacked by the puritans in Prynne's *Histriomastix* 1632. It was performed on 3 February 1634 and cost £20,000. Inigo Jones provided scenery and costume designs. Six months later *Comus* was first performed at Ludlow. The other was Thomas Carew's *Coelum Britannicum*, also 1634, and also a spectacular and expensive affair. The overblown and increasingly expensive production costs marked the beginning of the end for these wish-fulfilling symbols of an ordered, hierarchical and peaceful state. The state itself did not survive the civil war of the 1640s, and masque was not revived at the court of Charles II, except in its new form of opera. The first English opera was Sir William Davenant's *The siege of Rhodes* 1656.

In recent times, William Empson has written the script for a masque called *The birth of steel* which was performed in honour of a visit by the queen to Sheffield in 1954 (printed in his *Collected poems* 1955). The form continues to influence plays which demand ceremonial and ritual scenes: see the work of the modern French playwright Jean Genet, especially *The balcony* and *The blacks*; Peter Weiss's *Le Marat-Sade* can be seen as an extended anti-masque. See the essay 'Masques in plays' by Inga Stina-Ewbank in *A book of masques* ed. Spencer; and the masques in Shakespeare's last plays, *Pericles*, *Winter's tale*, *Tempest*.

FRANCIS BACON *Essay XXXVII Of masques and triumphs*

These things are but toys to come amongst such serious observations; but yet, since princes will have such things, it is better they should be graced with elegancy than daubed with cost. Dancing to song is a thing of great state and pleasure. I understand it that the song be in choir, placed aloft, and accompanied with some broken music; and the ditty fitted to the device [ie conceit of the plot]. Acting in song, especially in dialogues, hath an extreme good grace; I say acting, not dancing (for that is a mean and vulgar thing) . . . the alterations of scenes, so it be quietly and without noise, are things of great beauty and pleasure: for they feed and relieve the eye before it be full of the same object. Let the scences abound with light, specially coloured and varied; and let the masquers, or any other that are to come down from the scene [ie stage], have some motions upon the scene itself before their coming down; for it draws the eye strangely and makes it with great pleasure desire to see that it cannot perfectly discern . . . The colours that show best by candlelight are white, carnation [scarlet], and a kind of sea-water green; and ouches [gems] or spangs [spangles], as they are of no great cost, so they are of most glory . . . Let anti-masques not be long; they have been commonly of fools, satyrs, baboons, wild men, antics [monsters or clowns], beasts, sprites, witches, Ethiops, pigmies, Turquets, nymphs, rustics, Cupids, statues moving, and the like . . . Some sweet odours suddenly coming forth, without any drops falling, are, in such a company as there is steam and heat, things of great pleasure and refreshment.

ROY STRONG *Festival designs by Inigo Jones* International Exhibitions Foundation Washington 1967

At one end there was a stage, six or eight feet high, enclosed by a proscenium arch bearing figures symbolic of the theme of the masque. Before the proscenium projected three or four feet of stage; behind the proscenium and curtain came the stage proper, and beyond that a small upper stage for ultimate vistas. Behind this proscenium arch Jones created his pasteboard world of illusion in which the masquers lived; before it lay the world of actuality of King and Court. Bridging the two spheres were various combinations of steps or slopes that enabled the masquers, flanked by torchbearers to light their way, to flood down into the arena before them. The latter was a rectangular carpeted area where the masquers executed their special choreographed dances and then invited members of the audience to join them in general revels. Spectators sat on benches arranged in tiers around the arena, only those facing the proscenium seeing the perspective scenery properly, and of these, one pair of eyes, those of the King, had a perfect view, for in his pupils met the lines of painted perspective . . . The aesthetic structure of Jones' work for the masque depended on recession, layer after layer of scenery being peeled away, each set by use of perspective accentuating distance to infinity . . .

ANGUS FLETCHER *The transcendental masque* © 1971 by Cornell University Ithaca N.Y.

. . . the masque and its mixed media and their powerfully focused magical controls reflect the desire to invent a transcendental political rhetoric.

JOHN G. DEMARAY *Milton and the masque tradition* Harvard University Press Cambridge Mass. 1968

Since Milton wrote of the 'radiant feet the tissued clouds down steering' [*Nativity* 146], he probably knew that artificial clouds in masques were constructed of diaphanous materials and lighted from within. Such clouds were often made of oiled paper and calico. When the Banqueting House [in Whitehall] burned to the ground in 1619, it was because a masquing device constructed of oiled paper and dry fir was accidentally ignited. The fact that the clouds in Milton's poem are 'down steering' suggests that the poet realized that cloud machines like those in *Hymenaei* were often 'steered' in different directions over the stage. Masquers on these machines were bathed in light just as Mercy was when she descended 'throned in celestial sheen' [145] . . .

Circe, nature, chastity

What difference does the sex of the tempter make? Comus's
mother Circe was a witch:

> Bewitching siren, gilded rottenness,
> Thou hast with cunning artifice displayed
> The enamelled outside, and the honied verge,
> Of the fair cup where deadly poison lurks . . .
> Grief is the shadow lurking on thy steps . . .
> Yet thy Circean charms transform the world.

CAREW *Coelum Britannicum* 1634

Homer's Circe [*Odyssey* x] is by no means the lustful witch one finds in
Ovid [*Metamorphoses* xiv] . . . the whole relation [with Odysseus], though
it has customarily been taken as a story of temptation and abstention,
actually has in Homer more the feeling of a test of skill. Odysseus
renders Circe harmless, not by abstaining from any of her charms, but
by shrewdness combined with force. The sense is that if she is not
handled right Circe will either metamorphose or castrate the men who
encounter her; but for a good man . . . she is all pleasure and delightful
learning. Odysseus gains the ascendancy over her with the help of
Hermes, signifiying his own wisdom . . . he maintains it by combining
vigor with tact . . . as Sir Gawain was later to do . . . As the high priestess
of metamorphosis, Circe was bound to be a fascinating figure for the
writers of the Renaissance, before whom the wonderful possibilities of
psychic mobility were just opening up. The notion that man is inherently
a Proteus, a chameleon, an amphibious, multiform creature who can
make of himself what he will would have shocked Dante or St. Thomas
. . . Those mirror characters who pursue one another through the thick
underbrush of Spenser's elaborate heroic pattern are like masquers in
the new multiplex drama of the human ego.

ROBERT M. ADAMS ed. *The Circe of Giovanni Battista Gelli*
trans. T. Brown © 1963 by Cornell University Ithaca N.Y.

Spenser has several Circean figures, especially converging on
the Bower of Bliss in *Fairy queen* II xii, his version of corrupt
nature. Here is Excess:

> In her left hand a cup of gold she held
> And with her right the riper fruit did reach,
> Whose sappy liquor that with fulness swelled
> Into her cup she scruzed with dainty breach
> Of her fine fingers, without foul empeach,
> That so fair winepress made the wine more sweet:
> Thereof she used to give to drink to each
> When passing by she happenèd to meet;
> It was her guise, all strangers goodly so to greet.

168

The chief is Acrasia, who lives there in a parody of Venus and Adonis, Cupid and Psyche:

> That wanton lady with her lover loose
> Whose sleepy head she in her lap did soft dispose.
>
> Upon a bed of roses she was laid,
> As faint through heat, or dight to pleasant sin,
> And was arrayed – or rather, disarrayed –
> All in a veil of silk and silver thin
> That hid no whit her alablaster skin
> But rather showed more white, if more might be . . .

As Comus's stately palace is a corrupt version of Ludlow Castle, so Acrasia's Bower of Bliss is of the Garden of Adonis in *Fairy queen* III vi. These gardens are celebrated finally in *Comus* in the epilogue. Here is Spenser's version:

> And all about grew every sort of flower
> To which sad lovers were transformed of yore:
> Fresh Hyacinthus, Phoebus' paramour
> And dearest love,
> Foolish Narciss that likes the watery shore,
> Sad Amaranthus in whose purple gore
> Meseems I see Amyntas' wretched fate,
> To whom sweet poets' verse hath given endless date.
>
> There wont fair Venus often to enjoy
> Her dear Adonis' joyous company
> And reap sweet pleasure of the wanton boy;
> There yet, some say, in secret he does lie
> Lapped in flowers and precious spicery,
> By her hid from the world and from the skill
> Of Stygian gods, which does her love envý;
> But she herself, whenever that she will,
> Possesseth him and of his sweetness takes her fill.

Spenser goes on to include Cupid and Psyche, as Milton does in the epilogue. See Raphael's paintings in the Loggia di Psiche, Farnese Palace, Rome; and sculptures of Canova and Rodin.

ROSEMOND TUVE *Images and themes in five poems by Milton* Harvard University Press Cambridge Mass. 1957

'Circe, daughter of the Sun and of Oceanus's daughter, of heat and moisture, which engender physical pleasure, allures men to the indulgence of all intemperate appetites . . .' In this myth about the admixture of reason and unreason in the human psyche, her [the Lady's] godlike nature is seen as armor against her depraved nature – it is a myth about what *is* 'natural', and what is 'deformity' – and indeed about the *violation* of the soul's chastity by 'nature' in the Circean sense . . . The Lady's virgin state is not defined as her virtue; it is the 'armor' which provides 'a hidden strength' against the particular kind of assault upon the virtuous soul that is made by a Circe-figure.

Cupid and Psyche, with their twins, are implied in Milton's account in *Apology against a pamphlet* 1642 of the chastity he believed vital to the poet:

These reasonings, together with a certain niceness of nature, an honest haughtiness and self-esteem either of what I was, or what I might be (which let envy call pride); and lastly . . . modesty . . . all these uniting the supply of their natural aid together, kept me still above those low descents of mind, that can agree to saleable and unlawful prostitutions. Next . . . I betook me among those lofty fables and romances which recount in solemn cantos the deeds of knighthood . . . There I read it in the oath of every knight, that he should defend to the expense of his best blood, or of his life, if it so befell him, the honour and chastity of virgin or matron. From whence I learnt, even then, what a noble virtue chastity sure must be, to the defence of which so many worthies . . . had sworn . . . Thus from the laureate fraternity of poets, riper years and the ceaseless round of study and reading led me to the shady spaces of philosophy – but chiefly to the divine volumes of Plato, and his equal Xenophon, where if I should tell ye what I learnt of chastity and love – I mean that which is truly so – whose charming cup is only virtue, which she bears in her hand to those who are worthy (the rest are cheated with a thick intoxicating potion which a certain sorceress, the abuser of love's name, carries about); and how the first and chiefest office of love begins and ends in the soul, producing those happy twins of her divine generation, knowledge and virtue . . .

C. L. BARBER '*A mask presented at Ludlow Castle*: the masque as a masque' *The lyric and dramatic Milton: selected papers from the English Institute* ed. J. H. Summers 1966 and repr. in '*A masque at Ludlow*': essays on M's *Comus* ed. J. S. Diekhoff Cleveland Ohio 1968

In electing to make a Masque of Chastity and put Revel in the role of villain, Milton undertook a particularly difficult task . . . His sense of life prevented his using wholeheartedly one of the great resources of entertainment literature, the release sanctioned by seasonal or periodic holiday. On a tide of such mirth, Shakespeare could move out into magic woods with an implicit confidence in a return, after the holiday moment, with humanity intact . . . Milton has deliberately presented a figure of Revel who under the guise of refreshment tempts to dissolution from which there is no coming back. The whole historical development of English life . . . was giving ground from Milton's new vantage toward the pleasures of Merry England . . . The first response which the attitudes of our own time suggest is that Milton's project of celebrating Chastity is impossible. For we not only have no cult of chastity, we have a cult of defloration. Crazy Jane, 'Learned in bodily lowliness', tells the Bishop that 'nothing can be sole or whole / That has not been rent' [Yeats *Crazy Jane talks with the bishop*]. Much contemporary fiction is devoted to a mystique that spiritual exploration requires accepting one kind or another of rape by the world . . . When we look at Milton in our psychological perspectives, we cannot help feeling that he was vulnerable, and that in his idealization of chastity we have, clearly, a mechanism of defense . . . Through the ideal of chastity, Milton could reach to vital resources of his culture and religion. If Milton was vulnerable sexually, we should recognize that sexual vulnerability is just what his masque presents. If it is a defense, it is simultaneously a resource, a gathering of resources from a civilization which did not assume sexual invulnerability as an ideal. Milton fully recognized that unintegrated passion might destroy his particular complex sensibility . . . In [*Comus*] he presents the possibility of destructive release, and meets it by another sort of release, the release of imagination carried by rhythm out and up to other objects of love. This alternative release is in its way physical, and so can work to counter that which Comus offers. For poetry and song *are* physical, the whole body engaged in the rhythms of articulation, envisagement centred in physical utterance. It is notable that the images which suggest a benign sexual release refer to song: 'Silence / Was took ere she was ware'. In so far as the masque fails, it fails by a failure of rhythm. Where instead of poetry we get mere vehemence, mere assertion, and where our imagination is allowed to rest on the merely literal or merely intellectual contest, the defense of chastity lacks the final cogency of pleasure.

Songs and dances in Comus

By WINIFRED MAYNARD

A masque was designed to give several sorts of pleasure. With its rich and beautiful costumes and intricately patterned dancing and sometimes breathtaking transformation scenes it pleased the eye; its songs and dances pleased the ear; and often the aptness of the theme to the occasion pleased the mind, without presenting it with such solid food for thought as in *Comus*.

The part played by music in a particular masque depended on the balance to be struck between the various, often rival, kinds of attraction, and on the musical and financial resources the composer could call on. A masque for which Thomas Campion wrote the words and some of the music, *A Maske . . . in honour of the Lord Hayes and his bride* (1607), used considerable musical forces. The description of it[1] tells how on the right hand of the dancing area

were consorted ten Musitions, with Basse and Meane lutes, a Bandora, a double Sack-bott, and an Harpsicord,[2] with two treble Violins; on the other side somewhat nearer the skreene were plac't 9 Violins and three Lutes, and to answere both the Consorts (as it were in a triangle) sixe Cornets, and sixe Chappell voyces, were seated almost right against them, in a place raised higher in respect of the pearcing sound of those Instruments . . .

There were also oboe-players concealed under trees to play at the king's entrance into the hall; four 'Silvans' played lutes, bass-lute and bandora, a double chorus sang – altogether there were 42 voices and instruments. More than twice that number of musicians, about a hundred, took part in a masque in which Henry Lawes sang earlier in the same year that he wrote the music for *Comus*. This was *The triumph of peace*, with text by James Shirley, in which Lawes was one of five 'constellations'; some songs and instrumental music for it by his brother William survive.[3] But that was a very splendid affair, presented by the Inns of Court to Charles I and the queen as a demonstration of loyalty: before its presentation in the Banqueting House at Whitehall a procession including horses and chariots and lit by 2,400 torches paraded through London.

The masque presented at Ludlow Castle was on a more modest scale altogether, in terms of music and spectacle. No description or list of properties is known, but probably the council chamber at Ludlow did not make possible the use of elaborate scenic devices, and there is no record of the services of a masque designer. As for music, there would be some instrumentalists to accompany the dances, but the singers seem to have been just two, the Attendant Spirit and the Lady. Yet *Comus* makes its own musical mark because of the effectiveness and subtlety of its use of song. Its distinctiveness lay in the integration of song

[1] See Campion's *Works* ed. P. Vivian, Oxford 1909, 1967.
[2] See *The Oxford companion to music* for descriptions and pictures of instruments.
[3] These pieces, together with the songs for Lord Hayes's masque and for *Comus*, are printed in Andrew J. Sabol *Songs and dances for the Stuart masque* Providence R.I. 1959 (a total of 63 items of music for masques 1604–41); see also Diekhoff in Booklist for *Comus* here; J. T. Shawcross 'Henry Lawes's settings of songs for M's *Comus*' in *Journal of Rutgers Univ. Library* XXVIII 1964; Willa Evans *Henry Lawes, musician and friend of poets* 1941; Wilfrid Mellors *Harmonious meeting* 1965.

and speech so that they formed a continuous dramatic whole. When Campion introduces a song into his masque, it is clearly separated from the spoken dialogue, because it has its own formal musical structure, with a melody that is repeated for each verse. The melody is carefully shaped to fit the words, and the song is relevant to the action, but its effect is that of a 'set piece' inserted into the spoken action.

In *Comus* this effect is avoided by the use of a style of song which combines some of the attractiveness of melody with the close modelling of the vocal line on the words that characterizes recitative. In recitative, words, usually carrying forward the narrative of a story, as in opera, are delivered in a singing voice and the notes have definite musical pitch, but the length of the notes is determined by the way the words would be delivered in speech, and there may be little musical shapeliness. Since the late 16th century, there had been much interest in the relations between words and music in both Italy and France. In France a very stylized system was developed, in which long and short syllables were partnered by long and short notes, in 'musique mesurée à l'antique'. The Italians developed a much more flexible relationship in their search for a way to heighten words through music to gain added dramatic power. In the closing years of the century, a group of cultured amateur musicians, poets and theorists used to meet at the house of Count Bardi, in Florence, and discuss how best to try to re-create for their own day some equivalent to the Greek art of using music in the service of drama. Should they try to reproduce Greek declamation, so far as they could understand it (in 1581 one of the group, Vincenzo Galilei, father of the astronomer, had rediscovered a piece of Greek music but no one knew how its notation should be deciphered); or should they work out a new way to achieve the same end?

Caccini became the best-known spokesman of this group (who were called the Camerata, from the room they met in), because of his preface to his collection of pieces in the new style, *Le nuove musiche* 1601. He describes his aim as talking in music, or telling a story in music ('in armonia favellare'). This is what the early opera composers were aiming at, Peri, Caccini himself, and the greatest of them, Monteverdi. Monteverdi was able to combine musical eloquence and beauty with close faithfulness to the intonations and stresses of words; in the second act of his *Orfeo*, for instance, the scene of the messenger's arrival, and of Orfeo's reception of the news be brings, is one of extraordinary power.[1] The music poignantly expresses the intense emotions that the words alone only partly convey.

Masques differ from opera in that their dialogue is mostly spoken, whereas opera is sung throughout,[2] but they too began to use music to heighten their drama, and not as pauses or interludes in it. Nicholas Lanier and Henry Lawes were the first composers in England to develop masque-song on these lines (and they used a similar style for songs outside drama too). Both composers evolved a style that was more melodic than mere recitative, but still closely based on the natural rhythms and the implicit pitch of the words.[3] Lawes's settings for *Comus* show how adaptable this style was to the immediate dramatic purpose and context, for although they can all be described as 'declamatory song', that is, song in which the apt declamation of the words is the primary consideration, a sensitive listener will notice their differences. The songs with which the Attendant Spirit begins and ends the masque are close to recitative; 'Sabrina fair' and 'Sweet Echo' are more tuneful and shapely; and when the Attendant Spirit addresses the country dancers with 'Back, shepherds, back', and then the earl and countess as 'Noble lord, and lady bright', his words take on the rhythms and musical forms first of a country dance and then of the masque dance.

The first song owes its existence to the initiative of Lawes: Milton did not provide for an opening song. The masque would probably be heralded by instrumental music; then, in Milton's text, it opened with the Spirit's spoken announcement of his dwelling-place and his task. But Lawes must have wished to weave music and words together right from the beginning, and to avoid an abrupt transition from instrumental music to speech, and he achieved it neatly and simply by borrowing some lines

[1] Recorded on Archiv APM 14057, side 2. Music by Caccini and other Italian composers of monody (solo song) is recorded on side 1 of *Songs for courtiers and cavaliers*, L'Oiseau-Lyre OL 50128, and songs by Lawes on side 2.

[2] The distinction does not always apply: Matthew Locke's *Orpheus and Euridice* 1673 and John Blow's *Venus and Adonis* c. 1682 are both masques that are also operas, being sung throughout.

[3] Lanier was the earlier to practise it: see his song *Bring away this sacred tree* (Sabol p. 52) for Campion's *Squires' masque* 1613. Campion himself and Coperario wrote songs in the older lute-song style for the same masque.

from the epilogue.[1] Little change was needed; instead of saying 'To the ocean now I fly', the Spirit simply sang 'From the heavens now I fly'.[2] If Lawes had been able to obtain a 'cloud machine' and have it installed, he *would* fly down, descending slowly as hidden ropes lowered his chariot and singing from it as he came, and this would make a splendidly striking opening. The prefatory stage direction reflects some doubt about the practicability of this, since it says the Spirit 'descends or enters'. But even if flying could not be provided for in the castle, the Spirit could still make an effective entry, declaiming his words in musical phrases that partner both the shape and the sense of the lines; they seem simply to be the natural utterance of this ethereal being, distinguishing him from mere mortals, as he comes from his dwelling-place in the Hesperides. And, as if incidentally, they also enhance the total impact, of sound and spectacle together, of the masque's opening.

As he reaches earth, the Spirit drops from a singing voice to speech and explains why he has been sent. He has no sooner described Comus and his rout than they enter, and probably the musicians play clamorous music at this point, to add to the 'riotous and unruly noise' they are making.[3] But when Comus says 'Come, knit hands, and beat the ground, In a light fantastic round', very different music is called for, because they are going to dance 'the measure'. The term is often used in masques and can mean simply 'the dance', but it is also the name for a particular dance. In *Much ado about nothing* Beatrice says to Hero 'wooing, wedding, and repenting, is as a Scotch jig, a measure,

[1] Lines 975–82, 991–4, 997–8. The Bridgewater Ms (still in the Egerton family) gives the Spirit six more lines which Lawes did not set. It was edited by a later Lady Alix Egerton as *M's Comus : being the Bridgewater MS, with notes and a short family memoir* 1910; see also Diekhoff and Sprott in Booklist below.

[2] His last line was also altered, from 'Where young Adonis oft reposes' to 'Where many a cherub soft reposes'.

[3] Instrumental music was probably used at various points in the masque for added effect, particularly at moments when beings of a different kind from humans appear – the Spirit, Comus, Sabrina. Whether it was improvised, or composed, for the occasion, or chosen from existing music, as that for the dances probably was, Lawes did not think it necessary to record it. In the book in which he collected his own compositions, he entered only the five song-settings. His manuscript book, now in the British Museum, is described in *The Henry Lawes manuscript* by P. J. Willetts 1969. A selection of songs from it, edited by Elizabeth Poston, is to be published.

and a cinque-pace: . . . the wedding, mannerly-modest, as a measure, full of state and ancientry'.[1] The measure she has in mind is probably a kind of pavane called the *passamezzo*.[2] A courtly audience would not miss the point of giving this riotous crew a dance that is 'mannerly-modest'; indeed, even the term 'the measure' carries irony, because it is lack of measure, immoderateness of desires, that has transformed them into beasts. As they perform it, it becomes a blasphemous mimicry, a true antimasque, of the cosmic dance to which Comus compares it:

> We that are of purer fire
> Imitate the starry choir,
> Who in their nightly watchful spheres,
> Lead in swift round the months and years.
> The sounds, and seas with all their finny drove
> Now to the moon in wavering morris move . . .   111–16

The dance itself is graceful and seemly, but these monsters, clamouring and cavorting, make it into 'a wild, rude, and wanton Antick', in the words of the stage direction in the Bridgewater Ms.

The dance is broken off by Comus, who senses the presence of the Lady; and she, who has heard the riotous noise, enters and tells of her search for her brothers. Her apprehension is rising; she does not wish to encounter drunken merry-makers, but where shall she turn? Perhaps if she sings her voice will carry further and reach her brothers; especially if Echo will help her. So everything contributes to the naturalness of her song: the audience knows she is lost and fearful, she has said she will try to make her brothers hear her, and when she does sing, she addresses Echo and asks for her help. It is a beautiful and delicate

[1] II i 71.

[2] Music composed for this dance always used the same bass, the *passamezzo antico*. A detailed description of it, with instructions for performing it and a mid-16c example, are given in *Dances of Spain and Italy 1400–1600*, by Mabel Dolmetsch 1954, chap VII, and there are *passamezzo* pavanes by Byrd and Philips in the *Fitzwilliam virginal book*. It is sometimes suggested that wild, disorderly music should be used for Comus's dance, but this is to miss many points that Milton is making: it is the dancers who are wanton, not the music they dance to. For an amateur production, some of the dance-music, mostly by William Lawes, given in Sir Frederick Bridge's score for *Comus*, may be found useful, but a pavane should be used for this antimasque.

song; the words are uttered as naturally as in speech, but their rhythms are woven into a musical fabric:

tell   me but   where

she sings, and the phrase has its right intonation and accents, but its urgency is increased. At the lines 'Where the love-lorn nightingale Nightly to thee her sad song mourneth well', the music has a haunting mournfulness, which Lawes has produced by the quite simple musical means of a modulation of key from D minor to A major; and the song ends with a perfectly rounded closing cadence which seems to result inevitably from the graceful curve of the melody. This is typical of the unobtrusiveness of Lawes's craftsmanship; his music is partnering the verse so sensitively that the hearer is aware only of limpid, expressive, and seemingly artless melody. But it is the product of considerable art, and it calls for skill from the singer too: Lady Alice must have felt almost as apprehensive on her own behalf as her dramatic role required, as she made the tricky leap from F♯ to the E above, nine bars from the end, with her parents and brothers and their friends *and* her music-master all listening to her. Lawes can not have been easy to please; he did not trust anyone with a song except Lady Alice and himself, although Milton provided suitable verse for Sabrina to sing. But in compliment to his pupil, and to her parents, Lawes made her song the musical highlight of the masque.[1]

Within the masque, it is heard, with awe and admiration, not only by the Attendant Spirit from afar, but by a nearer, more sinister hearer, Comus (and we are meant to compare their responses to it). The next song comes much further on in the action, after Comus has put his spells on the Lady, and been routed but allowed to escape. The Spirit knows that he and the

[1] The reader should not pass by this song without singing it or hearing it. The music is in Sabol's *Songs and dances*, and in Diekhoff's volume cited in the *Comus* Booklist here; it is sung in the Argo recording of *Comus* RG 544–5. Lawes habitually composed only a vocal line and a bass line for an accompanying instrument (the theorbo-lute would be used, and sometimes a bass viol too); editors add inner parts for ease of performance, but Lawes does not indicate what harmonies he intended.

brothers cannot disenchant the Lady; but Sabrina, goddess of the river,

> can unlock
> The clasping charm, and thaw the numbing spell,
> If she be right invoked in warbled song.

The audience is thus again prepared for a song; and this one too, like the Lady's, arises from the situation, because it is the proper way to invoke Sabrina's aid. So the Spirit raises his voice to call her; and whenever we raise our voice to call someone – try it – we are almost sure to use the same musical interval, a falling third.

Sabri - na, Sabrina fair,

It is an entirely natural transition into a song which gives extra eloquence to the plea for her help, letting us see her 'am-ber-drop-ping' hair as four quavers drop one after another on our ears, and rising to impassioned appeal with a melodic phrase repeated a tone higher as if to implore her attention.

List - en for dear hon - our's sake, God - dess of the sil - ver lake

Then the Spirit's voice sinks into incantatory speech for 'some adjuring verse'. Sabrina rises in response to the power of his musical summons; but to our surprise, and probably to Milton's too, she does not sing. The stage direction says she does, but Lawes seems not to have provided any music for her, although Milton has written verse that invites setting;[1] perhaps Lawes wished to compliment Lady Alice by leaving her the only female singer, or perhaps he knew that the person taking the part of Sabrina was not a sufficiently pleasing singer.

The Lady is freed, and as her brothers and the Spirit escort her from Comus's palace, the Spirit says, with the double refer-

[1] The Argo recording concocts a song for her, without explaining that it is not authentic.

ence that masques exploited and that their audiences would enjoy,

> not many furlongs thence
> Is your father's residence,
> Where this night are met in state
> Many a friend to gratulate
> His wished presence, and beside
> All the swains that there abide,
> With jigs, and rural dance resort,
> We shall catch them at their sport,
> And our sudden coming there
> Will double all their mirth and cheer . . .

The earl's friends are indeed gathered in his honour; it is within that context that the whole masque exists. Now the scene, which itself is set up inside Ludlow Castle, changes to represent Ludlow town and the castle. The more detailed stage direction of the Bridgewater Ms is important here: 'then come in Countrie daunces, and the like etc., towards the end of these sports the demon with the 2 brothers and the Ladye come in'. This makes it clear that before the Spirit enters, the country dancers 'and the like' are given some time for their 'Sports'; that is, they provide a second, rustic, antimasque.[1] When the Spirit and his charges come in, his words take up the jigging rhythm to which they are dancing as he waves them aside. Then, in a graver, stately rhythm, he addresses the earl and countess in song, presenting their children to them.[2] The children have come safely and nobly through their trials: now is the time to express their triumph 'in victorious dance' – in the grand masque dance.

At this point, many readers are puzzled, because Milton does not explicitly say the main dance follows. But the stage direction before the epilogue shows that dances have come between it and the Spirit's preceding song: 'The dances ended, the spirit epilogizes'. The Bridgewater Ms tells us a little more: 'They daunce, the daunces all ended the DAEMON singes or sayes'. The clue there is 'the daunces *all* ended'. For readers in Milton's day, this was indication enough that the masque dance and the revels came here. They would be expecting the masque dance by

---

[1] The significance of the various kinds of dancing is discussed in the chapter on Milton and music in *JM: introductions* in this series.

[2] One could learn a good deal by collecting and studying poems made with particular dance-rhythms in mind, such as Waller's poem made to a sarabande (*Hylas, O Hylas, why sit we mute*) and several pieces in Edith Sitwell's *Façade*.

now, because there had already been two antimasques, the grotesque one of Comus and his crew and the trippings of the rustics. After singing 'Noble lord, and lady bright', a song with firm and shapely musical phrases, the Spirit would lead the children into a stately, graceful dance, which mirrored and celebrated the triumph of virtue, 'measure', and order. Their return from the wood to Ludlow Castle had brought the masquers back, so to speak, into the audience's midst, and so, quite naturally and without tearing the delicate tissue of the masque fiction, they could now move out among those present and take partners for dancing, so that family and guests were drawn in to share in the celebration – of the children's triumph which promised well for their future, and of the earl's taking up his duties as Lord President of Wales which was the occasion of the festivities.

But the evening must not peter out in general revels; the whole event must have shape and significance, it is all to be enclosed in the masque which itself encloses references to the occasion. So after the guests and masquers have joined in various fashionable dances, such as allemandes, corantos and sarabandes, the masquers draw apart again and the spirit has a farewell song. Here, as at the opening, Milton did not provide for one, but again Lawes found a solution ready to hand: he simply set the last twelve lines of the epilogue for the Spirit to sing as he took his departure, urging the audience, who cannot fly, with him, 'To the corners of the moon', to love virtue and so ascend even higher, to heaven itself. So with a song that is close to recitative but holds the hearers' attention by variations of pace and rhythm and by illustrative details such as soaring up at the mention of heaven, the masque and the whole entertainment comes musically, morally, and artistically to its end.

Booklist for Arcades and Comus

Masques

CHAMBERS, E. K. *The medieval stage* Oxford 1903, espec. vol I, chap 17; and *The Elizabethan stage* Oxford 1923, espec. vol I, chap 5–6.
EVANS, HERBERT A. ed. *English masques* 1906. A collection.
GILBERT, ALLAN H. *The symbolic persons in the masques of Ben Jonson* Durham N.C. 1948

HERFORD, C. H. and P. and E. SIMPSON ed. *The works of Ben Jonson* Oxford 1941 vol VII.

NICOLL, ALLARDYCE *Stuart masques and the renaissance stage* 1937. Lavishly illustrated.

ORGEL, STEPHEN *The Jonsonian masque* Cambridge, Mass. 1965. ed. *Ben Jonson : selected masques* 1970.

SIMPSON, P. and C. F. BELL ed. *Designs by Inigo Jones for masques and plays at court* Oxford 1934. Lavishly illustrated.

SPENCER, T. J. B. and STANLEY WELLS ed. *A book of masques in honour of Allardyce Nicoll* 1967. 14 masques. Illustrated.

STRONG, ROY C. *Festival designs by Inigo Jones : an exhibition of drawings for scenery and costumes for the court masques of James I and Charles I* 1967. Brief and helpful introduction to masque. Illustrated.

WELSFORD, ENID *The court masque* 1927. Illustrated.

Comus (selected)

ARTHOS, JOHN *On 'A masque presented at Ludlow Castle'* Ann Arbor 1954. Advanced.

BARBER, C. L. '*A mask presented at Ludlow Castle*: the masque as a masque' in *The lyric and dramatic M : selected papers from the English institute* ed. J. H. Summers 1966; repr in Diekhoff cited below.

BLONDEL, JACQUES *Le Comus de M : masque neptunien* Paris 1964.

BROADBENT, J. B. *Milton : Comus and Samson* 1960. Introductory.

DEMARAY, JOHN G. *Milton and the masque tradition : the early poems, Arcades, and Comus* Cambridge Mass. 1968. Staging, casting etc; illustrated.

DIEKHOFF, J. S. ed. '*A masque at Ludlow*' : *essays on M's Comus* Cleveland Ohio 1968. The first essay, by the editor, is on staging, casting etc; the volume also contains Barber's essay on the masque, cited above; Jayne's essay cited below; the text of the Bridgewater Ms; words and music of the five songs; large bibliography.

FLETCHER, ANGUS *The transcendental masque : an essay on M's Comus* Ithaca N.Y. 1971.

JAYNE, SEARS 'The subject of M's Ludlow masque' in Diekhoff cited above and in *M : modern essays in criticism* ed. A. E. Baker Oxford 1965. Platonism.

KNIGHT, G. WILSON *The burning oracle* Oxford 1939. Chap on M.

SPROTT, S. E. ed. *A Maske: the earlier versions* Toronto 1973.

TUVE, ROSEMOND *Images and themes in five poems by M* 1957. Iconography, religious symbolism.

WILKINSON, DAVID 'The escape from pollution: a comment on *Comus*' *Essays in criticism* x 1960.

Art, iconography, history of ideas

DANIELLS, ROY *M, mannerism and baroque* Toronto 1963. Chap on *Comus*.

FRYE, NORTHROP *Fables of identity* 1963. Chap on Nature and Homer.

KERMODE, FRANK ed. *English pastoral poetry* 1952. Anthology with helpful introduction.

LEAVIS, F. R. *Revaluation* 1936. Chap on M.

LOVEJOY, A. O. *The great chain of being* Cambridge, Mass. 1936.

MANTEGNA and LORENZO COSTA *The realm of Comus* Louvre.

PANOFSKY, ERWIN *Studies in iconology* 1939. Espec. chap 5.

POINTON, MARCIA *M and English art* Manchester 1970. The following
figures reproduce illustrations to *Comus*: 63 Joseph Wright of Derby
(and see *JM : introductions* in this series), 130–2 Blake, 186–7 Etty,
188–95 various Victorian artists, 217 Samuel Palmer.

SEZNEC, JEAN *The survival of the pagan gods* 1953.

SPITZER, LEO *Classical and Christian ideas of world harmony* Baltimore
1963.

WIND, EDGAR *Bellini's 'Feast of the gods' : a study in Venetian humanism*
1948.

    Pagan mysteries in the renaissance 1950 rev 1967.

Lycidas

Edited by JOHN BROADBENT AND OTHERS

Introduction

This edition

This edition of *Lycidas* was partly composed by members of the
School of English and American Studies to which I belong who,
as lecturers and students, joined me in two attempts at the group
editing of the poem in the spring of 1971 and the summer of 1972:
Michael Bennett, Gareth Griffiths, Paul Hadfield, Elizabeth
Henderson, Michael Hollington, George Hyde, Sharon Joseph,
Olwen Lloyd, John Sivell, Judith Thorp, Ross Tomkins, Neil
Turner, Mary Wilding, Lawrence Wilkinson, Terry Woodhead,
Gregory Woods. I have incorporated their suggestions freely and
the commentaries include some student contributions.

One of those members, then in her second year, took on the
job of defining the difficulties of the poem. In the first place, she
had never heard of it. Then there were verbal problems:

I found myself confused by the words 'heavy change' (37) and none of
the editions had annotated it . . . Probably my puzzlement arose from
the two words being placed together in an unfamiliar phrase.

This was taken up by a member who had a PhD but found
'mitred locks' inexplicable: thinking of carpentry, he thought it
meant a locked lock. 'Gadding vine' also gave trouble. A good
start might be made by collecting problems of this sort, and
classifying them; I think these come into a category of words
adjacent but alien. One is then deep inside the meaning, for that
sort of clash is what the poem is about.

The 'difficulty' member reported that syntax is a problem. Of
39–44 she wrote:

The sentence construction confused me until I realized 'mourn' didn't
refer to 'echo' specifically but also to caves, woods etc. I also didn't see
how woods and caves could emit echoes.

She remarked elsewhere that general introductions are useless because 'once I had read the poem everything I'd read before it went out of my mind'. But now, faced with the problem of echoes, local help was useful:

At this point commentary was invaluable in that I discovered Milton was using the classical story of Echo . . . It may be useful to know that this device originated in the *Lament for Bion* where orchards and fruits wither and Echo mourns among her rocks.

Some problems, though, were not worth the bother – old-fashioned orthography in particular. Ignorance of single words didn't matter much, though we all noted how many guerdons and gaddings there are. On a larger scale, the variousness of the poem's materials and tone ('various quills') made readers uneasy; we wanted to stop and work out the plot. It became a question of learning to know and not know. Pronunciation and emphasis improved after one bold and effective reading aloud. Of written aids, Daiches's from his *Study of literature* and Wayne Schumaker's *Flowerets and sounding seas*, both reprinted in Patrides's volume *Lycidas : the tradition and the poem*, were found the most useful. But on the whole we did it ourselves.

Pastoral elegy

Lycidas, then, is an elegy in the pastoral convention, written to commemorate a young man named Edward King who was drowned at sea. The origins of the pastoral are partly classical, the tradition that runs through Theocritus and Virgil, and partly Biblical, the imagery of the 23rd Psalm, of Christ as the Good Shepherd, of the metaphors of 'pastor' and 'flock' in the church . . . In the classical pastoral elegy the subject of the elegy is not treated as an individual but as a representative of a dying spirit of nature . . . So King is given the pastoral name of Lycidas, which is equivalent to Adonis, and is associated with the cyclical rhythms of nature. Of these three are of particular importance: the daily cycle of the sun across the sky, the yearly cycle of the seasons, and the cycle of water, flowing from wells and fountains through rivers to the sea. Sunset, winter, and the sea are emblems of Lycidas's death; sunrise and spring, of his resurrection . . .

NORTHROP FRYE from *Literature as context : Milton's 'Lycidas'* first published 1959 repr in his *Fables of identity : studies in poetic mythology* (Harcourt Brace N.Y. 1963) and Patrides

Biblical materials

'The hireling fleeth, because he is an hireling, and careth not for the sheep. I am the good shepherd, and know my sheep, and am

known of them . . . and I lay down my life for the sheep' *John* x.
The whole chapter is relevant; see also *Psalm* xxiii, *Ezekiel* xxxiv,
Zechariah xi, *1 Peter* v and Abel, Jacob, Moses, David. To understand pastoral as a genre, don't read books about it but think about
sheep: their place in the economy of Israel, Greece, Italy, and
renaissance England; what are they valued *for*? Consider also
the symbolism of their characteristics – lambs, rams, following
and herding, wool and horn, size relative to a man (see the nativity play trick where they swop a sheep for a baby), folding,
enemies, growth seasons, relationship to the shepherd, his
crook, his wanderings . . . Why should they be sacrificial animals?
What is the majestic Lamb of *Revelation*? Most of these questions
need to be answered in terms of how sheep differ from other
creatures.

Classical background

The herdsmen of animals spend all day, and may spend weeks,
alone. To keep themselves company they make pipes, and sing,
like cowboys in musicals. At other times, they come together for
shearing, slaughtering; these times would be marked by economic
and religious rituals – competitions, sacrifices – and by parties,
concerts, and their own mating, as in *A winter's tale* IV (note there
too the sacrifice of Mamillius and Antigonus, and the symbolic
loss of Perdita and Hermione). As an autonomous literary form,
pastoral was invented by the 'Alexandrian' or 'Greek bucolic'
poets of the 3rd century BC, Theocritus, Bion and Moschus.
They lived in the Hellenistic civilization of the eastern Mediterranean, moving between the great cities of Syracuse, Alexandria,
of Cyprus and of Asia Minor, and the rural hinterlands in Sicily
and smaller islands such as Cos and Rhodes. Their poems were
called *eidyllia*, meaning just short poems of varied subject-matter;
though usually rural in setting they include – as their actually
rural originals did – songs, competitions, laments, epithalamions.
Of course the form became more specialized under the Romans,
and in the renaissance. See Appendix.

David

Pastoral, however, was regarded as a junior genre, and one suitable for a young poet to start on. The shepherd was not the model
for 'Blind Thamyris and blind Maeonides [Homer]' whom

Milton wants to identify with in *PL* III; nor, really, for Orpheus. It was David who added more lustre to the equation than it could have for Greece and Rome: shepherd, slayer of wild animals, harpist before the wild King Saul, rebel chieftain, anointed king, architect of the temple (he knew himself to build . . .), ancestor of Jesus, 'ruddy and withal of a beautiful countenance, and goodly to look to' (*I Samuel* xvi), author of the psalms still sung throughout the world; yet also a lover of men and women, a persistent sinner, guilty of sacrilege, a murderer, and broken by his son Absalom – a figure, again, of the margins, a mediator between the best of gods and the worst of men, between eternity and history.

Anthropological structure

The poem is a ritual conducted on the vital surface between air and water. The above and the below are explored but we return at the end to here and now, dry land. The ritual is performed by various figures and creatures who come from, or command, the above, the below or the surface. There is an ultimate command above, and an ultimate horror below; but the crucial figures are those who, like Lycidas himself, Peter, Christ walking on the water, perhaps the poet himself, move between worlds. They are mediators, able to redeem because they reconcile, because by partaking of the nature of both extremes they affirm the rightness of the norm. To put it in terms of a family, you might say that someone who both has a living parent and a living child is more surely 'there' as a person than either a great-granny who stands at the back of a line, or a child. Living is what happens between being born and dying; to live in the world you have to maintain a sense of both those exits. It is worth ritualizing the forces that drown, that push you over the edge, because to do so gives you their power.

Consider the shores and other margins of this poem. On p. 187 is the beginning of a chart of its world and inhabitants in these terms.

Of course there are several ways of doing it. You might regard the below as a lower dimension morally, and put the wolves there with the monsters; or you might do it chronologically. Note how many hierarchies there are, descending through such ranks as

Calliope and the Muses	goddesses
nymphs	demi-goddesses
Druids	priests
Damoetas	humans
satyrs, fauns, bacchantes (?)	half-animals

Each set of beings and things is represented by species from each level of the poem's world; this is a ritual way of affirming the plurality of the real world, of affirming that life includes death, that women are goddesses and intoxicated cannibals, that the Lamb of God is not to be isolated from a bloated sheep's carcase, nor that from the bloated corpse with its sacred head.

```
              bright Phoebus = Apollo = Christ = sun = art
            those pure eyes
            nectar pure
crowns
evergreens                    order
flowers                       oatenflute
                              song                          wolves
vocal reeds melodious tear    air
bier                          Orpheus  Camus Peter Michael dolphins
—  —  —  —  —  —  —  —  —  —  —  —  —  —  —  —  —  —
                              water
                              hideous roar                 monsters
                              bones
                              chaos
            oozy locks
              blind fury = death
```

Death by water

Drowning is the special death of poets because of these oppositions, presumably:

> O blessèd rage for order, pale Ramón,
> The maker's rage to order words of the sea

WALLACE STEVENS *The idea of order at Key West* 1936
in *Collected poems of Wallace Stevens* Faber

In water everything is 'dissolved', every 'form' is broken up, everything that has happened ceases to exist . . . Immersion is the equivalent, at the human level, of death at the cosmic level, of the cataclysm (the Flood) which periodically dissolves the world into the primeval ocean. Breaking up all forms, doing away with the past, water possesses this power of purifying, of regenerating, of giving new birth . . . Water purifies and regenerates because it nullifies the past, and restores – even if only for a moment – the integrity of the dawn of things.

MIRCEA ELIADE *Shamanism* Routledge and Kegan Paul 1964

The theme can be traced in many other works; see appendix.

'Where were ye Nymphs when the remorseless deep / Clos'd o'er the head of your lov'd Lycidas?' The visual image is that of a face sinking for the last time beneath water, the motor image that of a rejoining of fluid edges; and there is perhaps induced also a slight muscular strain, as of an effort to fight one's way up toward air . . .

WAYNE SCHUMAKER from 'Flowerets and sounding seas: a study in the affective structure of *Lycidas' PMLA* LXVI 1951 and repr Patrides

Take the hints of Schumaker and Eliade. Trace the water and anti-water language in the poem: distinguish between salt and fresh (but the salt is not always sterile, eg tears; nor the fresh always vital). Note the water cycle, its flow; and what is in or on it.

Parts of the body

These form a set, of which heads are only the most important. Eg 21 and as he passes turn [no face?]; 51 the head of your loved Lycidas [which turns into Orpheus's gory visage]; 112 he shook his [not head but] mitred locks [hair]; 119–25 Blind mouths . . . the hungry sheep look up [to be eaten by empty eyes?]; 147 [cowslips] hang the pensive head; 169 repairs his drooping head [whose?]. It is in this area, and especially via the more passive verbs (weltering, sinking, dreaming, tangling, hurled), that you might improvise an enactment of the poem as a sort of mimed masque. Reduce the characters to a minimum and poet = Lycidas, Muse = Amaryllis = Bacchante . . . ?

Days, seasons, vegetation

Take Northrop Frye's hint. What is the felt relationship between growth, time and death? Frye refers only to the sun but other heavenly bodies are active in the poem; pattern them.

A difficulty about animals and vegetables, especially flowers, is that we have emasculated them – Easter bunnies, bunny girls; even flower people, a reassertion of the virtue of flowers, are seen as meek. Can serious creature poetry, such as Ted Hughes's or Lawrence's, correct this? If, as I suspect, it can't be corrected, perhaps we could ask what the motives for the emasculation have been? and what objects external to ourselves do, in urban culture, hold symbolic value? They may not be natural things at all. Study a hyacinth, or grape hyacinth, or an iris, to see why it was so often used as a symbol of virility, and its decay. Flanders poppies?

Only experience as direct as possible of the second term of any metaphor provides both the peculiar pleasure derived from the 'translation' of terms and the capacity to follow out the suggestions other than sensuous which are thus drawn in. Even 'What time the grayfly winds her sultry horn' remains a poorer thing if one has never heard a horn, and the care-free languor and peace that come with the music (metrical skill suiting) have changed the thermal quality of *sultry*. In figures where many suggestions enter, the avenues to such 'direct experience' may sometimes seem odd enough. An example is in the passage which begins 'Ay me! Whilst thee the shores . . .' . . . Direct experience here involves not only the imagined wash and murmur of the cold seas down the whole western coast of Britain from the Hebrides to Land's End. It asks that we should have thoughts like those awakened in Milton by Drayton's *Polyolbion*, by legends of Cornish might and of Orphean druidic seers prefiguring Christianity, by Spanish strongholds seen on Ojea's map and recalling ecclesiastical tyrannies once escaped, by the events of the centuries during which the venerable unmoved Mount opposite had stood . . . It has proved almost impossible to avoid considering the whole theme of the poem whenever discussion of the functioning of any topically suggestive image was attempted.

ROSEMOND TUVE from *Images and themes in five poems by Milton*
Harvard University Press, Cambridge Mass.

Interruptions and contradictions

The rivers Hebrus and Alpheus both went underground and reappeared later. Orpheus was killed in mid-song but his decapitated head went on singing in the river. The fury slits the thinspun life. Against these interruptions the sun goes round and round; the poet foresees tomorrow. The poem is about a major contradiction, death before maturity. Contradiction appears in many details, eg laurels and myrtles as emblems of poetic fame, and also of death; flowers of joy and vitality, flowers of grief and abbreviated life; fame = spur and infirmity; hireling shepherds = blind mouths; white-thorn (48) as emblem of spring blossom cut by frost is itself a metaphor for frost: white-thorn = icicle.

Poem and poet

Where were ye? What boots it? Are there any answers? A way of approaching this theme is to consider 'who' is the asker and answerer of questions; and 'who' gives the assurances and commands such as 'Weep no more'? This theme may be related to the series of 'false surmises', and the demand for rewards, guerdons, meed.

The poem is partly a ritual gaze at, and defence against, chaos. He, who could build, must not welter; so the poet must build. Thus many of the poem's vignettes can be read as versions of poetic building. It may be itself destroyed, like Orpheus; or neutral, like sleek Panope; or a fantasy, like the quaint enamelled eyes; the question is, where does poetry acquire the mastery that is needed to resist chaos in this case? where does it get endowed with what kind of power?

Such is the power of reputation justly acquired, that its blaze drives away the eye from nice examination. Surely no man could have fancied that he read *Lycidas* with pleasure had he not known its author.

DR JOHNSON *Life of Milton* in his edition of *The works of the most eminent English poets* 1779

Often we choose to think of it as the work of a famous poet, which it was not; done by an apprentice of nearly thirty, who was still purifying his taste upon an astonishingly arduous diet of literary exercises . . . any triteness which comes to mind with mention of the poem is a property of our own registration, and does not affect its freshness, which is perennial. The poem is young, brilliant, insubordinate. In it an artist wrestles with an almost insuperable problem, and is kinsman to some tortured modern artists. It has something in common with, for example, *The waste land* . . . Poets may go to universities and, if they take to education, increase greatly the stock of ideal selves into which they may pass for the purpose of being poetical. If on the other hand they insist too narrowly on their own identity and their own story, inspired by a simple but mistaken theory of art, they find their little poetic fountains drying up within them . . . Milton as a Greek shepherd was delivered from being Milton the scrivener's son, the Master of Arts from Cambridge, the handsome and finicky young man . . .

JOHN CROWE RANSOM from 'A poem nearly anonymous' (1933) repr in his *The world's body* Louisiana State University Press

Form

Form irregular but based on Italian canzone, like Spenser's *Epithalamion*. First paragraph a quasi-sonnet. Don't try to work out the rhymes, but give them full value, whether internal or external. Many are assonantal and reversed, eg 34–5 danced–sound–absent; 36–41 song–gone–mourn. Sometimes the rhymes are semantic: 13–14 parching wind antithetical to melodious tear.

There is a good deal of syntactical rhetoric, or 'schemes' as they were called. Here are a few, with their renaissance names (which don't matter but indicate that they were recognized patterns just as much as rhyme is):

1 Yet once more . . . and once more		epanalepsis
8 For Lycidas is dead, dead		epizeuxis
		anaphora
9 Young Lycidas		
37	now thou art gone,	
		anadiplosis
38 Now thou art gone		
180 That sing, and singing		traductio

That is usually in solemn ritualistic contexts; other passages are colloquial, eg 64–9; others dramatic, eg 58–62, St Peter's speech. In general, give the fullest value you can to each word, even each syllable; this will not only bring out richer meaning but push your embarrassments aside.

> The air was calm, and on the level brine
> Sleek Pánopë with all her sisters played.

The *air* was calm, not the sea – that is, no wind. We are not shown the sea at all, but the environment of the Nereids – 'the level brine'. Make it so, as you would with Wallace Stevens's more obvious rhythms and inquiring meanings:

> . . . Yet this is meager play
> In the scurry and water-shine,
> As her heels foam –
> Not as when the goldener nude
> Of a later day
>
> Will go, like the centre of sea-green pomp,
> In an intenser calm,
> Scullion of fate,
> Across the spick torrent, ceaselessly,
> Upon her irretrievable way.
>
> *The paltry nude starts on a spring voyage*

Don't read it as if it were 'Sleek Panope played with all her sisters'; it is 'Sleek Panope (her skin sleek as the smooth water it's wet with) and all the equally sleek sisters of Panope (of whom there were 49) *played* (not being little children but demi-goddesses who play because the universe is not a workhouse)'.

So much for the technicalities; the issue is, how do these repetitions and returns relate to the structure, to the cycle of the seasons or the waters? Is life a series of repeated but unanswered questions and incidents? or is it a Second Coming?

Most of the repeated terms in *Lycidas* are of common importance for the poets of Milton's day . . . *gentle, old, high, sad, come, go, lie, sing, hear, shepherd, flower, muse, power*, in the pastoral tradition, and *eye, tear, dead, weep* in the elegiac tradition.

Some, on the other hand, were brought into strong use first by Milton, and these particularly help define the singularities of *Lycidas*: *fresh, new, pure, sacred, green, watery, flood, leaf, morn, hill, shade, shore, stream, star, wind, fame, ask, touch* . . . the physical bodily force of earth and water dominates the inventive substance, then to be subdued by the triumph of significant structure, the rising from low to high, from sea and land to heaven . . . Thus the special vocabulary . . . while extremely rare as dominant vocabulary before *Lycidas*, becomes dominant in the mid-eighteenth century . . . Especially in America . . . the liberal and natural Protestant spirit continued its poetizing in these terms of scope and sacred feeling, one of the most characteristic American poetic adjectives being the *pure* of *Lycidas* . . .

> JOSEPHINE MILES from *The primary language of poetry in the 1640s* (*University of California publications in English* XIX 1948) rev in Patrides

When lilacs last in the dooryard bloomed,
And the great star early drooped in the western sky in the night,
I mourned, and yet shall mourn with ever-returning spring . . .

> WALT WHITMAN *Memories of President Lincoln* 1865–6

Text

The text of *Lycidas* exists in three main forms, all made in M's lifetime:

1 Manuscript, still visible in the library of Trinity College, Cambridge (called the Trinity or Cambridge Ms) with working versions of his early poems, plans for epic and tragedy etc, in his own handwriting. Many alterations to the version of *Lyc*; dated Nov 1637.

2 As published in the commemorative volume for which it was composed, *Justa Eduardo King naufrago, ab amicis moerentibus amoris &* μνειας χαριν with second part separately titled *Obsequies to the memory of Mr Edward King* Cambridge 1638, still visible in the University library. The first part contains 23 poems in Latin and Greek, the second 13 in English; M's is the longest. There is a Latin preface explaining that King's ship struck a rock off the coast and sank as King kneeled praying on deck.

3 As revised for publication in *Poems of Mr John Milton, both English and Latin, composed at several times* 1645. The effective 2nd ed. of this was *Poems upon several occasions* 1673.

For this edition I have taken the words of 1645 (giving a few of the 1638 variants in the notes), the simpler punctuation of 1638, and some of the simpler orthography of the 1637 Ms (eg no automatic initial capitals for lines – merely a printer's convention). I have modernized everything and added line and paragraph numbers.

Lycidas: the editorial arrangement

Lycidas

In this monody the author bewails a learned friend, unfortunately drowned in his passage from Chester on the Irish Seas, 1637; and by occasion foretells the ruin of our corrupted clergy, then in their height.

1   YET ONCE MORE O ye laurels, and once more
      ye myrtles brown, with ivy never sere,
      I come to pluck your berries harsh and crude,
and with forced fingers rude
shatter your leaves before the mellowing year.   5
Bitter constraint, and sad occasion dear
compels me to disturb your season due:
for Lycidas is dead, dead ere his prime,
young Lycidas, and hath not left his peer.
Who would not sing for Lycidas? he knew   10
himself to sing, and build the lofty rhyme.
He must not float upon his watery bier
unwept, and welter to the parching wind
without the meed of some melodious tear.

2   Begin then sisters of the sacred well   15
that from beneath the seat of Jove doth spring,
begin, and somewhat loudly sweep the string.
Hence with denial vain, and coy excuse,
so may some gentle muse

1 **laurels** all three evergreen leaves make poets' crowns, and stand for poetry.   2 **brown** dark, Ital. *bruno*. **sere** dry.   3 **crude** Ital. *crudo* = raw. Time has not yet ripened his poetic fruit.   4 **rude** rough.   5 **shatter** disturb. Try rattling laurels.   6 **constraint** compulsion.   7 **compels** until 18c verbs could disagree with subject.   9 **peer** equal.   10 **knew** knew how to.   11 **rhyme** verse.   13 **parching** withering.   14 **meed** due reward.   15 **sisters** the nine Muses, who lived by the well of Aganippe on Mt Helicon. It sprang with inspiring water; beside it was an altar to Zeus (Jove).   17 **string** of the lyre. Accelerate this line.   18 **Hence with** away with. He rejects the excuse of immaturity. **vain** pointless. **coy** meant something more like self-concerned.   19 **muse** poet. Read it as if he turns his head from now to future. He hopes that,

Prologue

Noise of dry unripe vegetation	lofty rhyme
parching wind	melodious tear
nature's sterility, poets' unreadiness	consummated emotion, art
(to die or write)	in 10
Yet once more	Weep no more 165

M's motto for the whole 1645 volume was *baccare frontem/ cingite, ne vati noceat mala lingua futuro* from Virgil *Eclogue* VII: crown my forehead with foxglove to ward off evil tongues from the poet that I will be. The motto of the first edition of *Comus*, published the year he wrote *Lyc*, was *Heu heu! quid volui misero mihi? floribus austrum/perditus* from *Eclogue* II: O O what have I asked for? I have let the sirocco in to ruin my flowers . . . Rituals of propitiation, warding off the evil tongues; it would be reasonable to define each section as a ritual of some sort.

Trace the crowns and heads passim.

Are young people afraid of dying young? if not, what are they afraid of?

Trace rewards from meed to guerdon in 73ff.

Invocation

Power to transcend unripeness invoked of the Muses, mistresses of a divine source that does not drown but inspires. The poem will consummate on another holy mountain, 'other groves and other streams along'. But immortal fame means you're dead; their altar reminds him of his urn. He reverts to youth, community, and so enters the pastoral world of a more realistic spring, stream etc; yet one that is still conventional and will be left in 11.

with lucky words favour my destined urn   20
and as he passes turn
and bid fair peace to be my sable shroud.
For we were nursed upon the selfsame hill,
fed the same flock by fountain, shade, and rill.

3   Together both ere the high lawns appeared   25
under the opening eyelids of the morn
we drove afield, and both together heard
what time the grayfly winds her sultry horn,
battening our flocks with the fresh dews of night,
oft till the star that rose at evening bright   30
toward heaven's descent had sloped his westering
    wheel.
Meanwhile the rural ditties were not mute,
tempered to the oaten flute
rough satyrs danced, and fauns with cloven heel

as he laments Lycidas, so will another poet bless his own future grave
with a few words of good omen. The passage is a bit confused: the muse
could be one of the sisters; 'my destined urn' does not fit Lyc; shrouds
are not black; the transition to the next para. is uncertain (no break in
1638); is the urn's location known? Treat it as attempt at ritual to ward
off anxiety lest writing about death while immature will call down death
on oneself? Perhaps urn and shroud do well to contrast with Lyc.
22 Stress *my* shroud.   **23 we** M and Lyc. Asserts the pastoral convention: they were together as shepherds = poets, and potential priests, and
students at Cambridge.   **24 fountain** spring. Distinguish in reading
between spring, shady place, stream: shepherds always on the move,
seeking fresh pastures.   **25 high lawns** downs. Note *together* here
and in 27 assert unity of human friendship (consummated in sweet
societies of heaven).   **26 opening** 1638 glimmering.   **27 drove** their
flocks.   **28 what time** when.   **28 grayfly** some insect. **winds** blows.
Natural music.   **29 battening** feeding. Probably means they fed sheep
on the dewy morning grass; but that leads him into the coming night.
30 star the evening star, Hesperus, which appears each evening and
soon sets in the west; it is also called the folding star because it warns
shepherds to fold their sheep. It is the same as Lucifer, the morning
star; both are actually the planet Venus. Trace to the next star or rise-
sink item. Instead of star . . . bright 1638 ev'n star bright; and instead of
westering 1638 burnisht.   **31** A slow line.   **33 tempered** tuned;
suggests Orphic taming of the wild. Read in dance rhythms. There is
singing on panpipes (actually made of thicker stalks than oats, usually
hemlock or fennel) – more natural music; and dancing by the goat-men
of Greece (satyrs) and Rome (fauns). The Latin for a goat-man was

Pastoral youth : the dance of nature

Asserts the pastoral norm: young, harmonious, innocent. Why is the Shepherd Good? But the shepherds in 8 are not. Each day securely begun and ended, 'in time'. (Compare the form of this section with those adjacent.) Each day brings food; contrast 4, 8. Consider the sort of music and dancing it is, and how related to the lyre in 2, the celebrations in 10.

from the glad sound would not be absent long   35
and old Damætas loved to hear our song.

4   But O the heavy change now thou art gone,
     now thou art gone, and never must return.
     Thee shepherd, thee the woods and desert caves
     with wild thyme and the gadding vine o'ergrown,   40
     and all their echoes mourn;
     the willows, and the hazel copses green
     shall now no more be seen
     fanning their joyous leaves to thy soft lays.
     As killing as the canker to the rose,   45
     or taint-worm to the weanling herds that graze,
     or frost to flowers that their gay wardrobe wear
     when first the white-thorn blows:
     such, Lycidas, thy loss to shepherd's ear.

5   Where were ye nymphs when the remorseless deep   50
     closed o'er the head of your loved Lycidas?
     For neither were ye playing on the steep

semicaper, halfgoat; hence caper meaning prance, prank etc. See M's Latin *Elegy V* 119–22; cf Eliot's rustic dancers in *Burnt Norton* and Yeats *What magic drum?*, and *News for the Delphic oracle*.   **35** Semantically therefore rhythmically throwaway line – collapse of sweating satyrs after dance?   **36 Damætas** conventional pastoral figure; see Virgil *Eclogue* II.   **39 desert** deserted.   **40 gadding** straggling. The first flower passage; cf 135.   **41 echoes** instead of primary music.   **44 lays** songs.   **45 canker** name given to insects that spoil rose buds (now refers to a disease of plants) as in Blake's *Sick rose*. Young calves may be killed by an intestinal worm.   **47 wardrobe** clothes. As the rosebuds and calves are young, so these flowers bloom early in the year when it's still frosty.   **48 blows** blooms – standard poetic use but you may link it into a music-flower pattern with the grayfly's horn in 28.   **49 ear** why ear?   **50 nymphs** may be the Muses again; more likely the localized demi-goddesses of mountains (Oreades), trees (Dryades), fresh water (Naiades), sea (Nereides). Nymphs were also seen as beautiful girls, half merged with their natural habitat. They could be like guardian angels, or mischievous fairies, or just girls. The Greek word *nymphe* also=bride; nympha is used in science for the labia minora, and for the chrysalis of an insect.   **52 steep** slopes of a mountain – either Kerig y Druidion in Denbighshire, where there were Druid sepulchres, or the sides of Mona=Anglesey, as opposed to its summit (then all thickly forested). But this section also feels vertiginous.

Pastoral death : the lament of nature

Nature, which brings the grayfly's horn, brings the cankerworm too. The lament is for the destructiveness inherent in natural life: what the Elizabethans called mutability. There is sterility in 'desert'; vacuum there and in 'caves'; a blind darkness where the sun (which in *PL* III 584 'to each inward part With gentle penetration, though unseen, Shoots invisible virtue even to the deep') can't reach; more emptiness in the echoes, a hollow lifeless sound; chaos in the wild gadding overgrowth. Heavy change, heavy repetitions – more weight than can be borne. The tight rhyme green-seen glimpses the lost nature, then it is gone.

Natural death and disease here: man-made in 8.

Dead flowers here: artificial flowers in 9 ?

Orpheus: appeal to female powers rejected

In 2 he appealed to the Muses. Now to more female figures (perhaps as the supposedly lifegiving and beneficent in nature ?). But the nymphs are helpless; the Muse who is also a mother is

where your old bards, the famous Druids lie,
nor on the shaggy top of Mona high,
nor yet where Deva spreads her wizard stream.   55
Ay me, I fondly dream!
Had ye been there – for what could that have done?
What could the Muse herself that Orpheus bore,
the Muse herself for her enchanting son
whom universal nature did lament,   60
when by the rout that made the hideous roar
his gory visage down the stream was sent,
down the swift Hebrus to the Lesbian shore.

6   Alas! what boots it with uncessant care
       to tend the homely, slighted shepherd's trade   65
       and strictly meditate the thankless muse?
       Were it not better done as others use,
       to sport with Amaryllis in the shade,
       or with the tangles of Nëæra's hair?
       Fame is the spur that the clear spirit doth raise   70

53 Druids priestly magicians and prophets of Celtic Britain; little known
about them except association with oak and mistletoe, and that the Romans
liquidated them. As David = king-priest-poet, so Druid = bard. **55 Deva**
river Dee, its course winding but also perhaps wizard like a Druid or like
Moses's snake-rod. All these places face the sea where Lyc drowned.   **56
fondly** foolishly; the first false surmise: cf 153.   **57 Had ye** even if you
had.   **58 Muse** Callïöpë, mother of Orpheus [orfoos]: she bore him.
He could enchant wild animals to be tame, make stones and trees move,
and nearly rescued his dead wife from Hades by enchanting the monsters
there; but after finally losing her he became a homosexual and so enraged
the Maenads (women of Thrace) that they tore him up and ate him, and
threw his head into the river Hebrus; still singing, it floated out to sea
and landed on the isle of Lesbos where the poetess Sappho and her
lesbian companions lived; it was taken to the temple of Dionysus there.
If this is what the Thracian women did to the archetypal poet, what is
the good of asking the nymphs why they failed to protect Lyc?   **61**
Angry rhythms. Note the vowel in *roar* as motif here.   **64 boots** what's
the good?   **65 trade** ie poetry.   **66 meditate** study, practise, get into
one's head. Muse here = poetry, not goddess. **thankless** unrewarding.
67 use as other, ordinary people usually do – not try to become a poet
but play with girls. Amaryllis (lily) and Nëæra (pron. as in M's original
spelling Nëera) are conventional names for shepherdesses. See Holman
Hunt's painting of *The hireling shepherd* doing this.   **69 or with** 1638
hid in.   **70 clear spirit** pure, unworldly soul. Seems to mean that the

helpless; and the Bacchantes (nymphs and mother in their savage aspect) are as murderous as nature itself. Where will help come from? First movement of the poem ends with this section.

Fame : rejects other female powers ; Phoebus

Pretended rejection of pastoral as symbol for poetry, and female muse as symbol for inspiration, in favour of real nature with real women in it: ie a proposal to exchange art (which killed Orpheus, via legendary wild women) for life (which might be vitalized by real tame women). Yet there are, in the poem's terms, dangers even in these shepherdesses – dark, tangles.

At line 70 the excuse is stated in a different tone – the cold ferocity of spur, burst, blaze, shears, slits. Either this does not

(that last informity of noble mind)
to scorn delights, and live laborious days;
but the fair guerdon when we hope to find,
and think to burst out into sudden blaze,
comes the blind Fury with the abhorrèd shears   75
and slits the thinspun life. 'But not the praise',
Phoebus replied, and touched my trembling ears:
'Fame is no plant that grows on mortal soil,
nor in the glistering foil
set off to the world, nor in broad rumour lies,   80
but lives and spreads aloft by those pure eyes
and perfect witness of all-judging Jove;
as he pronounces lastly on each deed,
of so much fame in heaven expect thy meed.'

7   O fountain Arethuse, and thou honoured flood   85

clear spirit is spurred by desire for fame (itself a weakness, but at least a
noble one) to rise above pleasure. But the shift of imagery from Nëæra's
hair (and next to blaze, shears etc) is so abrupt that you may wonder how
the question of 68 is being answered? At any rate it is about 'drive';
what does drive people who have drive?   **73 guerdon** reward – ie
fame; cf meed 14, thankless 66.   **74 blaze** of glory, with sense of
being 'blazed abroad', made famous overnight.   **75 Fury** Atropos,
one of the three Fates: Clotho chose each man's thread, Lachesis spun
it, Atropos cut it to length. Actually not a Fury and not blind but the
blindness and metallic force link with the spur, the bark in 100, the keys
in 110 etc.   **77 Phoebus** Apollo, god of sun, intellect, poetry, music;
taken as classical equivalent of Christ. To touch the ears was a Roman
gesture of reminding. Fame does not die, for it belongs to heaven. It's
not clear how fame becomes a plant; then said not to grow in the gold or
silver leaf under a gem; then a tree. The imagery dislocated again, or
forced?   **80 broad rumour** wide reputation.   **81 by those pure eyes**
do the eyes make it grow? or does it grow beside them? The eyes have no
logical place here: they must belong to the larger set of eyes in the poem,
or to the quite different image of using his talents 'As ever in my great
Taskmaster's eye' in the sonnet *How soon hath time*, also about unripeness but written 5–6 years before *Lyc*.   **82 witness** either judgement, or in the eyes of God (Jove).   **83 lastly** finally.   **84 meed**
proper share. Does the couplet clink, or convince?   **85 Arethuse**
spring in the island of Ortygia off Syracuse near where Theocritus was
born; stands for pastoral poetry, which M returns to now after the
solemn fame section. It stands also for reunion and return: Alpheus, the
chief river of southern Greece (cf Alph in Coleridge *Kubla Khan*), flows
underground in several places; he tried to make love to the nymph Elis,

202

fit the poem, or its argument is false. The blind Fate is another destroying female: she castrates, she is blind like the false priests. The poem's enemies tend to be sightless and to take things away.

Then Phoebus Apollo interrupts, the god opposed to whelming waters and Dionysiac women. But his sermon does not really transplant into the poem. The heavenly praise does not convince for its terms are alien – ears, eyes, foil, tree. Certainly ears and eyes and trees belong in the poem, but these are extraordinary species.

Perhaps being extraordinary is the point: we are forced to see that there are different orders of things and of truths. The everlasting growth of the undying tree, watched over by all-seeing but all-purity-imputing eyes, these belong to an order of being which recurs in section 10 with 'the blest kingdoms meek of joy and love'.

Pastoral resumed : the sea

Returns to the innocent nature of 3, in terms of the sea (which is usually chaotic). We come back via rivers that flow past the birth-

smooth-sliding Mincius, crowned with vocal reeds,
that strain I heard was of a higher mood;
but now my oat proceeds
and listens to the herald of the sea
that came in Neptune's plea, 90
he asked the waves, and asked the felon winds
what hard mishap hath doomed this gentle swain?
And questioned every gust of rugged wings
that blows from off each beakèd promontory;
they knew not of his story, 95
and sage Hippótadës their answer brings,
that not a blast was from his dungeon strayed,
the air was calm, and on the level brine
sleek Pánopë with all her sisters played.
It was that fatal and perfidious bark 100
built in the eclipse, and rigged with curses dark
that sunk so low that sacred head of thine.

or Arethusa, as she bathed in his waters; she fled, but turned into a river
too; untainted they flowed through the sea and came up together in
Ortygia in the spring Arethusa; it is still there (Fontana Aretusa) but
muddy and salt. **86 Mincius** river Mincio, tributary to the Po near
Mantua where Virgil was born; stands for Latin pastoral. The vocal reeds
connect with the evergreen crowns at the beginning, and the pipes of 33.
Virgil writes of the 'green plain' of Lombardy, 'tardis ingens ubi flexibus
errat / Mincius et tenera praetexit harundine ripas' *Georgics* III 14.
87 strain tune. **mood** style. Now he proceeds with pastoral. **89 herald**
Triton. Like the grayfly, he blows a horn: see *Comus* 873. He comes in
defence of Neptune, god of the sea. **91 felon** fierce, violent (not
criminal). **92 swain** shepherd. **93 . . . wings** that had wild stormy
wings. The winds used to be pictured as winged (as the rhyme suggests);
the beaked promontory implies a larger picture. **96 Hippótadës**
Aeolus, god of the winds (son of Hippotes); a rare name, with a vague
epithet. He kept the winds in a huge cavern. **99 Pánopë** a Nereid or
sea-nymph; one of the 50 daughters of Nereus. Actually the ship probably sank in a storn; so why this section? **100 bark** ship; or body of
sinful mankind? Another contributor wrote: 'The fatal bark's dark
cabin must enshrine That precious dust which fate would not confine
To vulgar coffins'. Auden's *Musée des Beaux Arts*, a companion poem to
Lyc, presents 'the expensive delicate ship' as an emblem of technical
genius that is indifferent to drowning; it 'Had somewhere to get to and
sailed calmly on'. **101 eclipse** astrologically a bad time. The curse-
dark rigging may be another version of the shade and tangles at 68–9.
The sacred head repeats the fate of Orpheus from 62–3.

places of poets (instead of drowning them). The waves and wind are law-abiding, the sea-nymphs innocent; death then was rigged into the ship itself? In spite of sleek Panope, ends with dark violence again; yet the section holds a pause. A student writes that the 'mixture of a pastoral ode with a tragedy in water is more distinct here than anywhere else in the poem'.

8 Next Camus, reverend sire, went footing slow,
his mantle hairy, and his bonnet sedge
inwrought with figures dim, and on the edge   105
like to that sanguine flower inscribed with woe.
'Ah! who hath reft,' quoth he, 'my dearest pledge?'
Last came, and last did go,
the pilot of the Galilean lake,
two massy keys he bore of metals twain   110
(the golden opes, the iron shuts amain);
he shook his mitred locks, and stern bespake,
'How well could I have spared for thee, young swain,
enow of such as for their bellies' sake
creep, and intrude, and climb into the fold!   115
Of other care they little reckoning make,

103 Camus river Cam; he appeared in various Cambridge poems of the
time; Phineas Fletcher used him to speak the prologue to a pastoral drama
acted at King's and published 1631. But it is the Granta, name of a
higher reach of the river, that has survived in this sense, as title of a
literary magazine. **sire** father, as in Father Thames. **footing** often used
for flow. **104 hairy** furry like the hood of the Cambridge BA; but cf
the satyrs, Næra etc. **bonnet** man's hat. Headgear for academic doctors
is still called bonnet. Crowns of sedge usual for river-gods in masques,
statues etc; cf the reeds of Mincius, and other items cited at 86n. **105
inwrought** first recorded use of the word; changed from 'scrawled
o'er' in Ms. Means the reeds are woven into faded patterns; *or* refers to
the fact that each rush or flag has dark streaks in the middle and serrated
edges. The figures or teeth look like AIAI, Greek alas! Hyacinthus was
a beautiful boy whom Apollo loved; when they were playing together,
Apollo accidentally killed him with a discus; from his blood sprang a
flower (ὑάκινθος in ancient Greek, actually some kind of iris or flag)
marked AIAI on its petals. **106 sanguine** bloody. **inscribed** is woe
'written in' into the natural world? **107 reft** bereft, bereaved. **pledge**
child (as token of parents' love). **108** One of several lines you might
ask the function of; there might be no answer. **109 pilot** St Peter,
fisherman of the Lake of Galilee (though Jesus usually called pilot).
Jesus said he would give Peter 'the keys of the kingdom of heaven'
(*Matthew* xvi), to bind and to loose. This is taken as the founding of the
church and St Peter is regarded as the first pontiff – bishop of Rome and
pope; hence mitred hair. A bishop's mitre is like a fish head. **113
spared for thee** . . . done without, instead of you, plenty of those who
creep . . . **115 fold** the church; these shepherds are not poets but
priests, treating the church with greed, as a career. This is the puritan
objection to the professionalization of religion. It was based on hundreds
of NT texts eg *1 Peter* v, 'Feed the flock of God which is among you,
taking the oversight thereof, not by constraint, but willingly; not by

Appeal to the guardians of inland waters brings on another storm, of anti-clericalism topical to the reactionary counter-puritan policies of Archbishop Laud (and fairly conventional as interlude in pastoral). Parallels the evil lurking in nature in 4.

Camus = Cambridge, learning, art, Church of England. Peter = Galilee, the Church of Christ. Both are aged figures. Camus is hairy (but not as the satyrs and the girls of 6 are hairy) and literary; Peter is also hairy, and accoutred with metal (but not as Atropos); he asserts power. Classify the imagery; put the pastoral items, and the music, up against others in the poem. Like 6, the section ends with violence (or rather its threat); like 8, it is

than how to scramble at the shearers' feast
and shove away the worthy bidden guest.
Blind mouths! that scarce themselves know how to hold
a sheep-hook, or have learned aught else the least   120
that to the faithful herdman's art belongs.
What recks it them? what need they? they are sped;
and when they list, their lean and flashy songs
grate on their scrannel pipes of wretched straw;
the hungry sheep look up and are not fed,   125
but swollen with wind, and the rank mist they draw
rot inwardly, and foul contagion spread;
besides what the grim wolf with privy paw
daily devours apace, and nothing said.
But that two-handed engine at the door   130
stands ready to smite once, and smite no more.'

9   Return Alpheus, the dread voice is past
that shrunk thy streams; return Sicilian muse,

filthy lucre, but of a ready mind; neither as being lords over God's
heritage, but being ensamples to the flock. And when the chief Shepherd
shall appear, ye shall receive a crown of glory that fadeth not away'.
The language of this passage was soon to overflow into M's anti-episcopal
pamphlets of the 1640s.   **119 Blind mouths** allow it to evoke what it
will by association – gaping birds and so on. Literally it refers to the
fact that shepherds are supposed to feed their sheep, not eat for themselves. The crozier carried by a bishop is an emblem of his 'pastoral'
office. But the Greek ἐπίσκοπος literally = over*seer*, super*visor*: who
should not be blind, ie in M's terms ignorant (education for the priesthood was irrelevant to the duties, though perhaps no worse than education for other professions then or since).   **122 recks** . . . what do they
care? . . . they're all right.   **123 list** like. **flashy** watery (related to
flask, not fire).   **124 scrannel** thin, reedy (dialect). Their pipes are
straw, not 'oat'. The music or preaching of the church? or chanted
liturgy, which the puritans wanted made more congregational?   **125
sheep** parishioners.   **127 rot** sheep-rot, fluke, causes intestinal wind
and enormous swelling. Mist was a standard metaphor for false teaching.
Cf killings at 45.   **128 wolf** Roman catholic church, especially the
Jesuits of the counter-reformation who were converting people back
again; the arms of their founder, St Ignatius Loyola, bear two grey
wolves.   **130 engine** could mean any kind of weapon, or simple machine. Nobody knows what is meant exactly. The image culminates the
first half of the poem with a threat of mechanical power; and anticipates
the 'Weep no more' (165) with which the poem begins to end. Every
syllable in 130 could take a stress.   **132 Alpheus** see 85n. The Sicilian

technological or manmade; to that extent, inadequate, so the poem can't end yet, though this section seems to close the second movement, and 9 opens by assuming that it's all over, the questions answered with force.

Pastoral resumed again : the wreath of flowers a false surmise

Nature is put to false use in the art of the pathetic fallacy; or perhaps it is a wreath of artificial flowers. Anyway, neither art nor

and call the vales and bid them hither cast
their bells, and flowerets of a thousand hues.   135
Ye valleys low, where the mild whispers use
of shades, and wanton winds and gushing brooks,
on whose fresh lap the swart star sparely looks,
throw hither all your quaint enamelled eyes
that on the green turf suck the honied showers,   140
and purple all the ground with vernal flowers.
Bring the rathe primrose that forsaken dies;
the tufted crow-toe and pale jessamine,
the white pink, and the pansy freaked with jet,
the glowing violet,   145
the musk-rose, and the well-attired woodbine,
with cowslips wan that hang the pensive head,
and every flower that sad embroidery wears;
bid amaranthus all his beauty shed,
and daffadillies fill their cups with tears,   150

muse also=pastoral poetry. Peter's voice has acted like a drought or
too-hot sun; now there will be a cool flower passage.   **135 bells** of
flowers.   **136 use** live.   **137 shades** shady places. **wanton** free.
138 star Sirius, the Dogstar, sunburnt because he appears in late
summer at a time of heavy heat, the dogdays; he hardly looks at these
valleys, so they are cool; then why is he introduced?   **139 quaint**
exquisitely wrought. **enamelled** glossily coloured; much decorative
metalwork was enamelled at this time and the word probably carried
less the sense of artifice than of polychromatic brightness. Still, these two
epithets push the eyes forward not so much as flower centres but more as
animated eyes, baroque emblems of grief; and also as part of the series
of strange eye images in the poem. They are thrown because behind the
mixed images lies a picture such as Botticelli's *Primavera* with the figure
of Flora scattering flowers onto the grass where they take root like
designs in a carpet.   **140 suck** complicates the image further.   **141
purple** redden, usually by bloodshed; which doesn't fit the preceding
images, or **vernal**=spring. Perhaps the myth of Adonis lies behind this?
see *Comus* 998 and *PL* 1 450.   **142 rathe** early (dialect). M may have
pron. primerose. They tend to grow where they can't be seen or picked.
143 crow-toe wild hyacinth, ragged robin; grows by water, was in
Ophelia's garland. **jessamine** white jasmine. Although common wild
flowers then, as the country names tell, most of these are strongly scented;
several have emblematic values.   **144 freaked** ... variegated with black.
Freaked in this sense probably coined by M. Heartsease (our pansy not
here then).   **146 woodbine** probably means honeysuckle.   **149
amaranthus** love-lies-bleeding; and the Greek mythical flower of
heaven which never fades.

emotion (an aesthetic culture, or a spontaneous one) is adequate. The fresh lap does not mean there is no monstrous bottom. It is necessary to be at the worst, like Edgar in Lear, to use art to harrow hell (as Orpheus did). This is the world's hell, as 8 was the hell of the Church of England in the 17c.

to strew the laureate hearse where Lycid lies.
For so to interpose a little ease
let our frail thoughts dally with false surmise.
Ay me! whilst thee the shores and sounding seas
wash far away, where'er thy bones are hurled,   155
whether beyond the stormy Hebridës,
where thou perhaps under the whelming tide
visit'st the bottom of the monstrous world;
or whether thou to our moist vows denied
sleep'st by the fable of Bellérus old   160
where the great vision of the guarded mount
looks toward Namancos, and Bayona's hold:
look homeward angel now, and melt with ruth,
and O ye dolphins waft the hapless youth.

---

151 laureate crowned with laurel because he was a poet. Links
the flower passage to the beginning of the poem.   **152 For so**
for in that way – but it is an illusion (cf 56) because he is not on
a hearse; and the flowers are not really mourning for him (just as
nature only conventionally mourns at 37); cf Eliot rejecting his flower
passage in *East Coker*: 'That was a way of putting it – not very satis-
factory'.   **156 whether** don't look for logical construction here: he
tries to abandon the fallacy and meet reality; but reality is full of whethers
and perhapses. **Hebridës** perhaps he has been washed out into the
Atlantic depths, to visit (!) the world of sea-monsters. Cf Jonah in
the whale, a symbol of resurrection.   **157 whelming** humming 1638.
159 moist vows tearful liturgy.   **160 Bellérus** Land's End. M has
invented a legendary Cornish figure, Bellerus, from the Latin name for
Land's End, Bellerium. The geography now turns southwest and fabulous. St Michael's Mount is off Penzance, said to be guarded by Michael
as captain of the heavenly host; monks who lived there had visions of
him.   **162 Namancos** NW Spain. **Bayona,** in the same area, was a
fortified post 50 miles from Cape Finisterre. They stand for the threat
of Roman catholicism.   **163 homeward** inland.   **164 dolphins** in
Greek mythology they several times rescue people in the sea; in reality
they respond to music and play; they symbolize natural power and
command of environment (Cleopatra says of Antony 'his delights were
dolphin-like and showed their back above the element he lived in') but
often in association with the spirit (see Yeats *Byzantium* and *News for the
Delphic oracle*). The closest myth is that of Arion, a musician who escaped from pirates by calling up dolphins with his lyre, throwing himself
into the sea and being carried home by one of them. Palaemon was a boy
whose drowned body was brought home for burial by a dolphin.

With the appeal to giants of the southwest, angels, dolphins, the stakes are raised from nymphs and even from Camus and Peter to semi-divine figures.

10 Weep no more, woeful shepherds weep no more, 165
for Lycidas your sorrow is not dead,
sunk though he be beneath the watery floor,
so sinks the day-star in the ocean bed,
and yet anon repairs his drooping head,
and tricks his beams, and with new-spangled ore 170
flames in the forehead of the morning sky:
so Lycidas sunk low, but mounted high,
through the dear might of him that walked the waves,
where other groves and other streams along
with nectar pure his oozy locks he laves, 175
and hears the unexpressive nuptial song
in the blest kingdoms meek of joy and love.
There entertain him all the saints above
in solemn troops, and sweet societies,
that sing, and singing in their glory move, 180
and wipe the tears for ever from his eyes.
Now Lycidas the shepherds weep no more:
henceforth thou art the Genius of the shore

---

166 Apply logical 'proof' to rhythm in this para: for . . . so . . . and yet . . .
so . . . but . . .   **168 day-star** sun.   **170 tricks** renews, rearranges.
ore gold.   **173 dear** beloved, precious, costly. Jesus walked on the lake
of Galilee in a storm; Peter tried too but sank till Jesus held him *Matthew*
xiv.   **174 where other** he is risen to another world, where . . .   **175**
nectar drink of the gods: but the ritual is more of anointing his muddy
hair with cleansing and regal oil.   **176 unexpressive** inexpressible,
and inaudible except to those above. Just as Lyc has an apotheosis, so
does poetry. Part of the train of ear images. **nuptial** marriage of the
Lamb with his bride the church *Revelation* xix and *Song of Solomon*; also
Platonic and Dantesque notions of the beatific vision as a sort of marriage
of the soul with the divine. Put strongly in *Epitaphium Damonis*: 'Deathless you go to the eternal wedding-feast, where angel voices sing enraptured by the lyre, and the ecstasy of the bacchantes marries the rod of
Zion in sacred orgy'.   **177 meek** see the beatitudes *Matthew* v.   **178**
entertain take him in. **saints** inhabitants of heaven.   **179 troops** . . .
societies the ceremony of heaven, and its fellowship (Latin *socius*
comrade, mate).   **180** Let the line ravish itself: accept erotic power of
moving like singing, the glory in 'move'.   **181 tears** 'And God shall
wipe away all tears from their eyes; and there shall be no more death,
neither sorrow, nor crying, neither shall there be any more pain: for the
former things are passed away' *Revelation* xxi quoting *Isaiah* xxv. The
last tears in the poem.   **182 shepherds** poets: they can end their
song. Completes line 165.   **183 Genius** local deity like a guardian angel.

Resurrection and apotheosis

Like the fundamental Christian doctrine of the Word made flesh, this section is paradoxical. Main paradox: Lycidas your sorrow is not dead (though he is). Subsidiary paradox: he has sunk through a watery floor (floors should be firm). Resolution: this is the sun's kind of sinking, and by implication Christ's; and they rise. The subsidiary paradox resolved in a similar yet acceptable metaphor, ocean bed (Christ's sepulchre?). At the end, a reversion: the solid world is seen now as a perilous flood, compared with the sure firmness of heaven.

Collect the materials which are here consummated – stars, waters, trees, hair, music etc.

The tenses assert an eternal present. The syntax builds, asserts 166–8, 173–7. The syntax enacts paradox – 172. Note accumulating clauses linked by so, and etc. – the figure of brachylogia.

in thy large recompense, and shalt be good
to all that wander in that perilous flood.   185

11 Thus sang the uncouth swain to the oaks and rills,
    while the still morn went out with sandals gray,
    he touched the tender stops of various quills,
    with eager thought warbling his Doric lay;
    and now the sun had stretched out all the hills,   190
    and now was dropped into the western bay;
    at last he rose, and twitched his mantle blue:
    tomorrow to fresh woods and pastures new.

184 recompense this is his great reward; cf 14 etc.   **185 flood** sea,
life, poetry? With *wander* we (not he) are back weltering, and lost.
186 uncouth not heard of; his only audience trees and streams.   **188
quills** pipes; various because of the mixture of styles in *Lyc*.   **189
eager** impetuous, impatient, mordant (not enthusiastic). **warbling**
singing, modulating. **Doric** Theocritus etc wrote in the Doric dialect
of Greek – simple, broad, rustic.   **190 sun** the epilogue runs for a
whole day, with a 'real' sun; now it has lengthened the shadows of the
hills, or silhouetted them, as it sets over the Atlantic (as Lycidas set).
192 blue colour of hope. He tucks it up for movement.   **193 woods**
often misquoted fields. Biblical backgrounds here, eg *Psalm* lxv, *Ezekiel*
xxxiv.

Epilogue

Pastoral for the third time resumed after the intrusion of a higher power, but now, being finished with as a strategy, resumed only to be dropped (and taken up again on a staggering scale for the Eden of *PL* iv–v). That was today's poem; now the poet sees himself out there, going to tomorrow. A day, the surest measure of time and assurance of continuity, encloses the poem. The landscape draws into the distance.

Appendix to Introduction to Lycidas

The pastoral tradition

The classical documents: GREEK: Theocritus *Idyl* I (Lament for Daphnis), VII (song of Lycidas the goat-herd, discussion of poetry) and XXVI (the bacchantes destroy Pentheus; cf Euripides *Bacchae*); Bion *Idyl* I (Lament for Adonis); Moschus *Idyl* II (myth of Europa: scenes of flower-gathering, and sea-gods); 'Moschus' (wrongly attrib.) *Idyl* III (Lament for Bion). ROMAN: Ovid *Metamorphoses* X–XI (Orpheus, Hyacinthus etc); Virgil *Eclogues* (ie Bucolics or Pastorals) II (Corydon's homosexual passion for Alexis), V (Lament for Daphnis, and his apotheosis), VII (pastoral details); *Georgics* IV (beekeeping, and the myths of Orpheus and Proteus).

The best introduction to these materials is via Gilbert Highet *The classical tradition* 1954, and by using one's own classical skills (eg Latin lessons at school) to translate some of this material. To translate even two lines of Latin so dire as

> restitit, Eurydicenque suam iam luce sub ipsa
> immemor heu! victusque animi respexit . . .
>
> *Georgics* IV 490

where the maddening word order and verb-endings are fully at work, to translate that into something that takes up the restitit . . . respexit structure, and the confused mindlessness of the middle clauses, to do that is worth a dozen exercises in the use of the ablative absolute, and a dozen books on 'classical background'. Theocritus, Bion and Moschus, if you know any Greek (I don't), still lack translations adequate to the burnt pastures of Sicily and the sexy elegance of Alexandria and the anthropology of their slaughtered gods. Much the best so far is *The Greek bucolic poets* by A. S. F. Gow, Cambridge 1953, excerpted below (there is also an excellent anonymous version published at Oxford in 1588 but it is not easy to reach).

THEOCRITUS from *Idyl* VII trans. Gow

. . . when, by the Muses' grace, we fell in with a wayfarer, a man of Cydonia and a worthy. His name was Lycidas, and he was a goatherd . . . On his shoulders he wore the tawny skin of a thick-haired, shaggy goat reeking of fresh curd, and round his breast an aged tunic was girt with a

218

broad belt . . . And with a quiet smile and twinkling eye he spoke to me, and laughter hung about his lip . . . And he bent his way leftward and took the road to Pyxa, but I and Eucritus and the fair Amyntas turned towards Phrasidamus's farm and laid ourselves down rejoicing on deep couches of sweet rush and in the fresh-stripped vine-leaves. Many a poplar and elm murmured above our heads, and near at hand the sacred water from the cave of the Nymphs fell plashing. On the shady boughs the dusky cicadas were busy with their chatter, and the tree-frog far off cried in the dense thorn-brake. Larks and finches sang, the dove made moan, and bees flitted humming about the springs . . .

If you have been in the country of any part of the Mediterranean (not on the coast) or even in the southern half of France, you will recognize this. If you haven't, read Lawrence *Sea and Sardinia*.

BION from *Idyl* I trans. Gow

. . . The fair Adonis lies upon the hills with wounded thigh, white thigh with white tush wounded; and as he softly breathes his life away brings grief to the Cyprian [Aphrodite]. Down his snowy skin the dark blood drips; dim grow the eyes beneath the brows; the roses fade from his lip, and on it dies the kiss that the Cyprian will never receive again. To her the kiss is sweet though the life is gone from him, but Adonis knows not that she kissed him as he died. *I cry 'Woe for Adonis' : 'Woe' in answer cry the Loves . . .*

Cf Yeats *Her vision in the wood.*

MOSCHUS from *Idyl* II trans. Gow

And the bull [Zeus transformed, bearing Europa on his back] reached the shore, and sped on like a dolphin treading the wide waves with hooves unwetted. Then as he came the sea grew smooth, and all round before the feet of Zeus the sea-beasts frolicked. The dolphin from the depths gambolled for joy over the swell. The sea-nymphs rose from the waters and advanced in rank mounted all on sea-beasts' backs. The thunderous Earthshaker [Poseidon] himself made smooth the waves over the main and led his brother on his briny road, and about him gathered Tritons, those deep-toned trumpeters of the sea, blowing on their tapering shells a bridal strain . . .

'MOSCHUS' *Idyl* III trans. J. M. Edmonds (Loeb Library *Greek bucolic poets* 1912)

Cry me waly upon him, you glades of the woods, and waly, sweet Dorian waters; you rivers, weep I pray you for the lovely and delightful Bion. Lament you now, good orchards; gentle groves, make you your moan; be your breathing clusters, ye flowers, dishevelled for grief . . . speak now thy writing, dear flower-de-luce, loud let thy blossoms babble aye: the beautiful musician is dead. *A song of woe, of woe, Sicilian muses.* You nightingales that complain in the thick leafage, tell to Arethusa's fountain of Sicily that neat-herd Bion is dead, and with him dead is music, and gone with him likewise the Dorian poesy. *A song of woe, of woe, Sicilian muses* . . .

You may be able to find a Biblical parallel.

The two best translations to use of Virgil's *Eclogues* and *Georgics* are exemplified now (eclogue means excerpt; it became the title accidentally in the middle ages; it should be *Bucolics*= pastorals):

VIRGIL from *Eclogue* II trans. Dryden (*Works of Virgil* 1697 repr 1961 ed. J. Kinsley)

> Come to my longing arms, my lovely care!
> And take the presents which the nymphs prepare.
> White lilies in full canisters they bring,
> With all the glories of the purple spring.
> The daughters of the flood have searched the mead
> For violets pale, and cropped the poppy's head,
> The short narcissus and fair daffodil,
> Pansies to please the sight, and cassia sweet to smell:
> And set soft hyacinths with iron-blue
> To shade marsh-marigolds of shining hue . . .

VIRGIL from *Eclogue* V trans. J. Lonsdale and S. Lee (Globe *Works of Virgil* 1894, with plentiful aids)

Oft in the furrows to which we have committed great grains of barley, unfruitful darnel and barren wild oats spring; instead of the gentle violet, instead of the bright narcissus, the thistle rises up, and the thorn with prickly spikes. Strew the ground with leaves, ye shepherds; curtain the fountain with shades . . .

VIRGIL from *Georgics* IV trans. Dryden (*Works of Virgil* 1697 repr 1961 ed. J. Kinsley)

> 'Twas noon: the sultry Dogstar from the sky
> Scorched Indian swains; the rivelled grass was dry;
> The sun with flaming arrows pierced the flood
> And, darting to the bottom, baked the mud;
> When weary Proteus from the briny waves
> Retired for shelter to his wonted caves.
> His finny flocks about their shepherd play
> And rolling round him spurt the bitter sea;
> Unwieldily they wallow first in ooze,
> Then in the shady covert seek repose . . .

Elegies for dead poets

WILLIAM DUNBAR *c.* 1460–*c.* 1520 from *Lament for the makaris* [makar is Scots for maker, the Greek meaning of poet]

Unto the deid gois all estatis,
Princis, prelatis and potestatis,
Baith rich and poor of all degree –
Timor mortis conturbat me.

. . . . .

I see that makaris among the lave   [the rest
Playis here their padyanis, syne gois to grave;   [pageants
Sparit is nocht their facultie . . .

He has done petuously devour
The noble Chaucer, of makaris flower,
The Monk of Bury, and Gower, all three . . .   [Lydgate

SPENSER from *The shepherd's calendar containing 12 eclogues proportionable to the 12 months.* Entitled to the noble and virtuous gentleman most worthy *of all titles both of learning and chivalry Mr* Philip Sidney 1579

April   . . . Bring hither the pink and purple cullambine,
                With gillyflowers;
        Bring caranations, and sops-in-wine,
                Worn of paramours;
        Strow me the ground with daffadowndillies
        And cowslips and kingcups and lovèd lilies;
                The pretty paunce
                And the chevichaunce
        Shall match with the fair flower-de-lis . . .

January   . . . All so my lustful leaf is dry and sere,
        My timely buds with wailing all are wasted;
        The blossom which my branch of youth did bear
        With breathed sighs is blown away and blasted,
        And from mine eyes the drizzling tears descend
        As on your boughs the icicles depend . . .

SPENSER from *Astrophel, a pastoral elegy upon the death of the most noble and valorous knight, Sir Philip Sidney.* Dedicated to the most beautiful and virtuous lady, the Countess of Essex 1586

[Astrophel = star-lover; Stella was Sidney's name for the girl of his own sonnets, Penelope Devereux, daughter of the first Earl and Countess of Essex; in 1580 she was married off to Lord Rich. Sidney died of wounds at the Battle of Zutphen in the Netherlands 1586.]

        . . . Break now your girlonds, O ye shepherd lasses,
        Sith the fair flower which them adorned is gone:
        The flower which them adorned is gone to ashes;
        Never again let lass put girlond on;
                Instead of girlond wear sad cypress now,
                And bitter elder broken from the bough.

. . . . .

        Ah no, it [his spirit] is not dead, ne can it die,
        But lives for aye in blissful paradise,
        Where like a newborn babe it soft doth lie

                    In bed of lilies wrapped in tender wise,
                    And compassed all about with roses sweet
                    And dainty violets from head to feet . . .

Modern American poets, notably Berryman and Lowell, are
prolific of elegies for each other.

Adonis and death by water

You will have noticed, as Frye does (quoted in the Introduction),
how the myth of Adonis, the annually dying and resurrected god
of fertility, mingles with pastoral, and with Daphnis the dead
poet. Renaissance celebrations of Adonis culminated in Shakespeare's *Venus and Adonis*, many paintings of the 16–17c (eg
Titian, Veronese, Poussin), and the epilogue to *Comus*. In the
17c it began to mingle more widely with the theme of death by
water; that theme came together with Adonis again in Eliot's
Waste land.

SIR JAMES FRAZER from *The golden bough : a study in magic and religion*
1890 ff abr 1922 chaps 29–33

The myth of Adonis was localized and its rites celebrated with much
solemnity at two places in Western Asia. One of these was Byblus on the
coast of Syria, the other was Paphos in Cyprus. Both were great seats of
the worship of Aphrodite, or rather of her Semitic counterpart, Astarte;
and of both, if we accept the legends, Cinyras, the father of Adonis, was
king. Of the two cities Byblus was the more ancient; indeed it claimed
to be the oldest city in Phoenicia, and to have been founded in the early
ages of the world by the great god El, whom the Greeks and Romans
identified with Cronus and Saturn respectively . . . The city stood on a
height beside the sea, and contained a great sanctuary of Astarte . . . [in
which] the rites of Adonis were celebrated . . . [there was another sanctuary inland] at the source of the River Adonis, half-way between Byblus
and Baalbec . . . the river rushes from a cavern at the foot of a mighty
amphitheatre of towering cliffs to plunge in a series of cascades into the
awful depths of the glen. The deeper it descends, the ranker and denser
grows the vegetation . . . At Alexandria images of Aphrodite and Adonis
were displayed on two couches; beside them were set ripe fruits of all
kinds, cakes, plants growing in flower-pots ['gardens of Adonis'], and
green bowers twined with anise. The marriage of the lovers was celebrated one day, and on the morrow women attired as mourners, with
streaming hair and bared breasts, bore the image of the dead Adonis to the
sea-shore and committed it to the waves . . .

Different parts of the theme can be traced in elegies for Sidney,
Shakespeare, Ben Jonson, Donne, and especially in epitaphs by
Herrick. Also in the 35 elegies of *Justa Eduardo King* was one by

Henry King, author of the great elegy for his wife, *The exequy*, later bishop of Chichester, who erected the monument to Donne in St Paul's; and John Cleveland, who was at Christ's with Milton (his father was a royalist minister but he was educated in Leicestershire by a presbyterian; he became a fellow of St John's College, and a minister himself, but was ejected from his post by parliament so joined the king's army at Oxford). Here is part of his contribution *On the memory of Mr Edward King, drowned in the Irish Seas*:

> I like not tears in tune, nor will I prize
> His artificial grief that scans his eyes;
> Mine weep down pious beads, but why should I
> Confine them to the Muses' rosary?
> I am no poet here: my pen's the spout
> Where the rain-water of my eyes runs out
> In pity of that name whose fate we see
> Thus copied out in grief's hydrography.
>
> .   .   .   .   .
>
> When we have filled the rundlets of our eyes
> We'll issue't forth, and vent such elegies
> As that our tears shall seem the Irish Seas,
> We floating islands, living Hebrides.

Here is part of a poem by Capt Thomas James who lost four of his crew of 22 when trying to find the northwest passage in his 70-ton ship the *Henrietta Maria*, in the winter of 1631–2; it is called *Lines on his companions who died in the northern seas*:

> . . . Why drop ye so, mine eyes? Nay, rather pour
> My sad departure in a solemn shower:
> The winter's cold, that lately froze our blood,
> Now were it so extreme might do this good
> As make these tears bright pearls, which I would lay
> Tombed safely with you till doom's fatal day;
> That in this solitary place, where none
> Will ever come to breathe a sigh or groan,
> Some remnant might be extant of the true
> And faithful love I ever tendered you . . .

Problems of excellence and sincerity face us with Cleveland and James; yet it was of *Lycidas* that Dr Johnson declared, 'It is not to be considered as the effusion of real passion; for passion runs not after remote allusions and obscure opinions. Passion plucks no berries from the myrtle and ivy, nor calls upon Arethuse and Mincius, nor tells of rough satyrs and fauns with cloven heel. Where there is leisure for fiction there is little grief.'

In July 1818 Keats visited the basalt islet Staffa off the west coast of Scotland and wrote a poem called *Staffa* in which he sees Lycidas:

> . . . Lo! I saw one sleeping there
> On the marble cold and bare;
> While the surges washed his feet
> And his garments white did beat
> Drenched about the sombre rocks . . .

Three years later Keats died, aged 24. In his elegy for him, Shelley adopted the name of Adonis; and starts by evoking Milton:

SHELLEY from *Adonis, an elegy on the death of John Keats* 1821

> Most musical of mourners, weep again!
> Lament anew, Urania! He died,
> Who was the sire of an immortal strain,
> Blind, old, and lonely; when his country's pride
> The priest, the slave and the liberticide
> Trampled and mocked with many a loathed rite
> Of lust and blood; he went unterrified
> Into the gulf of death; but his clear sprite
> Yet reigns o'er earth, the third among the sons of light.

He goes on to evoke 'the quick Dreams, The passioned-winged Ministers of thought, Who were his flocks . . .'

> And others came . . . Desires and Adorations,
> Winged Persuasions and veiled Destinies,
> Splendours, and Glooms, and glimmering Incarnations
> Of hopes and fears, and twilight Phantasies;
> And Sorrow, with her family of Sighs,
> And Pleasure, blind with tears, led by the gleam
> Of her own dying smile instead of eyes,
> Came in slow pomp – the moving pomp might seem
> Like pageantry of mist on an autumnal stream . . .

> Lost Echo sits amid the voiceless mountains
> And feeds her grief with his remembered lay
> And will no more reply to winds or fountains
> Or amorous birds perched on the young green spray,
> Or herdsman's horn, or bell at closing day . . .

Next year Shelley was drowned from a sailing-boat off the Italian coast, aged 29. Eleven years later, in 1833, Tennyson's friend Arthur Hallam died in Vienna – his corpse was shipped home and Tennyson started to write *In memoriam*, published 1850.

In memoriam is often presented as a document in the history of Victorian ideas. It is a poem of anguish, fearing that with the over-loved undergraduate friend, and fiancé of his sister, now dead, the poet's genius, and his potency, have died. Here are some of the passages which illuminate *Lyc.* The Orphean face without a body – 'And on the depths of death there swims The reflex of a human face' cviii – which is also the image of oneself. The dead friend as demi-god, hence a being of the margins (such as the surface air–water): 'The man I held as half-divine' xiv and various ghost passages. The horrors of watery chaos:

LXX

And crowds that stream from yawning doors,
   And shoals of puckered faces drive;
   Dark bulks that tumble half alive,
And lazy lengths on boundless shore . . .

The lost friend as Jesus in the storm-tossed ship on Galilee: 'The man we loved was there on deck, But thrice as large as man he bent To greet us' ciii. The lost friend as sexually virgin, or the virginal aspect of Tennyson:

XC

He tasted love with half his mind,
   Nor ever drank the inviolate spring
   Where nighest heaven, who first could fling
This bitter seed among mankind . . .

He is Tennyson's bride, hence Tennyson is a widower (xiii) or Tennyson is the bride (xcvii); death merges with marriage and rebirth (xcix).

Matthew Arnold's *Thyrsis* is a more pastoral elegy, for his friend the poet Arthur Clough who had died in Florence. It is set ostensibly in the hills round Oxford, actually in a Victorian garden where the poet sees his own middle-age: 'the year's primal burst of bloom is o'er'; then a flower-passage astoundingly different from Milton's – the false hope of 'Soon will the high Midsummer pomps come on'.

HERMAN MELVILLE from epilogue to *The Haglets* in his *John Marr and other sailors* 1888

Embedded deep with shells
And drifted treasure deep,
Forever he sinks deeper in
Unfathomable sleep –
His cannon round him thrown,
His sailors at his feet,
The wizard sea enchanting them
Where never haglets beat.

> On nights when meteors play
> And lights the breakers' dance,
> The Oreads from the caves
> With silvery elves advance;
> And up from Ocean stream
> And down from heaven far,
> The rays that blend in dream
> The abysm and the star.

The last two lines seem important to the entire tradition.

Then: Hopkins *Wreck of the 'Deutschland'* 1888 about drowned nuns and how to embrace Christ as life or as death; Paul Valéry *Le cimetière marin* 1921 trans. C. Day Lewis as *Graveyard by the sea*; T. S. Eliot *The waste land* 1921. The doyen of more recent poetry on this theme is Robert Lowell's *The Quaker graveyard in Nantucket* (1950 in *Poems 1938–1949* Faber):

> . . . Sailors, who pitch this portent at the sea [sailor's corpse
> Where dreadnoughts shall confess
> Its heel-bent deity,
> When you are powerless
> To sandbag this Atlantic bulwark, faced
> By the earth-shaker, green, unwearied, chaste   [Poseidon
> In his steel scales: ask for no Orphean lute
> To pluck life back . . .

Sylvia Plath has several on the theme, eg *Full fathom five*, Brecht's *Vom ertrunkenen Mädchen* is in the Ophelia tradition. *The white ship* by Geoffrey Hill in *For the unfallen* (Deutsch 1971) comments on the hopes of the tradition:

> Where the living with effort go,
> Or with expense, the drowned wander
> Easily: seaman
> And king's son also
>
> Who, by gross error lost,
> Drift, now, in salt crushed
> Polyp-and-mackerel-fleshed
> Tides between coast and coast,
>
> Submerge or half-appear.
> This does not much matter.
> They are put down as dead. Water
> Silences all who would interfere;
>
> Retains, still, what it might give
> As casually as it took away:
> Creatures passed through the wet sieve
> Without enrichment or decay.

For novels on the theme see Melville's *Moby Dick*, the flood scene in Lawrence's *Rainbow*, the drowned neanderthaler in Golding's *Inheritors*, and the whole of his *Pincher Martin*; and Lawrence Durrell's *Clea* Faber 1961, in which the heroine is accidentally nailed to an underwater wreck, in a pool already peopled with dead but unrotted sailors, by a fish-spear; but is rescued and given an artificial hand. The crisis is described with a wealth of simple rituals and symbols; the conclusion is an interesting apotheosis in the form of a letter from Clea:

It is the first serious letter I have attempted, apart from short notes, with my new hand . . . Of course I was frightened and disgusted by it at first, as you can imagine. But I have come to respect it very much, this delicate and beautiful steel contrivance which lies beside me so quietly on the table in its green velvet glove! . . . I have been totally absorbed in this new hand-language and the interior metamorphosis it has brought about. All the roads have opened before me, everything seems now possible for the first time . . . it's as if the whole composition of our lives were being suddenly drawn away by a new current . . .

Appendix to text of Lycidas

1 Prologue

Immortality and unripeness. In a Latin letter to Charles Diodati 23 Sept 1637 M wrote: 'What am I thinking about? you ask. So help me God, of immortality. What am I doing? Growing wings and learning to fly.' See also the sonnet *How soon hath time* 1631 and the Latin poem *Ad patrem* excusing his poetical studies to his father 1636–7 – both in the *Samson and sonnets* volume of this series:

and if the poems and the toy-poems that I write while young have a chance of living, of seeing the light beyond my own grave, of immortality, O if they are not crowded down into the unremembered shadows of Orcus –

then his father too will be immortalized. Eliot, middle-aged in *East Coker* (*Four quartets* Faber 1944), is less sanguine:

So here I am, in the middle way, having had twenty years –
Twenty years largely wasted, the years of *l'entre deux guerres* –
Trying to learn to use words, and every attempt
Is a wholly new start, and a different kind of failure
Because one has only learnt to get the better of words
For the thing one no longer has to say . . .

A commentary

Milton is being forced to write a poem before he is ready to do so. He is a young poet who has already started his career. 'Yet once more . . .' in single syllables expressing urgent forcefulness he plucks the berries of his art . . . Within the powerful urgency oppositions are contained which give the sense of seasonal death followed by seasonal rebirth. Life and death coupled with the cyclical movement of nature's changing seasons.

Opposition A 1. Leaves broken and shattered, berries harsh, unripe.
             2. Ripeness, mellowing year, fulfilment.

Not over-emphasized but an underlying feeling beneath that of conflict. Achieved by use of rhyme eg sere (brown, unripe) / year (sense of fulfilment); also by rhythm of language. Shatter and bitter jangle together giving an impression of forceful poignant anguish and bitterness that things must die before they are mature. The more gradual and decorous 'Mellowing year' and 'sad occasion dear' balance out the bitterness and, while lamenting the fact of premature death, leave the feeling that the sadness of things is also the fitness. Also, the evergreen garland of the poet which never dies seems to suggest that the poem is an act of mediation between two irreconcilable polarities.

The explosiveness now somewhat controlled leads to the quieter 'disturb' then the assertion of the fact that Lycidas is dead. The breaks of the caesura provide a solemn drumbeat of grief and challenge.

Opposition B 1. sea and wind; a bier, parching, weltering (both tossing
              and withering).
             2. tears and music; hope, harmony, melodious, rounded
              sounds.

Although a tear and the sea are so immensely different in size, one gets the impression that the former can triumph over the latter. The oppositions A and B influence each other so that hope for the future contained in the first accentuates a feeling that the 'melodious tear' (the poem) can win through in the second. Also a sense of hope within the poem itself, of melody and lyric chorus in the final three lines, lead to an anticipation of serenity to be brought about by the tear (poem). Born out of conflict it is the hope for the future – the poem itself is born and comes to maturity during one whole day. It is 'built' and 'lofty' being above the water where the dead youth floats, but simultaneously it is a tear. Thus it mediates between civilized and elemental forces. The movement to melody suggests that a poem's beauty can lessen the pain of death and help men to accept the fact that he must die.

These notions are underlying and anticipatory of outcome. The main impression is one of conflict. This prologue is declamatory and oratorical with harsh consonants, open vowel sounds and techniques of repetition. Syntactic and phonetic tightening in the language gives the impression that Milton is writing a fugue rather than a tone poem at this point. The assertion of the fact that Lycidas is dead is like the sounding of a challenge, a call for explanation. Why should man die before he has made his creative contribution? Lycidas could sing; all men can sing. 'Young' is stressed by its metrical position – what is the point of trying to be creative when one dies young? The main tone is anxious and urgent not just because Milton is a young poet writing before he is ready to, but because he is questioning the meaning of order within life and in doing so his 'forcing fingers' are forcing ultimately the poem itself. It has an extraordinary rhyme-scheme, and is very free, remembering that it is in an age-old tradition of pastoral elegy. The decorum of the very order man creates is forced. The assault is upon the poem's own assumptions – upon its tradition but also upon its survival.

TERRY WOODHEAD East Anglia 2nd year

2 *Invocation*

Poets dead. See the quotation from *Ad patrem* in 1 and Yeats's epitaph in *Under Ben Bulben*:

> Cast a cold eye
> On life, on death.
> Horseman, pass by.

Muses. See *PL* I–II in this series.

3 *Pastoral youth*

Poets = shepherds. See section on Moses p. 14 of *PL* I–II in this series.

Satyrs. See Jordaens's *Apollo and Marsyas* (a satyr who competed on the pipes against Apollo's lyre) and *Marsyas ill-treated by the Muses*; Titian *Flaying of Marsyas*; and some of the pagan paintings listed in *PL : introduction* p. 162 in this series.

4 *Pastoral death*

Echo. A nymph who lived in a cave and haunted rocks and woods. She loved Narcissus but could only reply, not start a conversation; and could only repeat what was said to her. Narcissus was lost and called 'Is anyone here?' 'Here!' replied Echo. But Narcissus rejected her, and eventually fell in love with his own reflection in a pool, and killed himself because he couldn't reach it. Echo pined alone till only her disembodied voice remained.

Echo	Narcissus
follows, approaches	initiates, rejects
hearing	sight
voice	eyes
reflection in air	reflection in water
frustrated of other-love	frustrated of self-love

Neither is consummated; compare the heavenly consummations of *Lycidas* and *Epitaphium Damonis*.

Mutability. See Broadbent *Poetic love* 1964 chap 9; Shakespeare *Sonnet* 60.

SPENSER in *The ruins of time* 1591 foresees the devastation of London:

> There also where the wingèd ships were seen
> In liquid waves to cut their foamy way,
> And thousand fishers numbered to have been
> In that wide lake looking for plenteous prey
> Of fish which they with baits used to betray,
> Is now no lake, nor any fishers' store,
> Nor ever ship shall sail there any more.
>
> They are all gone, and all with them is gone,
> Nor aught to me remains but to lament
> My long decay, which no man else doth moan,
> And mourn my fall with doleful drfeariment.
> Yet it is comfort in great languishment
> To be bemoanèd with compassion kind,
> And mitigates the anguish of the mind.
> .   .   .   .   .   .
> Whilst thus I looked, lo adown the Lea
> I saw an harp strung all with silver twine
> And made of gold and costly ivory,
> Swimming, that whilom seemèd to have been
> The harp on which Dan Orphëus was seen
> Wild beasts and forests after him to lead,
> But was the harp of Philisides now dead . . .

Cf the painting of Orpheus's head as a floating harp by Odilon Redon.

5 Orpheus

Druids

Two rivers are mentioned in paragraph 5, the Hebrus and Deva. They link the Druids to the story of Orpheus. Among the main tenets of the Druids was the belief that the soul of man is immortal and that the universe is indestructible, although from time to time it could be temporarily consumed by fire or water. The human head was regarded as being symbolic of divinity and immortal powers. The head was the centre of the life-force. Even when severed from the rest of the body it was capable of a continued, independent life . . . In Celtic mythology, the cult of the severed head was fundamentally associated with sacred water, especially in the form of rivers or springs. Such waters were symbolic of fertility, of divine motherhood, of strength, the power of destruction, the giver of life. Deva was such a river. Yet Hebrus too gives strength and life to Orpheus's head. Water is the giver of life. Yet it can also take away, as Lycidas is taken.

MARY WILDING East Anglia 2nd year

MILTON from *The history of Britain, that part especially now called England: from the first traditional beginning, continued to the Norman Conquest* 1670 Book I [Roman invasions; BC 55–AD 59]

Suetonius Paulinus, who next was sent hither esteemed a soldier equal to the best of that age, for two years together went on prosperously, both confirming what was got, and subduing onward. At last over-confident of his present actions, and emulating others of whose deeds he heard from abroad, marches up as far as Mona, the isle of Anglesey, a populous place. For they, it seems, had both entertained fugitives, and given good assistance to the rest that withstood him. He makes him boats with flat bottoms, fitted to the shallows which he expected in the narrow frith; his foot so passed over, his horse waded or swam. Thick upon the shore stood several gross bands of men well weaponed, many women like furies running to and fro in dismal habit, with hair loose about their shoulders, held torches in their hands. The Druids (those were their priests, of whom more in another place) with hands lift up to heaven uttering direful prayers, astonished the Romans; who at so strange a sight stood in amaze, as though wounded; at length awakened and encouraged by their general not to fear a barbarous and lunatic rout, fell on, and beat them down scorched and rolling in their own fire. Then were they yoked with garrisons, and the places consecrate to their bloody superstitions destroyed.

M seems to have thought the Druids spoke Greek. See William Collins *Elegy on Thomson*; Thomas Gray *The bard*; Blake *The voice of the bard*; Robert Graves *The white goddess*; Michael Drayton *Polyolbion* song IX lines 415–29, 436.

Orpheus. In Greek mythology, Orpheus was son of the muse of epic poetry, Calliope. Apollo, god of poetry, healing, prophecy, the sun, gave him the first lyre. The muses taught him to play it. With his music he moved stones and trees and tamed wild beasts.

Orpheus loved the nymph Eurýdicë. Aristaeus (hunter, beekeeper, conqueror of the Dogstar) tried to rape Eurydice; she ran away, trod on a snake, was bitten and died. She went down to hades. Orpheus went down to get her back. With his music he

enchanted Charon the ferryman of hell, Cerberus the guard-dog
with many heads, and the judges of the dead; his music suspended
the tortures of the damned and with it he persuaded Pluto to let
Eurydice go if he did not look back until she was in the sunshine
again. They went up to the world of the living, Orpheus first;
but he looked back at the last moment to see if Eurydice was
following: she disappeared back into hades.

After that Orpheus mourned. He neglected to honour Dionysus
the god of wine. He preached his own mysteries; he preached the
superiority of Apollo over Dionysus; he favoured homosexuality;
he preached the evil of sacrificial murder.

The Maenads or Bacchantes were women who worshipped
Dionysus in the mountains of Thrace. They were angered by
Orpheus. One day when their husbands were at a service taken
by Orpheus in a temple of Apollo, they stole their husbands'
weapons from outside, and massacred them. They tore off
Orpheus's head, dismembered his body, and threw the head into
the river Hebrus. Still singing, it floated across the Aegean Sea
to Lesbos where, though attacked by a serpent, it was placed
safely in a cave sacred to Dionysus. There it continued to pro-
phesy till Apollo told it to stop.

Meanwhile the Muses collected Orpheus's limbs and laid them
at the foot of Mt Olympus, where the nightingales sing sweetest
to this day. The blood-stained river Hebrus flowed underground. The Maenads were turned into oaktrees. The Thracians
tattooed their wives.

The *Lycidas* version of the myth is one of the most furious.
M also treats it in *L'allegro* and *Il penseroso* in this volume, and
PL VII 32–8; see *PL introduction* in this series, pp. 81ff for a student
essay on M's Orpheus. There is a list of other redactions in
Caroline W. Mayerson 'The Orpheus image in *Lyc*' *Publications
of the Modern Language Association of America* (*PMLA*) LXIV
1949, pp. 189–207. The myth of the poet who can tame wild
nature, and even death, but cannot tame the Bacchantes or keep
Eurydice on earth, yet remains the emblem of immortal song,
has been important to many ancient and modern artists. Any of
the following would start a valuable investigation: Moschus
Lament for Bion 116–26; Ovid *Metamorphoses* X–XI (note the
homosexual stories also in this context); Virgil *Georgics* IV 504 . . .
(and see his *Eclogues* III 46, IV 55, VI 29, VIII 55); Dürer *Death of
Orpheus* (engraving); Monteverdi *Orfeo* (opera); Poussin *Landscape with Orpheus and Eurydice*; Matthew Locke *Orpheus and*

Eurydice (opera 1673); Glück *Orpheus and Eurydice*; Leighton *Orpheus and Eurydice* (Victorian painting); Browning *Eurydice to Orpheus*; G. F. Watts *O and E* (painting); Liszt *Orpheus* (symphonic poem); Offenbach *Orpheus in the underworld*; Rodin *O and E* (sculpture); Rilke *Sonnets to Orpheus*; Oscar Kokoschka *O and E* (play); Edwin Muir *O's dream*; Anouilh *Eurydice* (play); Apollinaire *Orphée*; Auden *Orpheus*; Stravinsky *Orpheus* (ballet); Valéry *Orphée*; Yvor Winters *Orpheus : in memory of Hart Crane*; Wallace Stevens in section 'It must change' of *Notes toward a supreme fiction*; Lowell trans. Rilke's *Orpheus, Eurydice and Hermes* in *Imitations*. See Marcuse's chapter on Orpheus and Narcissus in *Eros and civilization*.

6 *Fame*

The spreading tree. Consider Yeats's blossoming tree in *Among schoolchildren* and *Prayer for my daughter*; rooted in hell, standing on earth, blossoming like candles in the sky, it asserts the unity of existence: 'O chestnut-tree, great-rooted blossomer, Are you the leaf, the blossom or the bole?'

7 *Pastoral resumed : the sea*

Milton and Stevens on the sea. Compare Wallace Stevens's *The paltry nude starts on a spring voyage, Infanta marina, Sea surface full of clouds, The idea of order at Key West, An ordinary evening in New Haven.*

The cursed bark. Cf Dalila who 'Comes this way sailing Like a stately ship' but brings curses in her rigging to tangle Samson, perhaps like the hair of Amaryllis and Neaera.

8 *Satire on hireling shepherds*

Milton on this subject in his prose. *Eikonoklastes* justifying regicide to Europe – in this passage, by the state of the national church of which the king had been head for the 24 years 1625–49:

For our religion, where was there a more ignorant, profane and vicious clergy, learned in nothing but the antiquity of their pride, their covetousness, and superstition? whose unsincere and leavenous doctrine, corrupting the people, first taught them looseness, then bondage: loosening them from all sound knowledge and strictness of life, the more to fit them for the bondage of tyranny and superstition.

Considerations touching the likeliest means to remove hirelings out of the church

. . . for now commonly he who desires to be a minister looks not at the work but at the wages; and by that lure or lowbell may be tolled from parish to parish all the town over . . . To whom it might be said, as justly as to that Simon [Simon Magus, who trafficked in church jobs, hence simony, *Acts* viii], 'Thy money perish with thee, because thou hast thought that the gift of God may be purchased with money' . . .

Next, it is a fond error, though too much believed among us to think that the university makes a minister of the gospel; what it may conduce to other arts and sciences, I dispute not now; but that which makes fit a minister, the scripture can best inform us to be only from above, whence also we are bid to seek them: *Matthew* ix 38 'Pray ye therefore the Lord of the harvest, that he will send forth labourers into his harvest'; *Acts* xx 28 'The flock, over which the Holy Ghost hath made you overseers'; *Romans* x 15 'How shall they preach, unless they be sent?' By whom sent? by the university, or the magistrate, or their belly? No, surely, but sent from God only, and that God who is not their belly.

Of reformation in England and the causes that have hitherto hindered it

Then was baptism changed to a kind of exorcism, and water, sanctified by Christ's institute, thought little enough to wash off the original spot without the scratch or cross impression of a priest's forefinger; and that feast of free grace and adoption to which Christ invited his disciples to sit as brethren and coheirs of the happy covenant, which at that table was to be sealed to them, even that feast of love and heavenly-admitted fellowship, the seal of filial grace, became the subject of horror, and gloating adoration, pageanted about like a dreadful idol . . . which indeed is fleshly pride, preferring a foolish sacrifice, and the rudiments of the world . . . before a savoury obedience to Christ's example.

. . . for if the life of Christ be hid to this world, much more is his sceptre inoperative but in spiritual things. And thus lived, for two or three ages, the successors of the apostles. But when, through Constantine's lavish superstition [emperor who endowed and established the church], they forsook their first love and set themselves up two gods instead, Mammon and their belly: then taking advantage of the spiritual power which they had on men's consciences, they began to cast a longing eye to get the body also, and bodily things, into their command; upon which their carnal desires, the spirit daily quenching and dying in them, knew no way to keep themselves up from falling to nothing, but by bolstering and supporting their inward rottenness by a carnal and outward strength . . . Of courtesy now let any man tell me, if they draw to themselves a temporal power out of Caesar's [the king's] dominion, is not Caesar's empire thereby diminished? But this was a stolen bit, hitherto he [an early pope] was but a caterpillar secretly gnawing at monarchy; the next time you shall see him a wolf, a lion, lifting his paw against his raiser, as Petrarch expressed it, and finally an open enemy and subverter of the Greek empire.

. . . Next, what numbers of faithful and freeborn Englishmen and good Christians have been constrained to forsake their dearest home, their friends and kindred, whom nothing but the wide ocean, and the savage deserts of America could hide from the fury of the bishops? O sir, if we could but see the shape of our dear mother England, as poets are wont to give a personal form to what they please, how would she appear, think ye? but in a mourning weed, with ashes upon her head, and tears abundantly flowing from her eyes, to behold so many of her children exposed at once, and thrust from things of dearest necessity, because their conscience could not assent to things which the bishops thought indifferent?

To grasp what M felt we should have to transpose the terms into attack on some other institution that we disapproved of. Wherever we transpose, though, and however much we believe in our own brand of puritanism, we have to answer the suggestion that we may be motivated by fear of our own accumulative, bodily, anal tendencies; see Norman O. Brown *Life against death* part 5 on 'The excremental vision', 'The protestant era' and 'Filthy lucre', and Erik Erikson *Young man Luther*.

Dante on simony

Inferno XIX

> O Simon mago, o miseri seguaci
> che le cose di Dio, che di bontate
> deon essere spose, voi rapaci
>
> per oro e per argento avolterate;
> or convien che per voi suoni la tromba,
> pero che nella terza bolgia state . . .

Now Simon Magus, you and your miserable disciples who lusted so much after money that you trafficked in the priesthood like ponces, turning the bride of Christ into a prostitute – now the trump sounds for you: you belong in the third bowel of hell . . . The pumice-stone of the entire ditch was pitted with deep round holes . . . out of each hole one of these sinners' legs stuck as far as the bulge of his calf; the rest was inside. All of them had the soles of their feet on fire: their ankles writhed so fiercely they would have snapped any rope that bound them. The fire flickered over the skin from heels to toes like flame licking over oil.

9 *Pastoral resumed again: the wreath of flowers . . .*

SHAKESPEARE from *The winter's tale* IV iii

Perdita   . . . bold oxlips and
     The crown imperial; lilies of all kinds,

> The flower-de-luce being one. O, these I lack
> To make you garlands of; and my sweet friend,
> To strew him o'er and o'er.

Florizel   What, like a corse?

Perdita   No, like a bank for love to lie and play on,
> Not like a corse; or if – not to be buried,
> But quick, and in my arms . . . Come, take your flowers.
> Methinks I play as I have seen them do
> In Whitsun pastorals . . .

The flowers' eyes. There is an unconscious stratum shaped something like this:

black star	bright eyes
looks	suck
gushing brooks	honied showers

It is a question of fitting in the wanton winds, fresh lap etc; then interpreting the substratum; then relating it to the overt meaning.

Dolphins. Traditionally guides (like guardian angels, like the genius of the shore, like the nymphs should have been). Called 'the shepherds of the sea'. They are ambivalent, standing both for Christ, and the spirit world; and for the potency of nature: Cleopatra says of Antony, 'For his delights were dolphin-like, they showed their back above the element he lived in.' Yeats sees them as carnal creatures bearing spirits through the water: 'Astraddle on the dolphins' mire and blood, Spirit after spirit!' (*Byzantium*); and in *News for the Delphic oracle*:

> Straddling each a dolphin's back
> And steadied by a fin,
> Those Innocents re-live their death,
> Their wounds open again . . .
> And the brute dolphins plunge
> Until, in some cliff-sheltered bay
> Where wades the choir of love
> Proffering its sacred laurel crowns,
> They pitch their burdens off.

See *The triumph of Galatea* by Raphael, and by Poussin, and Poussin's *Triumph of Neptune*.

Jonah. The Bible story will provide some valuable parallels, especially when you note (eg from Michelangelo's painting of Jonah's regurgitation on the Sistine Chapel ceiling) that his rescue was a type of the resurrection.

10 Resurrection and apotheosis

The theme of rising and falling ('So Lycidas sunk low but mounted high') recurs in the 'Death by water' section of *The waste land* (*Collected poems 1909–1962* Faber) about Phlebas the Phoenician:

> As he rose and fell
> He passed the stages of his age and youth
> Entering the whirlpool.

This, and the purgatory of Dante to which it alludes, are the basis for William Golding's novel *Pincher Martin*.

11 Epilogue

A commentary (based on an idiosyncratic reading of the text):

Once more the shepherd-poet sings his song: no more to Lycidas, who does not need it any longer (for he is not listening; he has ceased to play his part as a mediator between life and death; he begins his new journey). Instead the poet sings to the empty oaks and rills . . . Takes up the optimistic (although 'uncouth') theme of 'blest kingdoms' and 'solemn troops and sweet societies', tones it down, and calms it to the lasting peace of 'fresh woods and pastures new'. The 'still morn' is seen as a great classical figure wandering the oaks and rills in a thin mist ('with sandals gray') – playing a kind of background tune to the poet's dying song. Eagerly but thoughtfully he pipes a heavy, pensive theme. In the same way (eagerly but thoughtfully) Milton draws his heavy, pensive theme to its conclusion. The sun is no longer Phoebus. It has lost its power, like everything else in the poem (including Milton and the poem itself – and excepting Lycidas). It simply 'was dropped into the western bay'. Contrast this with 23–31. Lycidas and Milton are parted now. Milton has to sing to the oaks and rills. The sun is stretched out in exhaustion, and drops . . . Even the shepherds weep no more. The sun drops – Lycidas rises, and Milton rises. The sun rises once more . . . 'Pastures new' are the evergreens of the opening passage. They will never die.

GREGORY WOODS East Anglia 1st year

Reading list for Lycidas

For other resources, and more general books, see list at end of *M's early poems : a general introduction* by Lorna Sage in *JM : introductions* in this series. See also works cited above.

The most useful editions for readers of this volume are:

HUGHES, MERRIT Y. ed. *JM : complete poems and major prose* 1957.

PATRIDES, C. A. ed. *M's Lyc : the tradition and the poem* with an anthology of critical essays 1961; in effect, a handbook for the poem. Cited as Patrides below.

PRINCE, F. T. ed. *M : Comus and other poems* 1968.

Selected studies

ADAMS, ROBERT M. chap in his *Ikon : JM and the modern critics* Ithaca N.Y. 1955.

ALLEN, DON CAMERON chap in his *The harmonious vision* Baltimore 1954.

BROOKS, CLEANTH and J. E. HARDY ed. *Poems of Mr JM* (1645) with essays in analysis 1951, part repr in Patrides (cited above).

DAICHES, DAVID chap in *A study of literature* Ithaca N.Y. 1948 repr Patrides.

GREG, W. W. *Pastoral poetry and pastoral drama* 1906.

HANFORD, J. H. 'The pastoral elegy and M's *Lyc*' *Publications of the Modern Language Association of America (PMLA)* XXXV 1910 repr Patrides.

HANFORD, J. H. 'The youth of M: an interpretation of his early literary development' in *Studies in Shakespeare, M and Donne* Michigan Univ. publications: Lang. and Lit. I 1925.

HARRISON, THOMAS P. ed. *The pastoral elegy*, with English trans. by H. J. Leon, Austin, Texas 1939. Anthology and discussion of the tradition.

KNIGHT, G. WILSON chap in his *The burning oracle* 1939.

MAYERSON, CAROLINE W. 'The Orpheus image in *Lyc*' *PMLA* LXIV 1949.

MILES, JOSEPHINE *The primary language of poetry in the 1640s: Univ of California publications in English* XIX 1948 revised in Patrides.

NORLIN, GEORGE 'The conventions of the pastoral elegy' *American Journal of Philology* XXXII 1911.

RANSOM, JOHN CROWE chap in his *The world's body* repr Patrides.

ROSS, MALCOLM M. chap in his *Poetry and dogma* New Brunswick N.J. 1954.

SCHUMAKER, WAYNE 'Flowerets and sounding seas: a study in the affective structure of *Lyc*' *PMLA* LXVI 1951 repr Patrides.

TUVE, ROSEMOND chap in her *Images and themes in five poems by M* Cambridge, Mass. 1957 repr Patrides.

Chronology for this volume

Forth then with huge pathetic force
Straight to the utmost crown of night he flew.
The nothingness was a nakedness, a point

Beyond which thought could not progress as thought.
He had to choose. But it was not a choice
Between excluding things. It was not a choice

Between, but of. He chose to include the things
That in each other are included, the whole,
The complicate, the amassing harmony.

WALLACE STEVENS from *Notes toward a supreme fiction* 1942
in *Collected poems of Wallace Stevens* Faber